UNIFORMS
OF THE
GERMAN SOLDIER

UNIFORMS
OF THE
GERMAN SOLDIER

AN ILLUSTRATED HISTORY
FROM 1870 TO THE PRESENT DAY

Alejandro M. de Quesada

Frontline Books, London

Greenhill Books

A Greenhill Book

First published in two volumes in Great Britain in 2006 by Greenhill Books, Lionel Leventhal Limited
www.greenhillbooks.com

This single-volume edition published in 2013 by Frontline Books

an imprint of
Pen & Sword Books Ltd.,
47 Church Street, Barnsley, S. Yorkshire, S70 2AS.
visit us at www.frontline-books.com, email info@frontline-books.com or
write to us at the above address.

ISBN 978-1-84832-693-4

CIP data records for this title are available from the British Library.

Designed and typeset by Ian Hughes, Mousemat Design Limited

Printed and bound in India by Replika Press

CONTENTS

COLOR ILLUSTRATIONS

INTRODUCTION TO PART 1

The Kaiser's Army, 1870–1919

Germany's military history has captivated historians for generations. She went from being a strong military power to a vanquished nation only to rise again, like the phoenix, and become strong once more. The study of the uniforms of the German soldier during these periods of glory, defeat, and rebirth shows a gradual change, despite a steady trickle of influence from the past that permeates these decades.

While much has been written on the uniforms of the Kaiser's Army during World War I and on Hitler's Wehrmacht during World War II, virtually nothing has been done on German uniforms during the era of peace from 1871 to 1914, the Colonial and overseas troops, the Reichswehr, the Nationalen Volksarmee, and the Bundeswehr. Furthermore, in recent years no attempt has been made to show the continuation of uniform styles from the earliest days of the German Empire to the present, showing the steady changes of uniform and covering periods that are not familiar to the general public. The closest attempt was made over seventy years ago by Richard and Herbert Knötel and Herbert Sieg's *Handbuch der Uniformkunde*, published in 1937. While this book has become the main primer for anyone wanting to study military uniforms, its coverage stops prior to World War II.

The aim of this book is not to challenge this classic reference work but to complement it. The general history of the German Army and its uniforms presented here uses contemporary photography rather than drawings, showing the uniforms and equipment as they really appeared. In addition, by including a general history and a description of the uniforms it is possible to understand the latter in their context and examine the reasons why particular styles were retained, replaced, or reworked during periods in the existence of the German Army. It was impossible to include every single type of uniform, insignia, headgear, and equipment used in the last 130 or so years; however, this work attempts to illustrate styles and traditions that have been handed down from the earliest days to today's German Army. Hopefully this book will be a useful reference to the novice as well as the advanced military historian.

Prussia's Emergence as a Military Power

In the decades following the decline of the Holy Roman Empire, the Kingdom of Prussia emerged as the dominant player in Central European politics. Prussia had first been settled and Germanized during the thirteenth and fourteenth centuries by the Teutonic Knights, a military Order of German monks that overran the Slavs in the region. The Knights were eventually defeated by the Poles and Lithuanians at the battle of Tannenberg in 1410; however, in the course of the next century the Hohenzollern dynasty that ruled Brandenburg (with Berlin its seat of power) came to dominate Pomerania, Silesia, West Prussia, and eventually much of the Rhineland and Westphalia.

Germany's military heritage was carefully created by a succession of Prussian rulers in the seventeenth and eighteenth centuries. The first of these was the great Elector, Frederick Wilhelm (1640–88), who recognized that a standing army with a professional officer corps was the key to the development of a powerful state in his remote part of the Empire. His grandson, Frederick Wilhelm I (1713–40), doubled the size of his professional army to ninety thousand and added a trained reserve of conscripted peasants, forming one of the most modern and efficient fighting armies in eighteenth-century Europe. The Army was supported through heavy taxation, which consumed 80 per cent of peacetime state revenues. Frederick II (1740–86), known to posterity as Friedrich der Große (Frederick the Great) or "Alte Fritz", raised the strength of the Prussian Army to 150,000 and fought a series of wars between 1740 and 1763. By wresting control of the province of Silesia from Habsburg Austria, Prussia had become one of the most powerful continental states and a rival to the Habsburgs for domination over the myriad of German kingdoms and provinces.

The officer corps and its aristocratic character were established early in the eighteenth century as Prussian kings tried to gain the support of aristocrats, known as *Junkers*, by permitting them virtual control over the selection of officers. A cadet school was established in Berlin in 1733 to train sons of *Junkers* to be officers. Eventually the officer corps was on its way to becoming the most privileged social class in Prussia.

The militarism of Prussia inspired a multitude of feelings – respect, fear and hatred – among other European states and peoples. Under the strong leadership of a self-perpetuating and career-oriented general staff, the Prussian Army rarely had to endure any interference in its affairs by the civil government. However, the Army's failure to reform and lack of preparedness after the death of Frederick II in 1786 led to its decisive defeat by Napoleon Bonaparte's forces at Jena in October 1806.

General Gerhard von Scharnhorst oversaw the revitalization of the Army in the years following Jena. Reforms included ending dependence on mercenaries and introducing compulsory military service. The officer corps was expanded to include commoners, and officers were encouraged to take greater initiative in battle. The new Prussian Army distinguished itself at the battle of Leipzig in 1813 and again at Waterloo in 1815, where, under the command of Field Marshal Gebhard von Blücher, the Army was instrumental in Napoleon's final defeat.

Prussia's reputation for military efficiency was re-established by the Army's final victories over Napoleon. The Prussian War College (Kriegsakademie) became a model for military staff colleges around the world in the early nineteenth century. A book of that era, *On War* by the Prussian general Karl von Clausewitz, became a classic, its theories of land warfare still studied by officers of many armies more than 160 years after its author's death.

Prussian-led victories over Denmark in 1864, Austria in 1866 and France in 1870–1 were followed by the unification of the various German states into the German Empire (1871–1918). Seeking recognition of equal status from Great Britain, France, Russia and Spain – the states that comprised "old Europe" – the new German Reich was characterized by a rising surge of patriotism, as can be seen in the creation of organizations such as the Pan-German League, the Colonial League and the Navy League. Powerful industrialists such as Krupp began to wield considerable influence with the German imperial government. Otto von Bismarck became imperial Germany's first chancellor and began to mastermind a series of aggressive policies. Following the formation of imperial Germany, the legendary Prussian General Staff became the German General Staff. This body was a center of great power in the highly militaristic regimes of Kaiser Wilhelm I (1858–88) and Kaiser Wilhelm II (1888–1918), ignoring Clausewitz's dictum that civilians should control the military. Within the first years of Kaiser Wilhelm II's reign the parliament (Reichstag) had lost all direct control over the military, and by 1914 even the Ministry of War had been reduced to an essentially administrative role. By the outbreak of war in August 1914, the German Army was one of the largest in the world, with well over 662,000 soldiers on active duty, and an additional fifteen thousand reservists and thirty thousand officers. The forces of Prussia, Bavaria, Saxony and Württemberg combined amounted to over twenty-four army corps. Their high standard of training, the widely held belief that other nations were preventing Germany from assuming its role as a world power, and the militarization of German society, toughened the population for a war. Germany was like a coiled spring.

Uniforms of the Kaiserheer, 1871–1918

Describing the uniforms worn by imperial German soldiers from 1871 to 1914 is a complicated business, since there were many variations across the different regiments and German kingdoms. Basically, Hessian, Prussian and Saxon infantrymen wore dark-blue, single-breasted tunics, while those from Württemberg were the same colour but double-breasted. The tunic sported scarlet piping on the skirts at the rear and down the front; on Saxon tunics it was round the bottom of the skirts. As a special distinction, Prussian Guard Regiments wore two bars of white lace (*Kapellenlitzen*) on their scarlet-colored collars. A number of other regiments, including those from Bavaria and Saxony, wore these bars in white or yellow lace. Sleeves might have Swedish or Brandenburg-style cuffs, the colors differing according to regiment. Brandenburg cuffs were normally worn by the infantry, while Swedish cuffs tended to be worn by the artillery, cavalry, and pioneers. There were, however, numerous differences and exceptions to the norm from kingdom to kingdom. For example, a Bavarian infantryman wore a light-blue tunic, whereas his Saxon equivalent, say a member of the 108th Saxon Regiment, wore a dark-green tunic. With the notable exception of Bavarian infantrymen, who wore light-blue trousers, most German infantry units wore dark-grey, almost black, trousers with scarlet piping down the legs. Infantry battalion and company distinctions were identified by the color of the cloth knot affixed to the bayonet frog.

Field artillerymen wore a uniform similar to that of the infantry. The coat was dark blue with black collars and cuffs with red piping. The shoulder-straps were scarlet, while the trousers were dark grey. Saxon artillerymen wore dark-green tunics with a scarlet collar, cuffs and piping. The foot artillery wore the same uniform as the field artillery, with the sole exception that their shoulder-straps were white. Saxon foot artillery wore scarlet shoulder-straps.

German cavalry uniforms were as varied as those worn by the infantry. There were three basic types of cavalry: Heavy (Cuirassiers), Medium (Lancers/Uhlans) and Light (Dragoons, Hussars and Light Horse). Each Cavalry Regiment wore a distinctive regimental uniform. The Cuirassier Regiments took their name from the cuirass they wore. The Guard Regiments' cuirasses were copper-colored, while those of other regiments were of black iron. Cuirassiers wore a white tunic with regimental stripe facings on the collar, down the tunic front and on the Swedish cuffs. The Guard Regiments wore the usual *Kapellenlitzen* of white lace on each side of the collar and miniature versions of the double bars on the cuff. Their pantaloons were made of white kersey and their overalls of dark-grey cloth with scarlet piping. When mounted, the men wore leather thigh-boots. Imperial German Dragoons wore a similar tunic to that of the Prussian infantry, with the difference that it was light blue in color. The tunic's front, skirts, shoulder-straps and Swedish cuffs were piped with the regimental colors. Their pantaloons were dark blue and their overalls dark grey with scarlet piping.

The Hussars wore a tunic, its color varying from regiment to regiment; it was cut short, with five rows of lace or braided cord on the chest. The collar and cuffs were the same color as the tunic, with trimming and, in the case of the Guard Hussars, yellow lace. The uniquely shaped buttons found on the lace or braided cord were of metal or wood. Only the 3rd, 15th, and Guard Hussars Regiments were entitled to the dolman-pelisse that was worn loosely over the left shoulder suspended by lace or chain. Their pantaloons were dark blue. A low busby of sealskin with a colored bag was worn by all Hussars, and white hanging plumes were worn as part of the full dress uniform. Most Uhlans or Lancers wore a dark-blue, double-breasted tunic with piping of the color of the facings and pointed Polish cuffs with a button near the point. However, the Bavarian Uhlans' tunics were dark green and those of Saxony were light blue. A pair of metal epaulettes with a cloth center and backing were a distinctive feature of the uniform. Regimental colors were featured on the tunic's collar, cuffs and turnback, and under the surface of the epaulette. As a regimental distinction, the 17th and 18th Lancers wore metal shoulder-scales.

At the outbreak of World War I airship personnel wore the uniform of the Prussian Guard Pioneer Battalion, with a shako and Guard *litzen* on the collar and cuffs. The Flying Troops, who were founded during the Great War, wore a large variety of uniforms, since many of the officers and men had been pulled from other sectors of the Army. However, standardization of uniforms was begun in the latter part of the war. Officers wore winged propeller insignia on their braided shoulder-boards with a light-grey underlay, while enlisted men wore a winged propeller over their unit number (Bavarian flying units had only the insignia without the unit number) embroidered or chain-stitched into their cloth shoulder-straps. Piping colors on the shoulder-boards designated the battalion – white for the 1st Battalion, red for the 2nd Battalion, yellow for the 3rd Battalion and blue for the 4th Battalion. In addition, some flying units wore their numerical designation in the form of an oval patch on the left sleeve of the tunic and greatcoat. The designation consisted of the group number in Roman numerals over the squadron number in arabic numerals for bomber units, and "F" over arabic numerals for flying detachments. Field airship detachments consisted of a script "L" over the depot battalion number. Anti-aircraft platoons consisted of a winged artillery shell or "MG" (for *Maschinengewehr* or Machine Gun) for Prussian units, and for Bavarian units "FLK" and "MG" in red chain-stitch on their shoulder-straps. While Bavarian flying units wore a plain collar, all personnel in Prussian and other flying units wore the *Kapellenlitzen* of Guard Regiments. Seconded officers wore the winged propeller insignia on the shoulder-boards of the original regimental uniforms of their previous service. Hence in some unit photographs we are treated to the interesting spectacle of a variety of officer uniforms – for example, *Litewka*, *Überrock*, *Attila*, and other field-grey uniforms – all in one sitting. Early in the war, a variety of cold-weather clothing was used by pilots and their crews, many donning civilian fur coats and motorcycle crash helmets. In 1917 field-grey flight coveralls were authorized.

Military chaplains and field rabbis were designated as senior military officials without rank distinctions. On 3 June 1913 a field uniform was authorized for them. It comprised a knee-length field-grey frock coat with stand-up collar, barrel cuffs and violet piping on the collar, tunic front and cuffs. A Red Cross armband – white-edged violet for Christian chaplains and white for Jewish rabbis – was worn on the left sleeve of the frock coat. Military chaplains and rabbis wore a colonial-style Model 1907 Wide-Brimmed Felt Hat with violet brim edging and band as well as the Model 1910 Officer's Peaked Cap with violet band and crown piping. For Christian military chaplains both hat and cap had a white enamelled cross between the state and national cockades, while Jewish rabbis wore no distinctive insignia. Military chaplains and field rabbis also carried visible symbols – the Protestant cross (silver), the Catholic crucifix (black with silver edging) and the Jewish Star of David suspended from a silver chain. In 1915 the eight buttons of the frock coat were changed from matt grey to matt white.

By the middle of the nineteenth century, royal ladies began to make official appearances in versions of military uniforms. The idea of noble ladies as honorary chiefs of regiments originated in Germany, where this distinction was conferred on royal personages and distinguished generals and statesmen. These ladies often donned the uniform of their corps and rode at the head of their regiments. Queen Victoria was the honorary chief of the 1st Dragoons of the Prussian Guard, but she never wore the light-blue tunic of the regiment. However, several princesses of her family held positions as chiefs of German regiments and wore their uniforms. The German Empress Frederick, a daughter of Queen Victoria, sported the uniform of German regiments, as did her successor, the last German Empress and wife of Kaiser Wilhelm, who was chief of the Schleswig-Holstein Fusiliers and also of a Circassian Regiment; looking particularly attractive "in the pretty white tunic of the latter, and with a three-cornered hat, her Majesty was often seen on parade". Queen Margharita of Italy, Crown Princess Sophia of Greece and Princess Frederick of Hesse followed suit, as did Russian royal ladies – both the Dowager Empress and the Empress, a grand-daughter of Queen Victoria. Crown Princess Marie of Romania, daughter of the Duke of Saxe-Coburg-Gotha (better known as the Duke of Edinburgh), was honorary colonel of the 4th Romanian Hussars, and wore their uniform. Queen Alexandra and the Duchess of Connaught both held honorary colonelcies of German regiments, but the Queen did not wear the uniforms concerned.

The ladies' regimental uniform usually consisted of the correct male-style tunic with high neck and epaulettes, but with left-hand buttoning, and a woman's skirt, riding-style in the case of mounted regiments. Headgear varied from feminine versions of military caps to the *Pickelhauben*, complete with spike and, for the Tsarina, resplendent plume. In addition, noble ladies were permitted to wear medals, decorations and orders on their regimental uniforms, thereby completing their militaristic appearance.

Officers' rank distinctions were found on their shoulder-boards with pips. Gefreite wore a small button on each side of the collar. Unteroffizier or non-commissioned officers wore lace around the bottom of the collar and cuffs. Feldwebel or Cavalry Wachtmeister wore a pair of large buttons over the Unteroffizier lace on the collar. Vizefeldwebel wore the same distinctions as the Feldwebel but with an additional band of lace above each cuff. The Offizierstellvertreter wore in addition to the Vizefeldwebel distinctions a metallic braid around their shoulder-straps with metal unit designations. A Fähnrich had Unteroffizier distinctions but with an officer's sword knot (portepee).

On 23 October 1842 Prussia adopted the leather helmet with a metal spike ornament known as the *Pickelhaube* for its armed forces, and soon afterwards for its fire and police organizations as well, which were run on military lines. The different German states began to adopt the helmet, beginning with Oldenburg (1843), and then Hansestädte (1845), Sachsen-Altenburg (1845), Sachsen-Weimar-Eisenachm (1845), Reuss (1845), Anhalt (1846), Sachsen-Meiningen (1846), Hessen-Kassel (1846), Mecklenburg-Schwerin (1848), Mecklenburg-Strelitz (1848), Schleswig-Holstein (1848), Hannover (1849), Nassau (1849), Baden (1849), Hessen-Darmstadt (1849), Sachsen (1867), Württemberg (1871), and Bayern (1886). This style of helmet was also adopted by some civil organizations in nearby Austria-Hungary.

The *Pickelhaube* replaced the bell-crowned shako that had been worn by all Prussian infantry and Guard units. The first model, the M1842 Helmet, was constructed of heavy leather with reinforced side panels. The front visor was squared and the rear visor covered the neck. It was tall, typically measuring about thirty-seven centimeters. A tall brass spike was affixed to a cruciform base on the crown of the helmet (the base was then secured by stud retainers, star-shaped for officers and round for enlisted men). A raised neckband (*perlring*) was secured around the narrow base of the spike proper. A leather rosette or cockade in the colors of the German state was affixed to the right side by the knurled bolt that also served as support for the scaled chinstraps.

The Prussian *Pickelhaube* was modified in 1856. The chinscales were flattened (although convex ones were still used by cavalry, administrative personnel and regimental officers). The knurled bolts were replaced with a new retainer for securing the chinscales to the body of the helmet, while the cockade was reduced and began to appear in metal. The helmet's ungainly height was reduced in 1857 and again in 1860.

After field experience in the campaigns against Denmark (1864) and the Austro-Hungarian Empire (1866), the design of the *Pickelhaube* underwent several further changes. In 1867 the squared front visor was replaced by a rounded visor for the infantry regiments. The base plate of the helmet, once cruciform in design, was now rounded. The Prussian cockade was reduced in size. The metallic spine was also removed from the helmet. Only Dragoon officers and generals continued to wear the squared visor.

After the Franco-Prussian War, the failure of helmets to retain their shape was addressed in a directive of 23 November 1871 which called for the replacement of the rear spine. It was to be secured by a rivet in the rear visor and a screw post in the crown of the helmet. The scaled chinstraps of enlisted men's helmets were to be secured by threaded and notched screws, while those of officers were to be mounted by push-through posts. It was not until 1887 that a new model of *Pickelhaube* with many significant changes was issued for enlisted personnel.

The *Pickelhaube* worn by imperial German field and foot artillery regiments differed from that worn by the infantry only in that the spike was replaced by a ball. In full dress, the Guard Artillery wore white horsehair plumes, the horse and Saxon Artillery black plumes and the Bavarian Artillery scarlet plumes.

Cuirassiers wore a special *Pickelhaube* of yellow metal or white steel that descended very low behind the head and curved backwards to cover the nape of the neck, with a square front peak and a metal-scale chinchain. All Cuirassier Regiments wore the spike, but for the two Guard Regiments in full dress the spike was replaced with a white metal crowned eagle.

Dragoons wore a similar *Pickelhaube* to the infantry, except that the front peak was cut square with metal binding and the chinscales were of metal. The Uhlans, however, wore a type of *Pickelhaube* known as a *tschapka* or *czapka*. This helmet had a lacquered leather body with a tall, raised, four-cornered mortarboard top. The cloth facings matched the epaulette uniform facings. The visor trim of the helmet was of brass or German silver matching the color of the plate. Officers' *czapkas* were trimmed with silver or gold piping on the mortarboard. Cords were worn, secured to a leather knot on the top of the helmet. The scale chinstraps were mounted by screw retainers or the Model 1891 Posts. The *Reichskokarde* was worn on the right post of the *czapka* and the *Landeskokarde* was worn on the mortarboard. In 1915 the chinscales were replaced with black leather straps, and the fittings were issued in a pewter-colored field-grey finish. A variety of Uhlan *czapkas*, from metal to felt, were made during World War I, until all such decorative forms of headgear were phased out of service in 1917.

Many German states in the years preceding and following World War I used the standard Model 1881/91 leather helmet shell; the ornaments made the headgear distinct from state to state. Each helmet had the *helmwappen* (helmet plate) of a province or a distinctive regimental plate. On some *Pickelhauben* a *Landeskokarde* showing the province's color was attached to the sides of the shell. The *Pickelhaube* was virtually obsolete by the time World War I broke out.

An interesting earlier type of headgear was the crested helmet known as a *Raupenhelm*, adopted around 1803 by Bavaria during the Napoleonic Wars. The black leather helmet was similar to an earlier model that had been adopted in 1789. The helmet had a small plate on the front with a crown above, and a small chinchain, fastened on each side by lion's-head bosses. The plate was later replaced with the royal cipher in 1848. By the time of the Franco-Prussian War Bavarian troops wore a modified crested helmet with a leather chinstrap, binding around the peak, and a crowned "L" cipher. The helmet was replaced with the *Pickelhaube* in 1886.

Another type of headgear that was considered to be distinctively German was the shako or *tschako*. The shako had been the standard form of headdress for the Jäger and Schützen units since the Napoleonic Wars. In an *Allerhöchste Kabinetts-Ordre* (AKO) of the Prussian Army in 1854 a new pattern of shako was introduced. Enlisted personnel wore a shako made of black leather, while officers wore one with a fine black cloth cover. A field badge or cockade, black and white in color (for Prussia), was worn on the peak of the headgear, and a helmet plate affixed to the front. At the time there were only three styles of plates worn with the shako. Jäger Battalions 1, 2, 5 and 6 wore a ciphered "FWR" device, while Guard units wore a German silver Guard star. Other Jäger units wore a device with a brass button securing a vertical bar of braiding or *litzen*. The shako was designed to take brass or (for officers) gilded chinstraps. A parade plume of black and red was authorized for Sunday and parade service. The plumes were secured behind the cockade and fanned out, dangling forward slightly to add a drooping effect.

In 1860 a new shako was introduced for use in the Prussian Army. The front and rear visors were reduced in size, a black leather chinstrap was authorized for enlisted personnel, and rosettes were added. A new brass shako plate for Jäger Battalions 1, 2, 5 and 6 was adopted, consisting of a heraldic Prussian eagle with the "FWR" cipher in a shield on the eagle's breast. A simple "FR" cipher on the eagle plate was to be used by the other Jäger units. In addition, a bandeau inscribed "MIT GOTT FÜR KOENIG UND VATERLAND" (With God for King and Country) was authorized and incorporated into the Jäger plate. Further additions to the shako were also made: ventilation holes were added in 1888, infantry-style chinstraps in 1892, post mountings for the enlisted *Pickelhaube*-style chinstraps in 1895, and the black, white and red *Reichskokarde*, to be worn on the right post of the shako, was authorized in 1897. While on field maneuvres, special cloth field covers that were cut specially to permit the wearing of the field badge were worn over the black leather shakos. In April 1915, during World War I, the fittings were switched to pewter trim.

The origins of the visorless field cap (*feldmütze*), resembling a "pillbox" and worn by enlisted personnel, date from the Napoleonic Wars. Before World War I the color of these caps was the same as the tunic, and they were piped with the color of the appropriate branch of service or regiment. By 1910 all field caps were field-grey in color, with a red band and piping on the crown for infantry and a black band with red piping for artillery, pioneer, and other specialist units. Commissioned and non-commissioned officers wore the same field caps as enlisted personnel, although theirs had a visor. By 1915 the officer's peaked cap had a grey-green visor and chinstrap. The Model 1917 Officer's Standard Peaked Field Cap was adopted for all branches of the Army, and consisted of a dark greenish-grey band and crown piping, while a field-grey band and piping were used by Bavarian troops. All styles were worn with state and national cockades. In addition, special unit insignia were worn with the enlisted and officer caps. Ski troops of the Alpenkorps wore an Austrian Army metal edelweiss flower on the left side of the green cap band, while military administration officials wore a Hohenzollern eagle between the state and national cockades, members of the Carpathian Corps wore a scroll between their cockades inscribed "KARPA-THENKORPS", with binding paired antlers and pine branches, and members of the 8th Bavarian Reserve Division wore a blue-and-white Bavarian shield on two silver holly leaves on the left side of the cap. Additionally, the 17th Brunswick Hussar Regiment and the 1st Life Hussar Regiment wore their distinctive regimental badges on the field-grey undress caps.

In essence, the German Army had a standard uniform by the time World War I began in August 1914. The introduction of field-grey uniforms for all German troops began as an experiment in 1907, and selected units were issued with the trial uniforms. The new uniforms were successful, and the German General Staff made them the official service dress of the German Army in orders of 23 February and 18 March 1910. The cut of the tunic was basically the same for artillery, infantry and train. The color of the early tunics was much lighter and less green than that which became typical during the war. The Jäger and Schützen Regiments received grey-green uniforms. The buttons and metal fittings, such as belt hooks, on the Model 1910 Tunic were made of dull brass or silvered metal. The tunics had their own distinctive piping or *Waffenfarben* – red for infantry, pioneer and machine-gun units; green for Jäger and Schützen (although the Prussian Guard Machine-Gun Unit was permitted to retain black piping for collar and cuffs); scarlet for artillery; and light blue for train. The uniform collar, *litzen* and so on were basically the same as the peacetime uniform. General officers had their traditional gold embroidery on red collar patches, while non-regimental (staff) officers wore plain collar patches in the color of their peacetime tunic collar. Field tunics continued to use the three cuff styles, Brandenburg, Swedish and Saxon. Company or squadron numbers were placed on the buttons of the shoulder-straps, while the tunic buttons bore crowns or heraldic emblems. Each of the cavalry branches (Uhlans, Hussars and Cuirassiers) retained their own distinctive characteristics in the newly adopted field-grey uniforms.

In 1915 a simplified version of the Model 1910 Uniform was first issued. The cut remained basically the same, as did the collar and shoulder-straps, but the distinctive cuffs were replaced by plain-back or barreled styles, and the piping on the rear skirt was discontinued. On 21 September 1915 a new, simplified field uniform was introduced. In addition, field-grey greatcoats without collar patches were issued, as were stone-grey trousers (field-grey for Bavarian troops). The new Model 1915 Field Blouse consisted of a fly front that concealed its buttons; rank distinctions were still restricted to the collar and, occasionally, the shoulder-straps. It was in essence the old *Litewka* Model 1893 of Boxer Rebellion vintage, slightly modified from dark blue to field-grey, and was issued in large quantities to Landsturm units at the outbreak of World War I. The same order also abolished the colorful distinctive regimental uniforms. A considerable number of full-dress uniforms in field-grey were made and stored away in order to be donned after the war, only to be worn later on by some officers and members of the Freikorps during Germany's post-War revolutionary period. The Model 1915 Field Blouse was modified with the addition of breast pockets, and used by ski companies as well.

The Model 1916 Steel Helmet or *Stahlhelm* was widely distributed, and soon replaced all other forms of protective headgear used by the imperial German forces during the war. This helmet and its variants would become the new symbol of Germany and its military from 1916 onwards. Covers for the M-16 Pattern Helmets were of grey or white cloth and had a reinforced leather ventilation hole through which the helmet "horn" fitted. In addition, the helmet was often painted with an angular camouflage pattern. In 1918 a "special" steel helmet was introduced with cutouts along the leading edge of the distinctive pattern helmet. The cutouts were designed to offer protection to telephone talkers in the trenches, allowing them to wear the bulky helmet while also holding headsets to their ears. In the Weimar era, this style of helmet seems to have been issued from old stock to Reichswehr cavalry and artillery units. A plain leather chinstrap was utilized in the 1916 and 1918 Pattern Steel Helmets.

After 1916 the *Pickelhaube* was no longer issued, and surplus quantities were later modified and issued to German fire-fighting units or *feuerwehr*. The shako was later adopted by the Prussian and other German state police forces after the war, and remained in service well through the Weimar and Nazi eras. After World War II both

East and West Germany continued to use the shako, until it was finally phased out in the 1970s. The shako, then, was one of the most versatile and enduring forms of headgear in German service.

Germany as a Colonial Power

Germany possessed four colonies in Africa – German East Africa (Tanzania), Togoland (Togo), Kameruun (Cameroon), and German Southwest Africa (Namibia). In addition, Germany maintained colonial interests in the Pacific region – New Guinea, Samoa, and Tsingtao (China). All were lost to Great Britain, France, the United States and Japan in the course of World War I. All four African colonies were the scenes of conflict between the natives that dwelled there and the German colonial troops, called *Schutztruppen*.

The *Schutztruppe* was one of the smallest colonial forces in the world, even smaller than the forces of Portugal and Belgium. In 1900 it numbered only three thousand officers and men, and in 1914 it had 6,461 officers and men, of which fourteen companies were stationed in East Africa, nine companies in Southwest Africa and twelve companies in Cameroon. Togoland, however, had a paramilitary police organization rather than a *Schutztruppe*. In times of need the *Schutztruppe* would receive aid from German Marines (*Seebataillon*) stationed abroad, from German warships patrolling in the area or from regular Army units sent to the colonies from Germany itself.

The officers and NCOs of the *Schutztruppe* were white, regular officers and NCOs from the German Imperial Army. There were considerable incentives to serve with the *Schutztruppe*. The pay was good, and it was a chance to see exotic lands and military action, which appealed to bored officers in peacetime Germany. The enlisted men, or *askaris*, were local natives. They generally enlisted for an initial five-year term and then re-enlisted on a yearly basis. The *askaris'* uniform was khaki, and they were armed with either the Mark 71 or 84 Model Single-Shot Rifle. They were very loyal and well trained. The Germans stressed discipline and marksmanship. In the field, the *askaris* were taught to fight as a company.

In 1884, German trading companies founded all four German colonies in Africa. Within several years they proved unable to cope with the problems of running a colony, so the Imperial German Government took over their administration. The Germans' desire to push inland and expand their holdings led to conflicts with the natives and the creation of the *Schutztruppe*. For the next twenty-odd years, there was almost always fighting in at least one of the colonies. The numerous and varied skirmishes, campaigns and wars with the native tribes are reminiscent of the American Indian Wars. Small groups of German troops patrolled and attempted to control a vast amount of land. As the colonial wars were numerous, only the more major conflicts will be described here.

Three principal campaigns were fought by the *Schutztruppe* in East Africa: the Abushiri Rebellion in 1888–90, the Hehe War in 1891–8 and the Maji-Maji Revolt in 1905–7. German involvement in Cameroon began in 1884, when trade treaties were signed with Dovala chiefs along the coast. Conflicts with tribes living in the interior ensued, and the Germans created a *Poliztruppe* in November 1891 to combat the hostile natives. The Dohomey troops mutinied against the new acting governor, Leist, a brutal man who had treated them badly and, when they had complained about poor pay and terrible food, ordered their wives to be publicly whipped. The government in Germany founded the *Schutztruppe* in Cameroon on 9 June 1895. Togoland's paramilitary police force was very similar to the *Schutztruppe*: the soldiers wore khaki dress, were armed with Model 71 Mauser Rifles, and their officers were regular German Army men who referred to them as soldiers, not policemen. The police force was divided into platoons based on the tribal background of the men. In 1914, it consisted of two officers, six NCOs and 560 enlisted men.

Events in Cameroon were typical – the fighting consisted of small wars against rebellious or independent-minded tribes. The most ardent opponents of the Germans were the Dagombe, who resented German control over traditional trade routes. In 1877, they rebelled against the Germans along with their allies, the Konkomba, who were aggrieved at the loss of tribal lands. In May, Lt Valentine von Massow and a force of ninety-one police marched into the area to quell the revolt. They were attacked at Adibo by between six and seven thousand Dagombe and Konkomba warriors. Again, it was the combined use of machine-gun and small-arms fire and discipline which saved the day for the Germans. Some five hundred natives were killed, and their forces scattered. Shortly after the battle of Adibo, Massow and his men took the Dagombe capital, Yenbli, and burned it. The rebellion soon ended.

Some of the heaviest fighting witnessed by German colonial troops was to take place in German Southwest Africa. Made a protectorate in 1884, because of its extensive plains and grazing lands Southwest Africa was viewed as an area for German settlement. The German *Schutztruppe* almost immediately began to move inland in order to secure lands for German farmers and settlers. Also in the colony were large numbers of natives, divided into several large tribal groupings. In the north were the Ovambi, in the central region were the Herero, and in the south were the Mama, or Hottentots. All of the tribes were semi-nomadic cattle raisers. The first real opposition to the Germans came from one of the Mama subdivided tribes, the Witbooi, led by Hendrik Witbooi. Hendrik refused to sign a treaty of peace and opposed further German encroachment into their lands. German officials in the colony called upon the *Schutztruppe* to force Hendrik Witbooi and his people to sign.

The *Schutztruppe* in German Southwest Africa had been created in 1890, and was commanded by Captain Curt von Francois. Eventually it would consist of nine field companies, one of which was mounted on camels, and three light batteries of artillery. However, at the start of the Witbooi conflict Captain Francois had few men, and required reinforcements from Germany before the campaign could begin. Reinforced, Captain Francois planned a surprise attack upon Hendrik Witbooi's stronghold at Hornkranz. On 12 April, Captain Francois's force arrived outside Hendrik's fortified city. Francois split his command, ordering the first company to attack the city from the east and the second company to attack from the north. After the defense, which lasted approximately three hours, Hendrik ordered the city to be abandoned. Behind them they left 150 Witbooi dead. The German forces returned to Windhoek in triumph, but their victory was short-lived. In retaliation, the Witboois attacked a German horse post and drove off or captured most of the German horses. For the time being the German forces were left on foot, and the well-mounted Witboois were now hard to catch. Even after a further hundred men arrived from Germany in June 1893, Captain Francois seemed unable to regain control over the situation. In August, the Witboois ambushed a supply train of twenty wagons and destroyed it completely. In the following six months after the battle of Hornkranz, Hendrik was stronger than ever, with six hundred men, four hundred rifles and three hundred horses at his disposal.

In August, the newly promoted Major Francois now felt he could move against the Witboois. He planned to surround the Witboois, isolate them, then draw them into a confrontation and defeat them. However, the mobile Witboois kept slipping away while skirmishing with the Germans and raiding their rear areas. Losing confidence in Major Francois, the German government decided to replace him with Major Theodor Leutwein. Leutwein arrived in German Southwest Africa in February 1894. He did not immediately move against the Witboois, instead spending time meeting with, negotiating with and winning over neighboring tribes. He began to regain German control over the region while at the same time severing aid and support to Hendrik. In May Leutwein persuaded Hendrik to agree to a truce which was to last until the end of July. Leutwein hoped he could negotiate the Witboois into surrender; if not, the break would nevertheless allow time for additional German reinforcements to arrive. The Witboois did not capitulate, and the final confrontation was now at hand. Hendrik and his followers had retreated to the Naukloof Mountains and fortified their positions there. Leutwein blocked off the various mountain passes, thereby stopping any possible escape, and advanced into the Naukloof Mountains. The battle of Naukloof started on 27 August and became wide-ranging, roaming over rough terrain. The control of waterholes and advance points on the high grounds were contested by both sides. Unable to retreat and having lost the last of the Witboois-controlled waterholes, Hendrik surrendered on 9 September 1894. The Witboois conflict had proven to be an unpleasant experience to the Germans, but nothing like the next campaign, which would rock the colony.

A number of factors had led to unrest amongst the Herero: there had been an epidemic in 1897 which had killed half of the Herero cattle herds, and German settlements were putting mounting pressure on various tribes to move. On 12 January 1904, the Herero, led by Chief Samuel Maherero, revolted at Okahandja. The *Schutztruppen* under Leutwein were taken completely by surprise by the revolt. Leutwein's forces consisted of forty officers and 726 soldiers divided into four companies of mounted infantry and one artillery company. He also had a reserve of thirty-four officers and 730 enlisted men, four hundred German settlers with no military training and 250 native scouts and auxiliaries. His troops were armed with the Gewehr 1888 Rifle, and in addition there were five quick-fire, five older artillery pieces and five Maxim machine guns. There were also a number of small walled forts consisting of an armory, barracks and watchtower. Major Leutwein and three companies were in the extreme southern part of the colony, over four hundred miles away, subduing a small revolt by the Bondelzwort, when the Herero struck. With little opposition from the overstretched German colonial authorities, the rebellion in the north spread rapidly, destroying isolated farms and ranches and attacking most of the German settlements and forts in the region. Okahandja and Windhoek were briefly placed under siege. Between 19 January and 4 February, German troops were able to relieve both cities, but were not strong enough to take the offensive. Reinforcements arrived, consisting of Marines from the cruiser *Habicht* on 18 January. Sufficiently reinforced for Major Leutwein to put 2,500 men in the field, the Germans began a three-column counter-offensive in April. The columns were named the eastern, western and main. However, the newly arrived German troops were not conditioned for the climate, and soon proved to be ineffectual against the seasoned Herero. With so little success, Leutwein finally called off the offensive to await more reinforcements; in the meantime, the German government removed him and ordered General Lothar von Trotha, a seasoned colonial officer who had fought in East Africa and China, to take command of the colonial forces.

Von Trotha arrived on 11 June. During the months of May and June, large reinforcements arrived until von Trotha had approximately ten thousand men and thirty-two pieces of artillery. General von Trotha was able to accomplish what Leutwein had been unable to do: encircle the Herero with a large force. The Herero began to dig defenses at the Waterburg Mountains and prepare for their final battle.

The battle commenced on 11 August, when the Germans advanced into the mountains. The artillery bombarded the Herero positions, causing heavy losses. The infantry converged on several fronts, thus making it hard for the Herero to fight everyone at once. Unable to resist any longer, the Herero finally broke out and retreated into the desert, therefore ending the rebellion.

Just as one uprising ended another had begun. The Mama revolted in October under Hendrik Witbooi, now eighty years old. The Mama numbered 1,000–1,500 men, with only one-third armed with rifles. German troops now numbered seventeen thousand. Despite the imbalance of numbers, a long and arduous guerrilla campaign was waged, with over two hundred skirmishes and engagements. During the course of the revolt, Hendrik Witbooi was killed near Tses, and leadership passed to Jacob Morenga. The revolt was eventually put down, and the fighting ended in 1907. With this final campaign, the German colonial wars in Africa ended. In fact, the Germans would control their colonies for only another ten years, until World War I ended their colonial empire.

Uniforms of the Imperial German Colonial and Overseas Troops

In German East Africa from 1889 to 1891, troops raised under the authority of the Reichskommissar wore white tropical helmets with the national cockade of black, white and red. The basic uniform was white for service and a dark-blue tunic with turndown collar and brass buttons for full dress. The full dress tunic also had twisted shoulder-cords of silver, black, and red, as well as between one and three gold rank stripes on the cuffs, with the top row in the form of a loop. Officers wore sashes and sword knots embroidered in silver, red and black. In addition, a khaki service dress of the same pattern was worn, and NCOs' ranks were denoted on the left upper arm with one to three chevrons. The *askaris* wore a red fez with a blue tassel or turban, single-breasted khaki tunics and blue puttees. All leather equipment of the *askaris* and *Schutztruppen* in the German colonies was brown. Following the incorporation of the colonial troops of German East Africa into imperial service, the following uniform was adopted from 1891 until 1896.

For full dress, the officers wore a *Pickelhaube* bearing an imperial German eagle plate and chinscale in yellow metal, and a dark-blue single-breasted tunic with gold buttons, white piping on the turndown collar, tunic front, Brandenburg cuffs and skirt-pocket flaps, and a gilt imperial crown at the end of each collar. The sash and shoulder-straps were similar to those worn by the *Seebataillon*. Dark-blue trousers with white piping were worn. The fatigue or daily uniform was a white tunic with dark-blue piping and breast and skirt pockets. Tropical helmets were white, and worn with a brass spike and imperial German eagle plate. In addition, a white cap with a dark-blue band and a national cockade was worn by all ranks. In the same style as the white uniform, a khaki service dress with yellow piping and imperial crowns at the ends of the collar were used by the troops when in the field. British-style chevrons were used to denote NCO ranks. The uniform of the *askaris* remained unchanged.

From 1889 to 1893, the troops of the Reichskommissar in German Southwest Africa wore jackets and trousers of grey cord. Between 1893 and 1896, when this force entered imperial service, a light-blue collar and pointed cuffs were added to this uniform, with a white loop of Guard lace (officers wore silver) on a red patch. Up to 1895 a small, French-style kepi made popular in the American Civil War was worn, with a blue band and piping around the top and a black rectangular leather visor; the German national cockade of black, white and red was affixed to the front.

In 1896 a general pattern uniform was introduced for the *Schutztruppen* and became standard for most of the troops stationed in the various German overseas colonies. The home service uniform was a tunic of light-grey cord with stand-and-fall collar, Swedish cuffs and piping in the color of the colony (white for German East Africa, light blue for German Southwest Africa and red for Cameroon). In addition, light-grey trousers with the colony's piping was worn with the tunic. A broad-brimmed grey hat with a band bearing the color of the colony became the symbol of the German colonial soldier. The hat was turned up at the right side, with a large black, white and red metal cockade fastened to the flap. On the collar and cuffs of the tunic white Guard lace (silver for officers) with a red patch was worn. The sword knot, shoulder-straps and sash were in the national colors, in styles similar to those used by the Kaiser's army in Germany. Officers wore a double silver aiguillette on the left shoulder of their full dress uniform. General officers had traditional Prussian-style red distinctions with gold embroidery, gilt buttons and gold hat binding.

The service dress of the German colonial troops consisted of a khaki jacket with a row of white metal buttons bearing the imperial "squared" crown, turndown collar and round cuffs – piped with the appropriate colony's colors, with no lace – khaki trousers and a khaki tropical helmet bearing a cockade on the front. The *askaris* wore a similar uniform, with dark-blue or khaki puttees. A khaki fez with a neck flap was adopted, with a silver or brass German imperial eagle plate affixed to the front. As the distinctive color of the *Schutztruppen* in Cameroon was red, it was found on their uniform's piping, rank chevrons, and the bandsmen's wings worn by the native troops. The police troops in Togo wore the same uniform. All leather equipment and footwear were brown.

In 1850 a *Marinirkorps* was raised in the Prussian Navy, and in 1854 it was renamed the *Seebataillon*. It was composed of infantry and artillery carried on board ship. From 1867, the German Imperial Marines were strictly an infantry unit. The *Seebataillon* survived the transition from confederation to imperial troops in 1871. The numbering of the units began with the 1st in 1883, followed by the 2nd in 1889 and the 3rd in 1898. The *Seebataillonen* began to see service in the German African and overseas colonies – the 3rd Sea Battalion was called in as part of the Allied Relief Expedition during the Boxer Rebellion of 1900, and after that was stationed in the German colony of Tsingtao, China. On 29 August 1914, the 1st and 2nd Sea Battalions, home-based in Wilhelmshaven, were assigned to a special Naval Division, which also included units of the Marine Artillery and some other naval formations. Throughout World War I the Naval Division fought in most of the battles on the Western Front, including Flanders. On 10 November 1914, the 3rd Sea Battalion surrendered to Japanese Forces after a spirited defense of Tsingtao – losing one-third of Germany's marine force in the process. With the Armistice on 11 November 1918, the *Seebataillonen* were no more. When the German armed forces were reorganized in 1919, no provision was made for Marine Infantry.

Beginning in 1850, the uniform worn by units of the *Seebataillon* consisted of a dark-blue tunic with self-colored collar and Brandenburg cuffs. The front of the coat, collar, and the three-button scalloped skirt pocket flaps were piped in white. Officers wore white-piped cuff patches and a loop of old Guard lace on the collar. On the officers' epaulettes and other ranks' white shoulder-straps was a foul anchor. The trousers were dark blue with white piping. From 1856 to 1867, there existed a special *Seeartillerieabteilung*. It wore the same uniform as the *Seebataillon*, but with black collar and cuffs. Anchors with two crossed cannon barrels above them were worn on the shoulder-straps. Until 1862, the *Seebataillonen* wore a *Pickelhaube* like that of the line artillery, with a brass plate. This was replaced with a blue-covered felt shako with a black leather peak, bearing a bronze anchor badge with the motto "MIT GOTT FÜR KOENIG UND VATERLAND". The shako plate was altered in 1875 with the addition of the imperial eagle over the anchor, and brass chinscales were added to the shako. In 1883 the shako was modified with leather front and rear peaks. Officers' shakos were of black cloth, while those of other ranks were of lacquered leather. For full dress a black plume – red for musicians – was worn on the shako. Initially, the dark-blue visored cloth caps with white piping around the top of the band were worn with the initials "KM" on the front. In 1875 white bands and piping around the top were introduced to the cap. From 1854 a cockade was worn, with the national colors of red, white and black becoming standard after 1871.

From 1875 white collars and cuffs were worn on the tunic, and in 1888 officers and men adopted two loops of Guard lace on the collar and three on the cuff patches. The Guard lace was in gold for officers and yellow for the men. An imperial crown over two crossed anchors was affixed to the men's shoulder-straps and the officers' epaulette crescent. After a while, battalion designations in Roman numerals were added below the crossed anchors. Officers wore a gold imperial crown on their shoulder-straps. From 1906 onwards the lapels for officers were faced with white. On the field-grey Model 1910 Uniform the *Seebataillon* wore white piping on the cuffs, shoulder-straps, front of the coat and collar, with yellow Guard lace on the collar and cuff patches. The shoulder-strap for enlisted men consisted of an imperial crown over crossed anchors and the battalion designation in yellow embroidery. With the adoption of the Model 1915 Field Blouse the men wore yellow Guard lace on a white collar patch. The *Seebataillon* wore the same greatcoat as the Army. Leather equipment and footwear were black. For service in China and other tropical climates, khaki uniforms were worn, with a stand-and-fall collar and shoulder-straps. In addition, a tropical helmet bearing the brass shako plate of the *Seebataillon* was worn with the uniform. A national cockade was fixed below the plate. Leather equipment and footwear were brown.

During the Boxer Rebellion, Germany provided troops for the Allied armies waging the various campaigns in China. At the start of the Rebellion in June 1900, there were sailors from the East Asian Squadron, the 3rd Sea Battalion, a Kommando detachment, and a battery of Marine Horse Artillery. The East Asia Brigade, consisting of two infantry brigades, was quickly established and sent off to China under the command of General Graf von Waldersee. In addition, there was a Field Artillery Regiment, a mounted regiment of Uhlans, and a pioneer battalion with railroad-engineer and telegraph companies. Sanitation, train, munitions, and other support troops completed the complement of the East Asia Brigade. General von Waldersee's forces arrived at Taku on 21 September 1900 and remained in China until 7 September 1901 and the official declaration of the end of hostilities. The remaining troops of the East Asia Brigade and of the 3rd Sea Battalion returned to Tsingtao.

The uniforms of the East Asia Brigade were officially field-grey, but a wide variety of materials, shades, and styles were worn by the troops. Generally, the *Litewka* or jacket was of a slightly darker shade than the trousers and the hat. The Model 1892 *Litewka* was of field-grey cloth and fastened down the front by six horn buttons. There were four large pockets on the front of the jacket and, unusually, two on the rear. To improve wear, the two lower pockets were lined with leather and were intended for carrying cartridges. For all branches the collar, front seam of the jacket, and pocket flaps were piped in poppy red. The Jägers' jacket piping was light green. Reversible shoulder-straps were used for both field and garrison duties. For garrison duty the shoulder-straps used the following colors and emblems: infantry had white with the unit's number stitched in red, Jägers light green, cavalry poppy red, artillery poppy red with a red grenade, pioneer poppy red with a red "P", and railroad troops poppy red with a red "E" and lightning bolt. When in the field, troops reversed their shoulder-straps to show the field-grey body piped in either light green for Jägers or poppy red for all other branches. In addition, the Model 1893 *Litewka* was used by some troops. The jacket was dark blue, a front flap concealing the six horn buttons, and was issued with and without four flap pockets on the front. The shoulder-straps previously mentioned were also used with this coat, although the reverse for field use was dark blue. This coat and its later variants would later influence the adoption of the Model 1915 Field Blouse during World War I. Khaki uniforms for summer service were basically the same styles used by the *Schutztruppe* and *Seebataillon*. Shoulder-strap colors remained the same for field and garrison duties when worn on the khaki uniforms.

The most common headgear worn by members of the East Asia Brigade and colonial troops was the tropical helmet or *tropenhelm*, a khaki cloth helmet with a cork body and removable ventilator. The frontplate was of imperial colonial style in brass. The *Waffenfarbe* coloration on the cap band denoted branch of service, white for infantry and black with red piping for artillery, and a national tricolored cockade was affixed to the right side of the helmet. The cloth neck flap or havelock was removable, and designed to protect the wearer's neck from the South China sun. Troops also wore a floppy straw hat with the brim turned up and pinned to the wearer's right side; it sported a large German national cockade and, immediately beneath, a small cockade of the soldier's home province.

In addition, enlisted members of the Imperial German East Asiatic Infantry wore a *Pickelhaube* consisting of a grey-green cloth cover over a leather body with grey leather-beaded front and rear visors. It had a brass-trimmed spike, base, and stud retainers, a brass colonial eagle and grey leather chinstrap with brass fittings secured to Model 1891 Posts. The frontplate was common to all imperial colonial units. A single *Reichskokarde* was worn on the helmet's right side. Contingents from the other German provinces that formed the East Asiatic Forces used this helmet, with their respective state helmet plates and cockade. The following brass plates have been observed with the East Asiatic *Pickelhaube*: Baden, 92nd Brunswick Regiment (1st and 2nd Battalions), Prussia (Regiments 74, 77, 78, 164 and 165) and Württemberg.

The Imperial German East Asiatic Jäger and other enlisted services wore a shako whose helmet body was composed of green leather with green cloth sides. The frontplate was the familiar brass colonial service eagle. A brown leather chinstrap with brass buckles was worn, secured to brass Model 1891 Posts. The field badge or cockade was in black, white and red, as befits colonial troop units. The Jägers adopted a flat-topped sun helmet for their tropical kit, apparently attempting to pattern it after their shako. The body was khaki over cork with a reinforced, stitched bead on the front visor and a flip-up rear visor. The helmet plate, in brass, was the colonial services eagle. The top of the helmet was a ventilator button, and a cockade was secured to the right-hand side of the helmet. A color band was also used.

With the outbreak of World War I in August 1914, Germany sent troops to aid her allies of the Austro-Hungarian and Turkish Empires. Regular German forces were sent to Palestine, Sinai, Bulgaria, Macedonia, and Greece. Many of the troops were issued with khaki drill uniforms, or had normal continental uniforms modified for hot climates.

Troops serving in Macedonia and Palestine wore tropical helmets in brown drill with or without the colonial-style imperial German eagle plates commonly worn by the *Schutztruppen*. In addition, a helmet band was worn with a large national cockade affixed to the front or side, similar to those worn during the Boxer Rebellion – many might have been surplus items from that conflict. The color of the helmet band was white for infantry and black with red piping for artillery. Later, General der Kavallerie Otto Liman von Sanders, commanding the German troops in Palestine, issued orders for the tropical helmet to be replaced by a brown drill cap, to avoid confusion with British troops who wore similar headgear. These caps were worn with or without removable havelocks and were fashioned with brown leather chinstraps and visors. The cap bands were black with red piping for artillery, plain drill for infantry, and blue with red piping for train troops. The caps were designated as the Model 1916 Tropical Cap with regular peak and the Model 1918 Tropical Cap with the larger peak.

The uniform was varied but consisted mainly of a lightweight khaki drill jacket. The brown drill jackets had turned-down collars, breast and hip pockets, and six metal buttons down the front. Another version was similar in construction but had only two hip pockets and no breast pockets. A notable feature of these tunics was the clear stitching of field-grey thread on the hip pockets and the front of the coat. This becomes even more distinctive when the tunic has faded, almost to a yellowish color, under the blazing desert sun of the Middle East. Today many military historians and collectors apply the term Model 1916 Tropical Tunic to the above-mentioned pieces in order to differentiate those used by the Colonial, Marine, Naval, and East Asia Expeditionary Forces. The following shoulder-straps were used with the khaki tunic: artillery had scarlet piping and red grenades or numerals; infantry had either piping in army corps colors with red numerals or plain khaki; medical troops had dark-blue piping; train had blue piping. Trousers were of the same material as the jackets and were worn with puttees and brown ankle boots. Surplus colonial uniforms and equipment were also utilized by these troops.

Troops serving on the Macedonian and Serbian Fronts wore a felt ersatz spiked helmet. It was an all-pressed-felt construction with pressed-felt visors. A field-grey "pewter" metal regimental unit plate was secured to the front of the helmet, bearing the designation "R 22" (22nd Infantry Regiment). It had field-grey Model 1891 Posts with a matching spike base and ventilation top, and a black leather chinstrap with grey metal lugs and buckles. In addition troops wore another modified *Pickelhaube* variant made of cork and with a white cloth covering. The fittings were of wartime "pewter", and consisted of a spike base with a lug mount showing and a grey metallic frontplate with a regimental designation only. A brown leather chinstrap was worn, secured by alated side-split brad retainers. The havelocks made for these helmets are particularly interesting.

As the German states were united and collectively became a colonial power in Africa and the Pacific, the German soldier became the symbol of the nation's prestige and honor. Many nations around the world, especially in Latin America, admired the professionalism of the Teutonic militaristic bearing of the Imperial German Army. Military missions from Germany were sent all over the world to train foreign armies, many of which adopted the military uniforms, equipment and even the military traditions of the German Army. To this day one can still see Chilean or Ecuadorean soldiers dressed in Imperial Prussian-style uniforms and *Pickelhauben*, as well as bandsmen carrying "Jingling Johnnies" and goose-stepping down the main boulevards during national events. Throughout the twentieth century the Mauser bolt-action rifle was the weapon of choice for most nations of the world, and was only replaced by the Russian AK-47/AKM-style assault rifles in the latter part of the century. The golden era of German influence on other countries' uniforms, equipment and weapons began with Germany's victory in the Franco-Prussian War and ended with the Armistice and the abdication of Kaiser Wilhelm II. Civil war and social upheaval followed, after which Germany's fledgling democracy emerged. The military itself underwent changes, reinventing itself several times, and appeared to be in search of its soul – looking for a clear purpose to its existence in a world its monarch had now departed. In less than two decades the German Army would find its long-awaited Messiah – Adolf Hitler.

ALEJANDRO M. DE QUESADA

COLOR ILLUSTRATIONS

Above. A Prussian soldier from one of the Guard Regiments with a Model 1860 *Pickelhaube*, photographed in 1866

Above right. A soldier from the 1st Bavarian Infantry Regiment wearing the Prussian-style uniform adopted in 1872. Note the *Raupenhelm* or "Caterpillar" helmet on the left

Right. A soldier from Hessen wearing the Prussian-blue uniform with Swedish-style cuffs prescribed for artillery and pioneers. Note the cockade colors of white and red for Hessen. He is wearing a crowned belt-buckle and black belt

Above. Prussian artillerymen posing with their fieldpiece. Note the ball on top of their *Pickelhauben*

METZ. - La Compagnie des Drapeaux
Abmarschieren der Fahnenkompagnie nach Frescaty
N° 497 - Edité par G. Forissier, Metz

Far left. Prussian infantrymen wearing the blue tunics that were adopted by most of the German Confederation after 1872. Note the straight French-style cuffs, often referred to as Brandenburg-style, even though they have a more "scalloped" appearance. They are wearing musicians' wings on their shoulders

Left. Bavaria adopted the *Pickelhaube* in 1886, although it differed slightly from those used by the other states. One distinctive feature was the squared front visor, similar to the type used by the Dragoons. This soldier is with the 2nd Bavarian Infantry Regiment

Above. Prussian musicians leading a detachment of standard bearers carrying their regimental standards. Note the use of gorgets by the standard bearers

Right. A soldier serving with the Prussian 7th Infantry Line Regiment

Above left. A guardsman from the 1st Prussian Guard Dragoon Regiment. He has yellow Guard lace on his collar and the crowned cipher "VIR" in yellow on his red shoulder-straps

Above. This soldier is from the 1st Guards Field Artillery Regiment, and is wearing parade dress. Note the Swedish-style cuffs with the Guards' double *Kapellenlitzen* on his cuffs, as well as on his tunic and greatcoat collars

Left. A soldier from one of the Guard Regiments

Above. Without braid around the collar, the color discs indicate that this soldier is a corporal. He is armed with the Model 1898a Bayonet. A bayonet is affixed with a bayonet knot, or portepee, bearing the distinctive colors of one of the companies of his regiment

Above right. A trooper of the Gardes du Corps in court gala dress. The ceremonial duties of the Gardes du Corps were restricted to specially selected officers, NCOs and troopers of the Leib-Kompanie and the Trumpet Corps. Special uniforms were required for these duties. The sailor is from the SMS *Vineta*, and is wearing the naval parade uniform commonly referred to as a "monkey suit" by the sailors

Right. A lance-corporal of the 3rd Hussar Regiment, as distinguished by the regimental colors of the soldier's cap and *Attila*

Kaiser Friedrich III wearing the uniform and cuirass of the one of the Guard Cuirassier Regiments. Amongst the awards, decorations and orders is the Pour le Mérite, commonly referred to as the "Blue Max", one of Prussia's and later imperial Germany's most coveted decorations

Left. Kaiser Friedrich III wearing the double-breasted *Leibrock* tunic prescribed for senior officers with the shoulder-boards for Field Marshal. He is wearing the Grand Cross to the Iron Cross and the Iron Cross First Class

Right. Major Leutwein of the *Schutztruppe* wearing the early French-style, Chasseur-style Kepi

Below. Soldiers serving in the colonial forces (*Kaiserliche Schutztruppen*) in Africa wore distinctive upturned-brimmed campaign hats and brown uniforms usually made of corduroy

Opposite above left. A major of the *Schutztruppe* wearing the Colonial Service Field Uniform. The blue band on his cap signifies German Southwest Africa

Opposite above right. A soldier from the East Asia Brigade wearing the upturned-brimmed straw hat and light-weight field jacket

Opposite below. Training new native recruits for an *askari* unit in German Southwest Africa

Above. *Askaris* serving in German East Africa. All are wearing the brown Colonial Service and Field Uniforms. Note the fez with havelock. They are armed with the obsolete Infantry Rifle Model 1871/84

Below. *Askari* field musicians in German East Africa wearing distinctive musician's wings on their shoulders. The Red Cross badge worn by the drummer on the right is that of the *Sanitätsunterpersonal* or enlisted medical personnel

Opposite above. *Askaris* of the *Schutztruppe* in German Cameroon wearing the distinctive red fez with the imperial German eagle plate on the front. Note the red chevrons of the seated *Unteroffizier* or sergeant

Opposite below. Chinese soldiers serving in the German colonial forces in China being supervised by a member of the East Asian Regiment. Note the mixture of native dress with German equipment

Right. Members of a Saxon Jäger unit wearing their distinctive shakos. Note the equipment being carried by these soldiers

Below. A Bavarian machine-gun company posing with their Maxim MG-08 Machine Guns on sled mounts

Above. Maxim Machine Guns with shields being used in the trenches. During World War I the *Pickelhaube* would be replaced by the steel helmet

Below. A fallen Dragoon trooper being assisted by a comrade. The Dragoon Tunic was cornflower blue for all except for the Hessian (23rd and 24th) Regiments. He is armed with a lance and a Model 1889 Cavalry Saber bearing the state emblem of Prussia on the hilt

Right. An artilleryman wearing his distinctive *Pickelhaube.* Note the black facing with red piping on the collar and cuffs of his service tunic

Above. A soldier's life. These infantrymen are wearing fatigue uniforms while doing their laundry and polishing their marching boots. The headgear being worn is sometimes referred to as a *Krätzchen* Field Cap

Below. A supply battalion's field bakery at work. A light-blue band and piping were worn on the field caps of the officers and men

FEEDING THE MEN IN THE TRENCHES—A GERMAN FIELD BAKERY
PHOTO © UNDERWOOD & UNDERWOOD, N.Y.

Above. A patriotic image showing a soldier wearing the Model 1910 Field Tunic with Saxon-style cuffs and bearing a flag. His oversized standard-bearer's gorget may be a photographer's prop

Above. An excellent view of the field cap worn by this enlisted man with his Model 1910 Field Uniform. The national cockade of black, white and red was placed over the state cockade, which bore its own colors

Below. Crown Prince Wilhelm inspecting captured French soldiers. Note the variety of uniforms being worn by the German officers and men

Above. A Military Policeman or Feldgendarm wearing the dark-green Model 1889 Police Tunic with Swedish-style cuffs. He has guard *litzen* and gold NCO collar-and-cuff edging braid. The infantryman on the right is wearing the Model 1910 Field Tunic with Brandenburg-style cuffs and is armed with a Gewehr 1898 Rifle

Below. French Dragoons with captured German Uhlans and Dragoons. Note the difference in uniforms

Above left. A soldier from a Landsturm Battalion guarding a pair of captured French Zouaves. Note that the soldier is wearing the dark-blue Model 1893 *Litewka* and is armed with a Gewehr 1888 Rifle

Above. Gefreiter Adolf Hitler, seated on the far right, served with the 16th Bavarian Reserve Infantry Regiment. Most are wearing the modified Model 1910 Tunics usually referred to as Model 1910/15 Tunics (Simplified)

Left. German officers in field uniforms serving in the Balkans

1

THE
GERMAN EMPIRE
(1871–1914)

Above left. A Prussian soldier of the 35th Brandenburg Fusilier Regiment in 1863. In the campaigns of 1864, 1866 and 1870–1, it had become usual to wear the trousers inside the boots while on service. The soldier is armed with a Dreyse Needle Rifle, Model 1862, and is carrying a Prussian Model 1860 Fusilier Bayonet

Above. A sapper of the 3rd Infantry Regiment Number 102 from Saxony in 1863. Wearing a similar uniform to that worn by Saxon artillerymen, his buttons are in silver instead of gold. He has his regimental number on the pompom situated on the top of his oilcloth-covered shako. Note the red, crossed pick-axes on his sleeve and the distinctive apron

Left. Kaiser Wilhelm I at the time of the Franco-Prussian War. He is seen wearing the Model 1860 *Pickelhaube* with regimental guard plate. The uniform is an officer's double-breasted frock coat, which was generally the same for all arms, being of the same color as the tunic, with a plain collar and piping on the cuffs and sometimes on the skirts as well

Above left. A Prussian infantryman in full campaign rig, *c.*1870. He is wearing the Model 1868 Line Infantry *Pickelhaube* with rounded visor

Above. A Prussian infantry NCO in 1870. His NCO lace can be seen around the collar and Brandenburg-style cuffs. To his side is his sword, which all NCOs were entitled to wear. Amongst his many decorations is a ribbon bar – the coveted ribbon of the Iron Cross Second Class, which is placed first as his highest decoration. Clearly visible is the belt-buckle or *koppelschloss* that is designated as the Model 1847

Left. A Bavarian field medic with oilcloth-covered cap in 1870. He is armed with a brass-hilted artillery short sword or *Artillerie-Faschinenmesser*. Note the Red Cross emblem on his overcoat's shoulder-straps and armband

Above. A member of an Oldenburg Infantry Regiment in 1866. His blue tunic has red-piped pointed cuffs with a button at the point. Russian-style soft caps with red piping were adopted in 1864. He is armed with an early-model Dreyse Rifle with the Model 1839 Socket Bayonet. To his side he is carrying an infantry short sword designated as the *Infanterie-Faschinenmesser* Model 1840. After 1867, Oldenburg troops wore Prussian line-infantry uniforms with light-blue piping around the cuff patches and white shoulder-boards with a red crowned "P"

Above right. A Posen Landwehr NCO in 1870. He is carrying his *Pickelhaube* with royal cipher plate. Note the distinctive early screw posts on both sides of the helmet used to secure the chinstraps. Partially visible is the brass hilt of his Model 1817/69 Infantry Sword, which was heavily influenced by the Napoleonic War-era French Model 1803 Infantry Sword

Right. A member of a Mecklenburg-Schwerin Regiment in 1870. He is wearing a Prussian-style tunic with the distinctive *Kapellenlitzen* and is carrying the Model 1817/69 Infantry Sword. Note the white horsehair plume on his Model 1860 *Pickelhaube*

Above left. Tintype image of a Prussian infantryman armed with a Gewehr 1888 Rifle. He is holding his canteen. We can also see the back of another soldier who did not get out of the way when the photograph was taken. We can clearly see his mess-kit, Model 1887 Knapsack and Model 1871 Bayonet. Initially made for the *Infanterie-Gewehr* Model 1871 Rifle, it was reissued with the Model 1888 Commission Rifle

Above. A soldier from a Prussian Guard Regiment in 1870. Black horsehair plumes on his *Pickelhaube* were used for special occasions and parades

Left. A Prussian artilleryman with a Model 1874 Artillery Saber. Note the Swedish cuffs, black with red piping, on his tunic. The horsehair plume for the *Pickelhaube* is typical of those reserved for Line Horse Artillery Regiments

Above. This Prussian artilleryman has the Model 1860 *Pickelhaube* with the distinctive ball spike, *c.*1866. Of interest are the Brandenburg cuffs on his tunic designating him as part of the Foot Artillery (*Fuss-Artillerie*). Partially visible on his left hip is the brass hilt of his artillery short sword (*Artillerie-Faschinenmesser*)

Above right. The Prince of Hesse in the uniform of the Guard Fusilier Regiment (known as the 2nd Guard Regiment after 1830). He is wearing the Prussian-type uniform adopted in 1872, a dark-blue tunic with red piping. The pointed cuffs, also piped in red, were of basic color. On each side of the collar were two white lace loops with buttons. The buttons were in white metal. Note the distinctive rampant lion plate on the Prussian-pattern *Pickelhaube*

Right. A classic image of a Bavarian soldier with his "Caterpillar" helmet or *Raupenhelm*. The red padded wings replaced the shoulder-straps in 1860. The uniform represented here remained regulation until 1872, when Bavaria adopted the Prussian-style tunic. The distinctive helmet was replaced by the *Pickelhaube* in 1886

Above left. A priest who probably served as a military chaplain for the German Army during the Franco-Prussian War. Clearly visible is the Iron Cross Second Class with the distinctive ribbon for non-combatant recipients

Above. A Prussian Hussar, with the distinctive tunic of that service, in 1870. He is armed with the Model 1867 Cavalry Saber

Left. This officer is wearing the Prussian-style double-breasted tunic which was adopted in 1856 and remained in service, with slight changes, until 1900. The barrel cuffs were piped in red. Rank was displayed with a series of star pips on the crescent-shaped epaulettes. The upper portions of the epaulettes have a lace edging. During the short reign of Kaiser Frederick III (1883) epaulettes were not worn

Above. The Gewehr 1871 Rifle was adopted by Prussia on 14 February 1872 and became the standard rifle for troops of the German Empire. As these rifles became obsolescent, many were issued to the native troops of the imperial German colonial forces (*Schutztruppe*) and saw extensive service during World War I. This weapon accepted the Model 1865/71 (*Pionier-Faschinenmesser*) and 1871 Bayonets

Above right. The Gewehr 1871/84 Rifle was basically the same as the Model 1871 Rifle, with the addition of an eight-round tubular magazine. The rifle was short-lived and eventually replaced by the Commission Model 1888 Rifle. This rifle accepted the Model 1871/84 Bayonet, whose blade was much shorter and would become the basic design for future German bayonets

Right. A member of the 10th Field Artillery Regiment from Oldenburg, *c.*1867. The service tunic is the same as for infantry, except that the shoulder-straps and piping are red. Note the distinctive pointed cuffs with the button at the point. The grey trousers, introduced in 1858, are piped in red. Across the soldier's lap is a Model 1817/69 Infantry Short Sword, which was used by members of the foot artillery as well

Above left. Kaiser Wilhelm I wearing the double-breasted *Leibrock* tunic that nearly reached his knees. The tunic worn by General Staff officers was dark blue with a crimson collar, cuffs, piping and background to the epaulettes. Note the Kaiser's Field Marshal's shoulder-boards

Above. Kaiser Friedrich III wearing the double-breasted *Waffenrock*. The service or field cap was worn as well as the normal infantry helmet, a white plume being added when in full dress. Note the Grand Cross to the Iron Cross and the Pour le Mérite

Left. Kaiser Friedrich III in the uniform of the Guard Cuirassier Regiment

Opposite. Various images of Paul von Hindenburg, from a cadet in Wahlstatt to a senior officer serving in the General Staff during the second half of the nineteenth century. The changes in uniform through the years and his rise through the ranks are evident

Als Kadett in Wahlstatt

Als frischgebackener Leutnant im 3. Garde=Regiment zu Fuß

Hauptmann im Großen Generalstab

So rückte er 1870 ins Feld

Als Bataillonsadjutant im 3. Garde=Regiment zu Fuß

Above left. Professor Wilms taught chemistry in the Prussian Military Academy in Lichterfelde near Berlin. Note the distinctive lace on the collar of his tunic

Above. Paul von Hindenburg as a cadet in Berlin. He first saw action in Königgrätz in 1866

Left. General Otto von Bismarck in undress or field uniform, 1870–1

Below right. An NCO from the 25th Field Artillery Regiment wearing musician's wings or "Swallow's Nests" (*Schwalbennester*). Note the regimental ciphers embroidered on his shoulder-straps

Left. Paul von Hindenburg in the uniform of Generalmajor and as Chief of the General Staff of the 8th Armee Corps, Koblenz, 1897

Above. A Bavarian infantryman wearing the Prussian-style dark-blue service uniform that was adopted in 1872. The 1st Bavarian Army Corps had white piping around the cuff patches of the Brandenburg-style cuffs. Note the new service cap with the cockade bearing the colors of Bavaria (light blue and white). The soldier is armed with a Model 1871 Infantry Dress Bayonet

Above left. An NCO musician with a Model 1874 Artillery Saber

Above. A Prussian soldier from a Guard Regiment. He has a plumed Model 1860 *Pickelhaube*

Left. A Prussian infantryman with the Model 1868 *Pickelhaube*

Above. An infantryman from the 88th Infantry Regiment (1st Battalion Mainz; 2nd Battalion Hanau) wearing the blue tunic with red collar, piping and cuffs. The buttons were of plain gilt

Above right. An NCO attached to Telegraph Battalion 2-6, 8th Company, stationed in Metz in 1885. Note the script "T" over the "8" on his shoulder-strap

Right. An NCO from a Guard Telegraph Battalion. Note the Guard double *Kapellenlitzen* on the collar and the distinctive Telegraph Unit's emblem embroidered on his shoulder-straps

Left. In 1872 Bavaria adopted the Prussian-style uniform, but retained the distinctive *Raupenhelm*. The single crown on the shoulder-straps and Guard double *Kapellenlitzen* on the collar and cuffs identifies this soldier as serving in the Leib-Grenadier Regiment. He is armed with a Model 1871 Infantry Dress Bayonet

Right. A Lancer from a Prussian Uhlan Line Regiment. The coat worn by the Uhlans was dark blue for the Prussian and Württemberg Regiments, light blue for Saxons and green for Bavarians. Note the unique *czapka* with Prussian helmet plate being worn. The field badge or cockade on the mortar-board is white and black for Prussia

Left. A trooper from the 13th King's Uhlans Regiment from Hannover. Uhlan Regiments with light-blue facings had white-piped collars, cuffs and pockets. The trooper is holding a Model 1889 Cavalry Saber

Above. A rare view of the cuirass and protective helmet used in bayonet practice in the latter half of the nineteenth century, worn here by Bavarian soldiers. They are armed with the Gewehr 1888 Commission Rifle fixed with the Model 1871/84 Bayonet. By 1886 the distinctive Bavarian *Raupenhelm* had been replaced by a *Pickelhaube* bearing the coat of arms of the Kingdom of Bavaria

Above. A Prussian Lancer with the Model 1849 Artillery Saber that was commonly used by Uhlan and Hussar Regiments. Note the cloth belt worn with the tunic

Above right. Erbgroßherzog Adolf Friedrich von Mecklenburg in the uniform of the 1st Guard Uhlan Regiment, *c.*1900

Right. A Lancer from a Saxon Guard Uhlan Regiment, possibly the 21st Uhlan Regiment. His Model 1889 Cavalry Saber has the Saxon coat of arms on the hilt's guard

Gruſs aus der Sommerfrische, Zeithain.

Left. A Saxon NCO Lancer from the 2nd Saxon Uhlan Regiment (18th Uhlan Regiment). The Lancer jacket was light blue with crimson collar cuffs and lapels – which were buttoned back for full dress – while the overalls had crimson stripes. The 2nd had loops of yellow Guard lace on the collar. The *czapka* had the Saxon star on the front and a crimson cover underneath the mortarboard. The field badge or cockade was white and green

Below. Prussian Lancers of the 3rd Guard Uhlan Regiment. They wore yellow facings and piping on their tunics and *czapkas*. The NCOs are wearing stone-grey greatcoats. The collar patches of the greatcoats were in the regimental facing color and the shoulder-straps in the color of the epaulette field. The Prussian Guard Regiments had the double *Kapellenlitzen* on the collar patch, while the woven ciphers and numerals on their shoulder-straps were in yellow on red and crimson material; in all other cases they were red

Above left. An NCO in the uniform of the 11th Uhlan Regiment. His regimental number can be seen clearly on his crescent-shaped epaulettes

Above middle. A trooper from a Bavarian Chevauleger (Light Cavalry) Regiment. These troops were dressed basically the same way as Uhlans; they wore a steel-green (*stahlgrün*) uniform but a different type of headdress – in this case, the *Pickelhaube* and not the *czapka*. Note the Bavarian Lion on the hilt guard of the trooper's Model 1889 Cavalry Saber

Above right. A Prussian corporal from a Dragoon Regiment wearing his stone-grey greatcoat over his regimental uniform. The Dragoon single-breasted tunic was cornflower-blue for all regiments except the 23rd and 24th (Hessian) Regiments. The collar, collar patches, Swedish-style cuffs and shoulder-straps were in the regimental facing colors

Right. A member of a Leib-Gendarmerie or Military Police Unit

Left above. The double *Kapellenlitzen* on his collar and the script "E" on his shoulder-strap indicate that this NCO belongs to a Guard Train Regiment

Above. An Army administration official serving in the *kriegsministerium* (War Ministry). Note the distinctive collar insignia. The uniform of the General Staff and War Ministry resembled that of the General Officers in its cut and dark-blue color. The collar, Swedish-style cuffs and all piping, however, were carmine. The collar and cuffs had two double loops of silver (General Staff) or gold (War Ministry) embroidery with bars of a leaf pattern on them. The buttons were white metal. The dark-blue trousers had triple red stripes

Left below. A Color Guard of the 17th Brunswick Hussar Regiment wearing service dress uniform. Note that he is wearing the distinctive regimental busby plate

Opposite above left. Archduke Ernst August of Brunswick in the service dress uniform of the 17th Brunswick Hussar Regiment

Opposite above right. A trooper of the 15th Hanoverian Hussar Regiment wearing gala uniform. Note the chevron on the corporal's right arm. The distinctive busby front plate of the 15th Hussars bears the battle honor "PENINSULA – WATERLOO – EL BODON – BAROSSA" on laurel leaves below the ribbon bearing the motto "MIT GOTT FÜR KOENIG UND VATERLAND"

Right. Standard bearers of a Prussian Hussar Line Regiment wearing the gala uniform with pelisses over their *Attila* (tunic). Note the use of gorgets by the troopers. All are wearing the "VATERLAND" ribbon on their busbies

Above left. A trooper from the 1st Prussian Leib-Hussar Regiment in gala uniform

Above. Crown Prince Wilhelm in the uniform of the 1st Leib-Hussar Regiment. Note the distinctive regimental skull plate on his busby and the pelisse coat hanging from his shoulders

Left. Crown Prince Wilhelm wearing the undress cap with its distinctive regimental skull insignia between the Prussian state and national cockades

Above. The Crown Prince wearing the pelisse of the Hussar Regiments

Right above. An excellent detailed study of the undress cap and pelisse. The undress cap was black with a red band and white piping

Right. A trooper from a Prussian Hussar Line Regiment. Note the distinctive black leather boots that are associated with the Hussars. The boots were ornamented at the top with white or yellow leather trim according to the button color, which formed a loop at the front. Officers wore patent-leather boots with gold or silver lace instead of braid. A rosette replaced the loop of the other ranks, who were also permitted to wear patent-leather boots for walking out

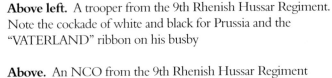

Above left. A trooper from the 9th Rhenish Hussar Regiment. Note the cockade of white and black for Prussia and the "VATERLAND" ribbon on his busby

Above. An NCO from the 9th Rhenish Hussar Regiment wearing the undress cap with regimental color and piping distinctions

Left. A trooper from the 9th Rhenish Hussar Regiment wearing the peakless undress cap

Opposite above left. This trooper is wearing the cornflower-blue *Attila* of the 9th Rhenish Hussar Regiment. The crown of his peakless undress cap was cornflower blue and the band was cornflower blue with yellow piping. He is armed with an 1879 Pattern Saber

Opposite above right. A Hussar trooper wearing the field-grey undress *Attila* that was instituted on 22 November 1909 and is usually referred to as the Model 1910 Hussar Field-Grey *Attila* Field Tunic. His sidearm is a Model 1884/98 Bayonet

Opposite below left. Crown Prince Wilhelm wearing the regimental gorget and uniform of the 2nd Queen's Cuirassier Regiment (Pomeranian). The gorget was presented to the regiment upon the 150th anniversary of the battle of Hohenfriedberg

Opposite below right. Regimental veterinarian in the uniform of the 4th Cuirassier Regiment, 1900

Above left. Colonel General Karl Einem in the white full-dress uniform of his *à la suite* commission to the 4th Cuirassier Regiment. The epaulettes of the former Minister of War bear the three stars of his rank

Above. An NCO from a Saxon Cuirassier Regiment wearing the white-plumed Pattern 1889 Enlisted-Style Cuirassier Helmet

Left. Bavarian Crown Prince Rupprecht wearing the uniform and distinctive regimental gorget of the 1st Great Elector Life Guard Cuirassier Regiment (Silesian)

Right. NCOs of the 3rd Baden Dragoon Regiment (22nd Dragoon Regiment) with an NCO of the Prussian Jäger zu Pferde Regiment. Dragoons wore cornflower-blue tunics with the regimental facing color on the collar. Dragoons wore *Pickelhauben* similar to those of the infantry, with a "squared" visor front and silver furniture on the helmet

Below right. As Germany approached the twentieth century, old and new were combined in the uniforms of the German Army. From the left, an artillery enlisted man in service uniform, as indicated by the distinctive ball on top of his *Pickelhaube* and the shoulder-strap of the 16th Field Artillery Regiment; a senior officer wearing the field-grey field uniform that was adopted in 1910; and an Uhlan wearing the distinctive *czapka*

Far right. A Prussian infantryman of the 4th Grenadier Regiment armed with the Model 1888 Commission Rifle. He is wearing the 1891 Pattern *Pickelhaube* with the visor trim in place. The chinscales confirm that this soldier is an NCO. He is wearing the dark-grey greatcoat (introduced in 1867) with collar patches and shoulder-straps

Above. Members of the 1st Guard Regiment of Foot wearing their parade-style helmets. All are armed with the Gewehr Model 1888 Commission Rifle

Far left. A Guard NCO in a stone-grey greatcoat. He is armed with the Model 1879 or Model 1883 Commission Revolver, and an officer-style sword used by NCOs

Left. soldier from one of the Guard Infantry Regiments wearing Brandenburg-style cuffs on his tunic

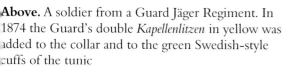

Above. A soldier from a Guard Jäger Regiment. In 1874 the Guard's double *Kapellenlitzen* in yellow was added to the collar and to the green Swedish-style cuffs of the tunic

Above right. An infantryman of the 115th Leib-Guard Infantry Regiment. His shoulder-strap has the initials "EL" for Ernst Ludwig. Note the distinctive belt-buckle for Hessen-Darmstadt

Right. Guardsmen of the 1st Dragoon Regiment and of a Guard Infantry Regiment. The soldier in the middle is wearing the green tunic with the Guards yellow Kapellenlitzen for a Guard Schutzen unit. The Guard Schützen units wore Brandenburg-style cuffs while the Jäger units used the Swedish-style cuffs

Above. An NCO from the 25th Dragoon Regiment in service uniform. The 17th, 18th, 23rd and 25th Dragoon Regiments had the distinction of wearing the Guard *litzen* on the collar and cuffs of their button collar. The 119th Grenadier Regiment wore a similar device on the shoulder-strap, but with different colors and facings

Above. An enlisted man from the 109th Leib-Grenadier Regiment. Note the use of the state and national cockades on the peakless field cap

Above. Men and officers from the 1st Tsar Alexander Guard Regiment marching through a Berlin street. The distinctive Miter Cap or Grenadier/Fusilier Cap for this regiment bore the Guard star under a king's crown. The 1st Foot Guards wore a similar cap

Right. A gathering of dignitaries and officers from the Guards Regiments. A senior officer of the 1st Foot Guards wearing the Miter Cap is seen conferring with a member of the Guard Infantry Regiment. The latter is wearing the Model 1910 Field-Grey Tunic

Below. Generalfeld-marschall August von Mackensen reviewing Saxon standard bearers of various regiments. Of particular interest is the Model 1890 Cavalry Guard's Helmet with a lion mounted on the top. The helmet's silver lion was awarded to the Garde-Reiter Regiment in 1907 and was to be worn when in full dress

Above left. A Bavarian Halberdier in full dress uniform with the outer vest of the Garde du Corps, serving in the royal palace of the Bavarian king, 1890s

Above. A trooper of the Prussian Garde du Corps wearing the distinctive Butcher Boots, which rose above the knee, adopted in 1856. He is wearing the red vest or *supraweste* bearing the Guard's star emblem on the front

Left. The 1889 Pattern Garde du Corps Parade Helmet had a tall, tombak Cuirassier-style body, with German silver trim on the visor. The front plate consisted of a silvered Guard star with the motto of the Black Eagle Order, *"suum cuique"* (Each to his own). The parade crowned eagle is of silver on an oval base secured with silvered plain retainer studs. Large convex tombak chinscales were secured to the helmet by Model 1894 Posts. Note that this soldier is wearing a cuirass

Above left. A Prussian soldier from the 2nd Squadron of the King's Gendarmerie wearing court dress, 1890s. The white tunic had red lapels and white lace patches with buttons

Above middle. A corporal of the Württemberg Royal Palace Company of Guards, 1890s

Above right. A Prussian corporal in the uniform of the Palace Guard Company. The uniform did not change much between 1829 and 1914

Right. A Prussian captain of the Palace Guard Company

Far right. A Prussian sergeant of the Palace Guard Company. During the nineteenth century Prussian kings had the same kind of fondness for their uniforms as they did during the era of Frederick the Great. Kaiser Wilhelm II had numerous court celebrations in the historical costumes of Frederick's day

Above. Members of a signals unit in service dress. Note the crossed signal-flag insignia on the soldier's sleeve on the far left

Below. Mounted artillerymen wearing ball-top *Pickelhauben*

Right. Artillerymen wore basically the same uniform as the infantry, but with some differences, such as the use of the Swedish-style cuffs instead of the Brandenburg-style cuffs, and the ball instead of the spike on the helmet. This soldier is wearing the white leather belt with the open-face buckle normally used by cavalry units

Below. A close-up of an artillery officer from Saxony. The white-and-green state cockade is clearly visible on the left side of his helmet. He is wearing the officer's undress uniform with his stone-grey greatcoat

Below right. A member of the Field Artillery wearing the peakless undress cap. He is holding an 1874 Pattern Artillery Saber

Right. An artilleryman from the 39th Field Artillery. Note the flaming bomb and regimental number embroidered in red on the black shoulder-straps

Below. A group of NCOs from the 75th Infantry Regiment. Of particular interest is the Prussian standard bearer with his distinctive gorget and arm-shield (*see inset*). The standard bearer's arm-shield and gorget were first introduced for use by the German Army in an *Allerhöchste Kabinetts-Ordre* (AKO) dated 15 June 1898. There were variations used by the German states and some elite units. The arm-shield ceased to exist in 1919 with the abdication of Kaiser Wilhelm II. Note the other soldiers with their shoulder-straps rolled, possibly for field maneuvers

FAHNEN & STANDARTEN DER METZER GARNISON
BEI DER PARADE AM 10. MAERZ - 1813-1913 - z. JAHRHUNDERTFEIER
ORIGINAL AUFN. V. FR. JOZIOR -METZ

Above. Regimental standard bearers of the Metz Garrison preparing for a ceremony, 1913. Note the use of the gorgets. The arm-shield for standard bearers is not worn on the greatcoat

Below. Soldiers of the 3rd Bavarian Infantry Regiment. Note the regimental standard bearer wearing his gorget and arm-shield (*see inset*). He would have had the Bavarian regimental standards and royal ciphers depicted on his badges of office

Above. A Prussian foot artilleryman armed with a Kar. 98a Rifle

Above right. A soldier from a Saxon Jäger unit wearing the unique shako and dark-green service dress. He is wearing the General Marksmanship Cord (*Allgemeine Schützenschnur*) that was introduced in 1894

Right. An enlisted man from the 73rd Fusilier Regiment Generalfeldmarschall Prinz Albrecht von Preussen (Hanoverian) wearing the "GIBRALTAR" cuff title (*see inset*). Other units entitled to wear the cuff title were the 79th Infantry Regiment von Voigts-Rhetz (3rd Hanoverian Infantry Regiment) and the 10th Hanoverian Jäger Battalion

Right. Prior to World War I, priests serving with the Army as chaplains normally wore their habits and an armband identifying their status. It was not until 1915 that a uniform for military chaplains was introduced. The chaplains wore a colonial-troop-style felt hat with the cross between the state and national cockades, and a distinctive field-grey frock coat without any rank insignia. In addition, the chaplain wore a chained cross of either a Catholic or Protestant style around his neck, and a violet armband

Below. King George V of Great Britain in the uniform of Colonel-in-Chief of the 8th Cuirassier Regiment Graf Gessler (Rhenish). Many senior officers, aristocrats and monarchs received *à la suite* commissions from elite regiments in various countries of Europe

Above. Princess Viktoria Luise of Prussia in the specially tailored uniform of Colonel-in-Chief of the 2nd Leib-Hussar Regiment. The Princess received her *à la suite* commission on 22 October 1909

Left. Kaiser Wilhelm II received many *à la suite* commissions from home and abroad. The Kaiser was a uniform enthusiast; he had many designed for himself and liked being depicted in the various uniforms in his collection. Here he is in the uniform of Field Marshal of the 1st Foot Guard Regiment. Note the specially tailored sleeve for his withered arm

Below. Kaiser Wilhelm II in the uniform of the 21st Uhlan Regiment (Kaiser Wilhelm II Koenig von Preussen 3 Saxon), for which he served as the Regimental Colonel-in-Chief. Note the Leib-Gendarme standard bearer with the Kaiser's personal standard, which was carried with him wherever he went

Above. An excellent study of the various styles of *Pickelhauben* and uniforms worn by senior officers surrounding the Kaiser

Right. A veteran Prussian Army Oberst in dress uniform. His gilt crescent-shaped epaulettes bore two rank stars and a regimental number. His decorations attest to his decades of service and campaigns, including fighting in the Franco-Prussian War

Above left. A Leutnant wearing the double-breasted Officer's Undress Uniform (*Leibrock*), 1880s

Above. Leutnant von der Linde wearing the service tunic. In time the tunic had been modified and new shoulder-boards were used. The new service tunic (*Waffenrock*) worn by this Leutnant remained in use well up to World War I

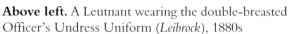

Left. A major of the 3rd Kgr. Elisabeth Garde Grenadier Regiment wearing the double-breasted *Waffenrock*. Of particular interest are the regimental insignia incorporated on the shoulder-board (*see inset*). Note the presence of the Pour le Mérite

Above left. Chief of the German General Staff Generaloberst Helmuth von Moltke's *à la suite* commission entitled him to wear this full dress uniform of the 1st Guard Grenadier Regiment

Above. A Saxon general's full dress gala uniform, worn by General der Infanterie d'Elsa

Left. Close-up of a Saxon general's full dress gala uniform, worn by General von Einem

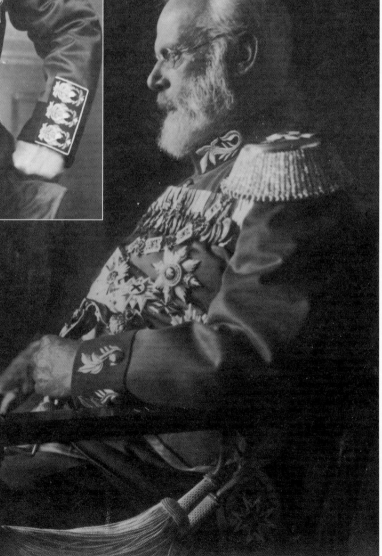

Left. Generaloberst Alexander von Kluck in the full dress uniform of his honorary commission in the 3rd Guard Grenadier Regiment

Right. King Ludwig III of Bavaria wearing his Bavarian field marshal's Model 1910 Parade Dress Uniform with the distinctive laurel-leaf pattern in silver bullion thread on a red patch. This distinctive Bavarian collar insignia and other variations were in use until 1916, when the Prussian Alt-Larisch pattern (in silver) was adopted by Bavarian generals

2

IMPERIAL GERMAN COLONIAL AND OVERSEAS TROOPS

Above. German *Schutztruppen* in various headgear and uniforms, c.1890. Clearly visible is the imperial German crown on the belt-buckle worn by the reclining sergeant. Note the use of a spike from a *Pickelhaube* by the NCO in the center

Right. Mounted troopers of the *Schutztruppe* wearing a variety of headgear, including the campaign slouch hat, the tropical busby of the Hussars, the spiked tropical helmets and the French-style kepis

Above left. *Schutztruppen* armed with Gewehr 1888 Rifles guarding a prisoner during the Herero uprising

Above. The Colonial Uniform Tunic in brown corduroy and the Colonial Service Uniform in brown drill. The piping of the campaign hat (as well as the band of the *feldmütze*), collar and cuffs were blue, denoting German Southwest Africa. Note the leather cartridge-belt rig for mounted troops and the mixture of the cotton drill uniform with the corduroy trousers of the standing Gefreiter

Left. A classic image of a member of the colonial troops serving in Africa. His leather cartridge-belt rig has a fixed bayonet frog. Note the bayonet knot (*Troddel*) on his left side, and a ring to attach a saber. He is armed with a Gewehr 1898 Rifle

Above left. A Feldwebel with removable chevrons. Most chevrons and insignia worn on the *Schutztruppe* uniform were attached with hooks on the back so that they could be easily removed. The buttons on the service uniform were also removable

Above middle. The brim of the grey felt campaign hat was hooked to the wearer's right side and a large *Reichskokarde* was then attached to the upturned brim. The sergeant's *feldmütze* was made of corduroy with a colored wool band denoting the colony in which the soldier was stationed. A single cockade bearing the national colors was worn on the field cap's band

Above right. While stationed in Germany, members of the *Schutztruppe* would wear a stone-grey *Waffenrock* or Uniform Tunic made of wool, commonly referred to as the *Heimatuniformen* or Home Uniform. Note the colored cuffs and collar as well as the Guard's lace. The Uniform Tunic was intended for parades, walking out, and for all ceremonial occasions

Right. A close-up of an NCO wearing the *Waffenrock*. Note the silver *litzen* around the collar

Left. Another view of the stone-grey Home Uniform, worn by a veteran NCO

Below. An excellent example of various uniforms used by the *Schutztruppe* in the African colonies. Next to the white fatigue uniforms is the colonial or tropical version of the *Litewka* and the stone-grey greatcoats with Guard-style collar tabs. All are wearing *feld-mützen*

Die Welt ist weit, die Welt ist schön.
Wer weiss, ob wir uns
Wiedersehn !

4437

Above left. A close-up of the tropical *Litewka* in brown corduroy. All shoulder-straps had a "V" pattern in black red, and white with or without a wool base in the color of the colony

Above right. Members of the *Schutztruppe* in greatcoat and Colonial Uniform Tunics

Left. An Oberleutnant in the *Schutztruppe*. The only visible signs of rank are his shoulder-boards and sword

Right. An NCO of the *Schutztruppe* in the Colonial Uniform Tunic and *feldmütze* of brown corduroy. The Colonial Uniform Tunics were usually used for parades, as walking-out dress, and for ceremonial occasions while serving in the colonies

Above. Artillerymen in various types of uniform and headgear servicing a cannon

Above. A senior officer in the *Schutztruppe* wearing the Colonial Officers' Service Uniform. He is wearing the stone-grey service cap worn with the Home Uniform Tunic. The cap's band and piping were in the colors of the colony where the soldier was serving, in this case German Southwest Africa

Below. A camel rider of the *Schutztruppe* serving in German Southwest Africa in 1905. Note his leather cartridge-belt rig and holster for his Gewehr 1898 Rifle

Above left. A mounted cavalryman in full rig that was basically the same as that of the camel riders

Above right. German police and colonial officials wore similar uniforms and headgear to those of the *Schutztruppe*. Seen here is a police officer (*Landespolizei*) serving in German Southwest Africa. Note his rank, displayed on the collar and shoulder-boards. Piping for police-force field caps and uniforms in the colony was green

Below. Officers and NCOs in the German colony of Cameroon wearing their white summer uniforms. Note the standard blue piping around the collar and down the front of the tunic. In Cameroon red piping was used for headgear, in Togo yellow piping

Above. The summer uniform was worn by the *Schutztruppe* in all of its African and tropical possessions. Colonial officials adopted variations of the uniform. Note the white shoes worn by the seated enlisted man

Below. A review of native troops or *askaris* of the *Schutztruppe* serving in Cameroon. The *askaris* are wearing the distinctive red-tasseled fez with the small colonial imperial German eagle plate. They are wearing khaki uniforms with red piping on the collar and cuffs. A red bar was worn on the collar as well. Native troops in Togo, or *Polizeitruppe*, wore the same headgear and uniform but with yellow piping. Note that the officers are wearing white tropical helmets and uniforms

Above. *Askaris* serving in German East Africa and German Southwest Africa wore similar uniforms to those in Cameroon, although they wore a taller fez in khaki. The khaki fez was made with neck flaps which protected the wearer from the sun

Right. This close-up of the previous photograph shows the khaki fez with neck flap in use. The *askaris* are armed with the obsolete Mauser M1871/84 Jägerbüsche Rifle that continued to see service throughout World War I. Note the puttees worn with brown leather ankle boots

Below. *Askari* regimental band in German East Africa. Some are wearing the distinctive "Swallow's Nest" on their shoulder, identifying them as military musicians

Above. When white colonial troops received new uniforms, their old tunics were handed down to the native troops. Seen here are native troops in German Southwest Africa wearing the old Colonial Uniform Tunics minus the Guard's lace on the collar and cuffs

Below. Another view of discarded Colonial Uniform Tunics being used by *askaris* in German Southwest Africa. On closer examination, the shaded areas can be seen where the Guard's lace had been on the collar and cuffs. They are all wearing the *feldmütze* in brown corduroy. It is believed that these uniforms were used for parades and special occasions in place of the khaki uniform issued only for field use

Above. Native police troops of Kaiser-Wilhelms-Land (German New Guinea). They did not wear much of a uniform, except for a visored cap with national cockade. When they were needed in the field the colonial authorities provided limited equipment consisting of an obsolete rifle, belt with cartridge box and a mess-kit

Below. A very interesting study of uniforms worn by the *Miokesen-Schutztruppe* in Kaiser-Wilhelms-Land (German New Guinea). They are wearing naval-style jumpers with khaki visored caps bearing the *Reichskokarde*. Note the NCO on the far right wearing a rank chevron on his left sleeve

Above. Police troops in German Samoa

Below. A native police officer in one of Germany's colonial possessions in the Pacific

Right. While a part of the Navy, the men of the *Seebataillonen* or Marines wore similar uniforms to their Army counterparts. Like the *Schutztruppe*, the Marines provided additional protection to the colonies as well as Germany's interests on the seas. A few officers, such as General Lettow von Vorbeck, had the distinction of serving in the Army, the *Schutztruppe* and the *Seebataillonen*. Note the imperial German eagle with anchor and the dark-blue parade dress uniform of the soldier. The collar tabs consisted of Guard lace in yellow gold on a white field

Above. German Marines wearing the Army-style dark-blue *Litewka* with the distinctive collar tabs. The dark-blue visorless field caps have a white band with the national cockade (*Reichskokarde*). Their shoulder-straps have an embroidered imperial crown over crossed anchors, with their battalion numbers in yellow thread

Right. German Marines, wearing khaki tunics without breast pockets, out on field maneuvers in the German colony of Kiautschou, China. Many have placed a band over the shako plates of their tropical helmets. The machine-gun crew is firing a Maxim MG-08 on a sled mount. In the distance is a gun crew carrying a machine gun in the field

Above left. During World War I the 1st and 2nd Sea Battalions served on the Western Front. They quickly adopted the Army's field uniforms based on the Model 1910 Service Tunic and the 1915 Field Blouse. The only distinctions from the uniforms of regular Army personnel were their collar tabs, shoulder-strap, and the white band with a single *Reichskokarde* on their caps

Above. Marines serving in tropical climates wore uniforms similar to those worn by colonial troops. However, there were differences in the style and cut, as well as the insignia. Note that his khaki tunic was made without breast pockets. He is wearing a shako plate on his tropical helmet

Left. A German Marine NCO of the 3rd Sea Battalion wearing musician's wings on his shoulders

Right. General Graf von Waldersee led the East Asia Brigade during the Boxer Rebellion of 1900–1. Here he is wearing the khaki uniform used by the German Expeditionary Forces. Of particular interest is his field cap, which shows very strong British influence, though with a *Reichskokarde* on the right side

Below. A bicycle troop from the 1st East Asia Brigade. They are wearing straw hats with the brim turned up and, attached to the side, the *Reichskokarde*, with the *Landeskokarde* immediately below it. Note the shoulder-strap with the numeral "1"

Below right. Members of the East Asia Brigade wearing the simple lightweight fatigue blouses and straw hats with *Reichskokarde*. Their stacked weapons are Gewehr 1898 Rifles

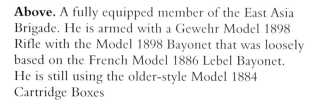

Above. A fully equipped member of the East Asia Brigade. He is armed with a Gewehr Model 1898 Rifle with the Model 1898 Bayonet that was loosely based on the French Model 1886 Lebel Bayonet. He is still using the older-style Model 1884 Cartridge Boxes

Above right. Prussian infantrymen of the East Asia Brigade preparing to be sent to China. In this excellent study of the field equipment used at the time of the Boxer Rebellion, the soldiers are all wearing the black leather Model 1895/1897 *Pickelhauben*. In 1895 a ventilator hole behind the spike base of the enlisted man's spiked helmet was added, and the use of both the national and state cockades became mandatory in 1897

Right. The black band with red piping around his tropical helmet identifies this soldier as an artillery-man. He is armed with the carbine version of the Gewehr Model 1898 Rifle (Kar. 98a) and a Model 1889 Cavalry Sword. Note the marksman lanyard on his *Litewka*

Above. This infantryman, as designated by the white band around his tropical helmet, is carrying the newer model cartridge pouch for the Mauser Rifle, adopted in 1898. Note the imperial German eagle plate on his tropical helmet. He is wearing the four-pocket field-grey *Litewka* with a concealed-button front flap down his tunic

Above. A review of the Allied forces in China by German and Russian officials. Of particular interest is the side view of the tropical helmets worn by the German infantrymen, with the white band and *Reichskokarde* affixed to the right side. The imperial Russian on the far left is armed with a Model 1891 Mosin-Nagant Rifle

Above. Imperial German engineers of the East Asia Brigade waiting to be sent to the field. Note how the long shovel is a part of their kit. Most are wearing just the *Reichskokarde* on their tropical helmets

Above. Members of the 1st East Asia Brigade wearing various styles of *Litewka* and headgear

Below. Members of the 2nd East Asia Brigade in khaki and field-grey *Litewkas*. The unique field-grey wool-covered leather *Pickelhaube*, made specially for the German Expeditionary Force to China, can be seen being worn by the soldier in the field-grey *Litewka* second from right. Note the musician's wings of the soldier standing to the rear of the group

Above. A group photograph of infantry and field artillery NCOs of the 2nd East Asia Brigade. Some of the artillerymen have black shoulder-straps with red piping and a chain-stitched script "F" on the straps. Note the distinctive cap bands – white and black with red piping – that designated the appropriate branches of service. The NCOs on the far right have the Model 1850 Artillery Officer's Swords, while the NCO second from left has a Saxon-style Officer's Sword

Below. An entourage of members of the East Asia Brigade and *Seebataillonen* watching German-raised Chinese troops fix bayonets to their Gewehr 1888 Rifles. Most of the obsolete equipment worn by the native troops, including the German-style belt-buckles and khaki uniforms, is of German origin. The uniforms worn by the Chinese soldiers are similar to those raised by the British (Her Majesty's 1st Chinese Regiment) during the Boxer Rebellion

Above left. This German senior NCO is serving with Turkish forces during World War I. He is wearing the German-influenced khaki uniform adopted by the Turkish Army. A former member of the *Schutztruppe*, he is wearing the imperial German ribbons for the Colonial Service and German Southwest Africa campaign medals. Note the distinctive Turkish helmet he is wearing: called a *kabalak*, it consists of a long cloth wound around a wickerwork base and resembles a sun helmet or solar topee

Above right. A German artillery officer serving with the Turkish Army. He is wearing the officer's version of the *kabalak* and the German-style Turkish officer's shoulder-boards. Note the flaming bombs device on his collars

Left. A German artilleryman serving in Palestine. He is wearing the Model 1915 Field Blouse and the tropical helmet with havelock. Note the imperial German helmet plate, the *Reichskokarde* on the side of the helmet and the distinctive black band with red piping for Artillery. He is armed with the Gewehr 1898 Rifle and the P.08 Automatic Pistol commonly known as the "Luger"

Above. Members of General Otto Liman von Sanders's Expeditionary Force to Palestine marching through the streets of Jerusalem. All are wearing khaki uniforms and tropical helmets with a large *Reichskokarde* on the front

Below. Another view of German troops in Palestine. Note the khaki visored field caps of the NCOs on the far right

Above. Burial of a comrade in the Holy Land. Note the various headgear worn by the German officers and enlisted men

Below. These two German soldiers are wearing lightweight khaki uniforms, and have adopted the standard headgear worn by the Arab population in Palestine

Right. Two enlisted men serving as field medics in Palestine. Both are wearing lightweight khaki uniforms and tropical helmets

Left. An enlisted member of a Guard Regiment serving in Palestine. Note the Guard's lace on the collars of his field-grey Model 1915 Field Blouse

Above. German troops serving in Macedonia. Most are wearing modified lightweight uniforms. Note the *Pickelhauben* covered with havelocks (*see inset*)

Right. German troops posing with a Bulgarian soldier on the Salonika Front. Many are wearing lightweight khaki uniforms based on the modified Model 1910 Tunics and the khaki field caps with havelocks of the type worn by the German Expeditionary Force in Palestine. Note the reissue of the Boxer Rebellion-era Straw Hats of the East Asia Brigade

Left. Of all the German troops that served overseas, General Lettow von Vorbeck's forces kept on fighting in German East Africa to the very end of the War and remained undefeated. In November 1918 he still had 1,500 active German troops and levies under his command. Still under arms, his *Schutztruppe* crossed the border into northern Rhodesia and surrendered a few days after the Armistice. He and his men were the only victorious army granted the privilege of marching through Berlin's Brandenburg Gate at the end of World War I. Seen here upon his return, many of his men are wearing a mixture of German and British headgear and uniforms. Note the distinctive white band for German East Africa on von Vorbeck's hat

Above. A veteran of the *Schutztruppe* wearing his Home Uniform Tunic in the 1930s. This former NCO had served in German East Africa. Many veterans continued to wear their uniforms at reunions, memorial services and special occasions

Above. When the veterans' uniforms were no longer serviceable or were lost, replicas of those worn by the *Schutztruppe* were made. This former member of the colonial troops is wearing the brown corduroy replica of the service uniform. As a member of a veterans' organization during the time of the Third Reich (1933–45), he was required to wear the armband of the Nazi Party. The badge below, adopted after World War I, was traditional of the German colonies. Known as the "*Kreuz des Südens*", the sleeve badge was also worn by selected German police units chosen to continue the "traditions" of the German police formations that served in the former colonies. In addition, a metal breast eagle of the German Veterans' League was pinned over the wearer's right pocket

3

WORLD WAR I
(1914–1918)

Above. War! German infantry marching to the front, August 1914. The men are wearing the Model 1910 Field Uniform and covers for their *Pickelhauben*. Note the NCO with Infantry Officer's Model Sword

Below. Prussian artillery officers and an NCO in a variety of greatcoats and headgear. The NCO at the far left is wearing the old dark-grey greatcoat that was introduced in 1867, while the officers are wearing stone-grey greatcoats, some with fur collars. Of particular interest is the shelter draped over with *zeltbahn* or shelter-half tents. Each soldier carried a shelter-half tent. It took two soldiers to make a tent, which they then shared

Above. A Prussian infantryman in full marching order wearing the Model 1910 Field Uniform in 1914. Note the Brandenburg-style cuffs. The twisted two-colored piping around his shoulder-straps indicates that he is a one-year volunteer (a scheme that was cancelled after 3 October 1914) for military service. His boots are the high-shaft natural leather enlisted men's Model 1866 Marching Boots

Above. A soldier wearing the Model 1910 Tunic with Swedish-style cuffs. He is wearing a cloth cover with unit designation over his spiked helmet. Note how the soldier's bayonet scabbard has been strapped to the shaft of his entrenching shovel

Left. Bavarian infantrymen wearing the Model 1910 Field Tunics with Brandenburg-style cuffs. The drummer is wearing musician's wings on his tunic. Because of limited supplies, substitutes or ersatz items began to appear, such as the felt *Pickelhauben* being worn by the soldiers. Note the difference between the black leather helmet worn by the musician and the ersatz felt helmets worn by the other soldiers

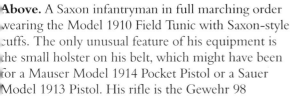

Above. A Saxon infantryman in full marching order wearing the Model 1910 Field Tunic with Saxon-style cuffs. The only unusual feature of his equipment is the small holster on his belt, which might have been for a Mauser Model 1914 Pocket Pistol or a Sauer Model 1913 Pistol. His rifle is the Gewehr 98

Above right. A Saxon NCO wearing the Model 1910 Field Uniform with Saxon-style cuffs. He has NCO braid on his collar and cuffs

Right. This soldier is wearing the shoulder-straps of a Saxon Regiment on his Model 1910 Field Uniform with Saxon-style cuffs, 1915. Note the ersatz *Pickelhaube* of pressed felt and without the metal visor trim

Above left. A Saxon Jäger wearing the distinctive shako with his Model 1910 Tunic with Saxon-style cuffs

Above. An NCO of the 24th Pioneer Battalion from the VII Army Corps District. Most pioneer units wore Swedish-style cuffs on their tunic and black piping on the shoulder-straps, cuffs, down the front of the tunic and on the field cap. He is wearing the 1910 Pattern Field Cap with his uniform. Note the collar disc for senior NCOs. He is armed with a P.08 (Luger) Pistol

Left. This Prussian infantryman is wearing the Modified Model 1910 Field Tunic that was introduced in 1915. Note the barrel cuffs that replaced the earlier and differing styles of cuffs. Of particular interest is the ersatz *Pickelhaube* made of metal and then painted field-grey. An ersatz Model 1915/16 Bayonet is fixed to his Gewehr 98

WORLD WAR I (1914–1918) • 125

Right. This soldier is wearing the Model 1915 Field Blouse and the Model 1916 Steel Helmet that replaced the *Pickelhaube*. He has a gasmask hanging from his neck. Dog's hide was initially used for gasmasks since dogs do not perspire through their skin, which is therefore suitable for preventing harmful gas or chemicals from penetrating the mask. Manufactured materials such as rubberized canvas were used later on

Far right. This NCO is in full marching order. A German soldier was expected to carry a comparatively heavy load consisting of a belt, three cartridge pouches (two up front, one in the rear), knapsack, ration bag, greatcoat, mess-kit, haversack, canteen, entrenching tool and rifle. In addition, this NCO is carrying a map case and sword

Above. A group of soldiers wearing the Model 1908 Greatcoats introduced on 1 February 1908. The soldier in the background is wearing a Model 1893 *Litewka* with collar patches and a pre-War visored undress cap. The NCO on the far right is wearing the old pre-War dark-grey greatcoat. The soldiers are armed with Gewehr 1888 Rifles, while the NCO on the far left is armed with the Mauser Model 1896 "Broomhandle" Pistol

Left. A sentry wearing the grey Model 1908 Greatcoat. He is armed with the Gewehr 1888 Rifle with Model 1871 Bayonet

Right. A foot artilleryman wearing the Model 1910 Field Tunic with Brandenburg-style cuffs. He is armed with a Gewehr 91, a variation of the Karabiner 88 and of its parent, the Gewehr 1888 Commission Rifle. In Prussia, and later in the other states of the Reich, foot artillery were equipped with 91 Rifles. Most were made by the Suhl manufacturers V. C. Schilling and C. G. Haenel, since the state factories were busy filling orders for the Gewehr 1888 Infantry Rifles. By 1892, these manufacturers had delivered a total of some 200,000 carbines to Prussia, Saxony, Württemburg and Bavaria

Above. German soldiers serving in the Carpathian Mountains wearing heavy sheepskin winter coats over their uniforms and equipment (as evidenced by the bulges in their coats). Most have a gasmask can strung from their necks and are armed with an assortment of weapons, from Gewehr 98 Rifles to Stick Grenades

Above left. An artilleryman of the 22nd Field Artillery from Münster wearing the Model 1910 Field Tunic with Swedish-style cuffs. His field-grey peakless field cap has the black band with red piping. Note the flaming bomb emblem over his regimental number on his shoulder-straps

Above. A Prussian Hussar wearing the field-grey Model 1910 *Attila*. His busby has a cover permitting his cockade to be shown. Since 1889 troopers from all the Hussar Regiments were armed with a lance, the shaft of which was wood for the Saxon Regiments and steel for the Prussian and Brunswick Regiments

Left. A Hussar from the 1st Life Hussar Regiment wearing the field-grey Model 1910 *Attila*. Note how the field cover of his ersatz busby of pressed felt has been lifted up and is supported by the cockade, revealing the distinctive regimental plate. He is armed with the Gewehr 98 Rifle with an ersatz Model 1915/16 Bayonet

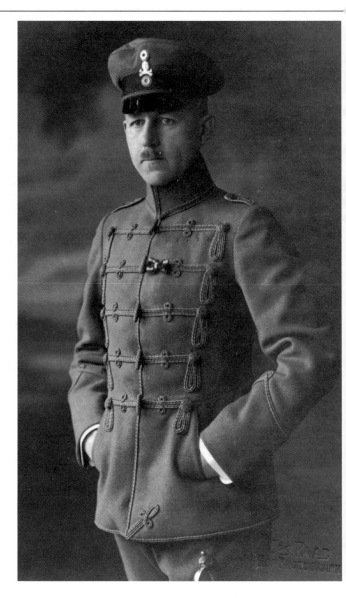

Above left. During the years of the War, the field-grey Hussar uniform was used as a walking-out uniform. Note the field cap and pre-War riding boots with distinctive white trim

Above. An Oberleutnant of the 17th Brunswick Hussar Regiment wearing the distinctive regimental badge on his field-grey undress cap

Left. Crown Prince Wilhelm, Commander of the 5th Army, with the regimental insignia of the 1st Life Hussar Regiment on his pre-War undress cap. He is wearing a tailored field-grey officer field tunic with four patch pockets. The pattern was similar in style to those worn by the Württemberg Ski and Mountain Troops. A few aristocrats and senior officers had specially tailored uniforms made that occasionally conflicted with uniform regulations. Rank does have its privileges

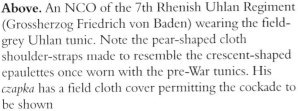

Above. An NCO of the 7th Rhenish Uhlan Regiment (Grossherzog Friedrich von Baden) wearing the field-grey Uhlan tunic. Note the pear-shaped cloth shoulder-straps made to resemble the crescent-shaped epaulettes once worn with the pre-War tunics. His *czapka* has a field cloth cover permitting the cockade to be shown

Above right. Three members of an Uhlan Regiment. The one in the center is wearing a lightweight drill jacket modeled on a *Litewka*, while the other two are wearing the Model 1910 Uhlan Tunics. Note that the soldier on the far left is wearing the normal shoulder-straps instead of the distinctive Uhlan pear-shaped shoulder-straps. The soldier on the far right is wearing the "camouflage" grey band on the lower part of his *feldmütze*, which nonetheless allows his national cockade to be shown

Right. The era of horses and men in combat are long gone, and this Uhlan is now reduced to fighting from a trench as an infantryman. He is wearing the Model 1916 Steel Helmet with his Model 1910 Uhlan Tunic

Left. A Bavarian Dragoon wearing the Model 1910 Tunic with Swedish-style cuffs. His ersatz *Pickelhaube* is made of metal and no longer has the squared front visor normally worn by Bavarian troops since its adoption in 1886. He has the NCO's and trooper's Pattern "Pallasch" Sword attached to his saddle

Below. German cavalrymen from a Dragoon Regiment in full rig. Note the Gewehr 98 Rifles in their leather carriers. All are wearing the Dragoon-style *Pickelhaube* with squared visor and cloth cover

Opposite above. Train troops (*Eisenbahntruppen*) wearing the Model 1893 *Litewka* with the script "E" on their shoulder-straps. Many are armed with Gewehr 1888 Rifles and Model 1871 Bayonets

Opposite below. French prisoners of war being led by a Gendarmerie of the Prussian Guard Regiment and guarded by a detachment of infantrymen from the 118th Regiment. Their regimental designations are clearly visible on their *Pickelhaube* covers. The soldiers are armed with Gewehr 1898 Rifles fixed with the Model 1898n/A Bayonet

Above. Soldiers of the 2nd Guards Railway Troops Regiment. All have double *Kapellenlitzen* on the collar and cuffs of their Model 1910 Field Uniforms, and are wearing the distinctive Model 1915 Field Caps with black leather chinstraps that were usually issued to supply and medical personnel. The shoulder-boards have a scripted "E" over a "2"

Left. A soldier from the Prussian 6th Jäger Regiment wearing the Model 1860/95 Shako and Model 1910 Field Tunic with Swedish-style cuffs. He has a scripted "J" over a "6" on his shoulder-straps

Right. NCOs from the 5th Jäger Regiment wearing covers that permit the shako's cockade to be shown. The stenciled unit numeral on the shako cover can clearly be seen being worn by the soldier on the left. Note the use of puttees and leather gaiters

Above. Soldiers from a Prussian Jäger unit wearing the ersatz 1915 Pattern Shakos of pressed felt

Below. An unidentified Prussian Jäger detachment patrolling the streets of Brussels in 1915. All the men are wearing covers for their shakos with the state cockade visible (white and black), and are armed with Gewehr 1898 Rifles

Left. An NCO from a Guard unit wearing a Model 1916 Steel Helmet and armed with a P.08 (Luger) Pistol

Right. Karl Heidenreich as a soldier of the 5th Reserve-Jägerbataillon (Hirschberg), wearing the distinctive insignia of the Karpathenkorps on his field cap

Below. Members of a Pioneer unit dressed in a combination of Model 1910 and Model 1910/15 Field Uniforms. The soldiers are using the straps from their breadbags to support the load from their cartridge pouches. Note the use of the Model 1893 Ankleboots and the Model 1866 Marching Boots. Note how the soldier on the far right has tucked his pant legs into his socks. All are armed with the Karabiner 98a

Above left. An enlisted man wearing the Karpathen-korps and Edelweiss insignia on his *feldmütze*. The metal "S" pinned to the collar of his Model 1915 Field Blouse identifies him as a member of the 1st Bavarian Ski Battalion

Above. Bavarian Ski Troops wore a modified Model 1915 Field Blouse with the addition of two breast-patch pockets. Note the "S" collar patches being worn by the soldier on the right (*see inset*)

Left. A soldier of a Württemberg Ski Company, 1915–16. Note the mountain cap (*Gebirgsmutze*), based on those worn by Austrian Mountain Troops (*see inset*). A certain Oberleutnant by the name of Erwin Rommel served with the Württemberg Mountain Battalion while campaigning in the Transylvanian Alps

Left. These artillerymen, as denoted by the flaming bomb devices on their shoulder-straps, are wearing the modified Model 1910 Field Tunics (Model 1910/15). Note the use of the *Gebirgsmütze*, possibly signifying an affiliation with a mountain troop unit

Right. Prior to 1915 most priests serving as chaplains wore their traditional habits with a violet armband identifying their status as non-combatants. This chaplain is wearing a black frock coat and *feldmütze*

Above. These recaptured German prisoners of war had been caught by the Americans as they were trying to return to their lines. The one on the left is wearing the German Army-issue undershirt, while the one on the right is wearing the Model 1895 Fatigue Jacket of twilled linen

Above right. An NCO wearing the gorget of the Gardes du Corps Regiment with his Model 1910 Tunic

Right. An excellent study of the differences between the Model 1910 and the modified Model 1910/15 Tunics, as well as the Field Caps

Left. In 1915 the Army introduced a special uniform for military chaplains. This Catholic priest – as denoted by his crucifix – is wearing the long field-grey chaplain's frock coat and hat. Note the lack of any rank insignia on the uniform, and the cross between the cockades on his colonial-style hat. The violet armband is retained with the uniform

Above left. An Obergendarm of the Feldgendarmerie or Military Police. The Military Police were made up of seconded Prussian Rural Police (Landgendarmerie) personnel and cavalry troopers. They wore dark-green Model 1889 Tunics, Dragoon-style *Pickelhauben* and a silver gorget. An Oberwachtmeister had two cuff braids and an Obergendarmen a yellow loop attached to the shoulder-board

Above. Two members of the Feldgendarmerie on duty. Note the use of the Swedish-style and Polish-style cuffs. Of particular interest is the Prussian eagle at each end of the gorget, either side of the soldier's personal number. Felgendarmerie from other states had the following: Bavaria – coat of arms with lion's heads at each corner; Saxony – coat of arms; Württemberg – coat of arms. Those serving in a Reserve Corps sported an "R" in addition to the personal number

Left. A Landsturmmann serving as a temporary Feldgendarm. Note the armband with "Gendarmerie" worn on the greatcoat

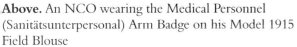

Above. An NCO wearing the Medical Personnel (Sanitätsunterpersonal) Arm Badge on his Model 1915 Field Blouse

Above right. The Totenkopf Unit Traditions Badge was also worn by the 92nd Brunswick Infantry Regiment, as can be seen on their field caps. Note the Red Cross armband being worn by the stretcher bearer

Right. Another soldier serving as a temporary Feldgendarm. He is wearing an armband with "Hilfsgendarmerie" on his field blouse

Above. A Group of senior NCOs from the 395th Infantry Regiment of the 18th Reserve Infantry Brigade. Note the double sleeve rings of the three holding the position of *"Der Spiess"*

Below. A member of an Airship Detachment (Luftschiffer-Abteilung) in pre-War uniform. Note the script "L" over "4" on his shoulder-strap

Below. This NCO from an Airship Detachment is firing a Maxim MG-08 Machine Gun

Right.
Members of the 1st Machine Gun Company of the 209th Infantry Regiment posing with a balloon. Note the MG-08 Machine Guns

Left. The winged propeller on this NCO's shoulder-strap identifies him as a member of a Flying Battalion. He is wearing the Model 1860/95 Shako and Model 1910 Tunic with Swedish-style cuffs. Note the Guard's double *Kapellenlitzen* on the collar and cuffs, and the marksmanship lanyard and wound badge in silver

Below. A soldier of the 228th Flying Battalion. We can see his shoulder-strap with the Aviation insignia worn on the Model 1915 Field Blouse

Above left. A German aviator in full rig, consisting of sheepskin-lined greatcoat, leather gloves, Model 1913 Goggles, leather flying helmet and Model 1913 Motor Transport Corps Crash Helmet

Above. A Leutnant wearing the field-grey Model 1910 Officer's Service Tunic. Note the Observer's Badge

Left. A Leutnant wearing a privately modified Model 1910 Officer's Tunic with additional breast-patch pockets. Note the Pilot's Badge

Above. NCOs of a Flying Battalion wearing a wide assortment of greatcoats of various shades and quality. All have the winged propeller on their shoulder-straps

Left. Hans Bauer wearing a modified Model 1915 Field Blouse with patch pockets similar to those worn by the Ski Troops. He is wearing officer-quality Guard-style double-*Kapellenlitzen* collar tabs, but no rank shoulder-boards. Note the Bavarian Pilot's Badge. Hans Bauer became Adolf Hitler's personal pilot in the decades following World War I

Right. Throughout the War the Model 1893 *Litewka* continued to be worn by some soldiers. By 1915 it influenced the creation of the field-grey Model 1915 Field Blouse. This artillery-man from a Guard Regiment is wearing a *Litewka* with pockets, showing the many differing styles that can be found with this jacket. Note the knot attached to the bayonet frog of his Model 1884/98 Dress Bayonet

Above left. An NCO of a Landsturm Infantry Battalion wearing the Model 1915 Field Blouse. The Landsturm was established during the Napoleonic Wars as a paramilitary unit to support the German Army when the homeland was threatened. During World War I many Landsturm Infantry Battalions were assigned to Reserve and Landwehr Infantry Regiments. The numbers of the parent infantry brigade were worn on the collar. In April 1915 it was replaced with the corps number above the battalion number

Above. The numerals (III B/10) on the collar of this Landsturmmann identify him as a soldier of the 10th Landsturm Battalion of the 3rd Bavarian Army Corps. He is wearing an ersatz 1915 Pattern *Pickelhaube* of pressed felt and the modified Model 1910/15 Tunic. Breadbag straps are used to hold his cartridge pouches and belt in place. He is armed with a captured and reissued Russian Model 1891 Mosin-Nagant Rifle

Left. A member of the 8th Landsturm Infantry Battalion of the 16th Army Corps wearing a Model 1915 Field Blouse. He is armed with a Russian Model 1891 Mosin-Nagant Rifle modified to accept an ersatz Model 1916 Bayonet

Above. Men of the 102nd Landsturm Infantry Battalion wearing the distinctive Model 1813 oilcloth peaked caps bearing the Landwehr Cross above the state cockade. All are wearing the Model 1893 *Litewka* and are armed with the Karabiner 98a Rifle

Below. Soldiers with the 57th Landsturm Infantry Battalion wearing the Model 1860 Shako and Model 1910 Tunic with Brandenburg-style cuffs. The distinctive Landwehr Cross can be seen on the shako. All are armed with the Gewehr 1888 Rifle. Note the musician's wings worn by the bugler on the far left

Left. Two soldiers from the Landwehr Infantry serving as temporary Feldgendarmerie. Both are armed with the Gewehr 1888 Rifle

Above. An early war scene showing a Maxim MG-08 Machine-Gun Crew from the 106th Infantry Regiment. Note the Luger of the kneeling soldier holding the binoculars

Below. A late war scene of a machine-gun crew. Note the mixture of uniforms and headgear. Most are wearing on their left sleeve the Machine Gunner's Marksmen Sleeve Badges that were introduced on 19 February 1916. Some of the men are wearing a field-grey band over the red band of their field caps

Above. Bavarian cooks preparing a meal for the troops in a mobile field kitchen or *gulaschkanonen*. All are wearing the off-white Model 1895 Drill/Fatigue Uniform made of herringbone twill

Below. A crewman sits next to German A7V Tank "Adalbert", which took a total of eighteen men. It carried a 57-mm gun and seven machine guns. A Tank Crew Badge was authorized at the end of the War. "Adalbert" went through various actions and was finally captured by the French after the Armistice

Left. A German soldier demonstrates a captured French flame thrower used to clear pillboxes and trenches

Right. An officer of a Guard Regiment wearing the Model 1910 Officer's Field Uniform

Above. Three officers out in the field. One is a member of the 92nd Brunswick Infantry Regiment. Note the tent made from various *zeltbahn*, and field equipment hanging from the trees

Above left. A Leutnant wearing the regimental insignia of the 25th Dragoon Regiment on his shoulder-board

Above. This general is wearing the Model 1910 General Officer's Field Tunic with breast pockets, Model 1900 "Alt-Larisch" Collar Tabs, and barrel cuffs

Left. An officer wearing the Model 1903 Officer's Undress Tunic *Litewka* with colored collar patch and the Model 1910 Peaked Field Cap

Above. An excellent view of the field marshal's shoulder-board, worn by Prince Leopold while reviewing Saxon Jäger and infantry troops

Left. Field Marshal Emil von Eichhorn wearing the Model 1903 Officer's Undress *Litewka* with colored patch and gold buttons

Right. A full view of a general wearing the Model 1910 General Officer's Field Tunic

Above. A group of Prussian general officers wearing their stone-grey Model 1903 General Officer's Greatcoats with red lapels

Below. A field marshal, senior officers and foreign dignitaries reviewing troops of a Guard Regiment, 1917

Left. A close-up of the previous photograph showing an excellent array of uniforms. Amongst the group is an officer of the *Schutztruppe*, Feldgendarmerie with their distinctive gorgets, Saxon Jäger, Cuirassier, Dragoon, Uhlan, Austrian, Bulgarian and Turkish officers

Below. War came to an end on the eleventh hour of the eleventh day of the eleventh month of 1918. These soldiers taken prisoner by the American Expeditionary Force show the condition of the German Army at the Western Front after fighting for well over four years

Bottom. The horrors of war. Much of this soldier's personal equipment is scattered about his remains – his Gewehr 98 Rifle, Model 1910 Mess-Tin, Model 1893 Water Bottle, Model 1892 Shelter-Quarter (*zeltbahn*), Model 1916 Steel Helmet, Model 1909 Cartridge Pouches, Model 1915 Gasmask and Model 1898/05 Bayonet

INTRODUCTION TO PART 2

Germany's Armies, 1919 to the Present Day

When the guns finally ceased firing in France and Flanders on 11 November 1918, the old Imperial German Army was still a cohesive fighting force but was beginning to be impregnated by the canker of revolution which was gripping the country as a whole. Under the terms of the Armistice it had to withdraw from the territory it had occupied for over four years. Although it had to accept the inevitable, the Army allowed itself one last flourish. On 11 December troops lately returned from France paraded in Berlin. The officers wore their full decorations, and the troops and heavy weapons were adorned with crowns of oak leaves signifying triumph rather than defeat. Yet, the grim expressions of the troops, the muted applause from bystanders, and the fact that the Imperial German flag was absent – the Kaiser having gone into exile – showed that this was no victory march. Thereafter the Army rapidly disintegrated, with many units being taken over by revolutionary soldiers' councils.

Germany now witnessed similar events to those that had occurred in Russia in 1917. Communists threatened to topple the Socialist government in Berlin and even to set up their own republic in Bavaria. In defence of the state, some officers raised their own forces from among loyal soldiers. These groups became known as the Freikorps and, with the encouragement of the government and support from those elements of the Army that were still untainted by the whiff of revolution, they crushed uprisings in many parts of the country. They were also active on Germany's eastern borders, defending the country's integrity against incursions by Poles and others who wanted to enlarge their territories. By mid-1919 some stability had been restored, but Germany now had to face a fresh indignity.

One of the prime Allied objectives when drawing up the peace terms was that German militarism, which they believed had been a major cause of World War I, should be crushed for ever. Accordingly, the Treaty of Versailles saw that the German Great General Staff, which was seen as the embodiment of this militarism, was abolished. The Army was to be limited to 100,000 Regular troops, with no conscription allowed, and the Navy to a strength of 15,000. Aircraft, tanks, submarines and other offensive weapons were prohibited. The left bank of the Rhine was demilitarised, with Allied troops remaining in occupation of it. In addition, the Allies dictated that Germany should suffer huge financial reparations for the damage it had inflicted during 1914–18, payments which were to cripple the country economically. All of this reinforced the notion among some sectors of the population that Germany had been "stabbed in the back" and that the Army had been betrayed in 1918 by political elements within the country. No one grasped this belief more eagerly than Adolf Hitler, recently demobilised as a Corporal, and he and like-minded individuals formed their own political party which vowed to throw off the shackles of Versailles and make Germany great once more.

The new Reichswehr, as Germany's armed forces were now called, absorbed some of the Freikorps. Others remained covertly in being, and it was not until after Hitler's abortive 1923 putsch in Munich that these were finally disbanded, many of their members joining Hitler's "private army", the Sturmabteilung or SA. The Army itself was careful to keep politics at a distance and concentrated on developing a framework for possible future expansion. To this end it adopted the principle of training every soldier to be able to operate at two ranks higher than their current one. It also retained some of the old traditions, especially with regard to regiments, and created a disguised General Staff in the shape of the Truppenamt (Troop Office). Yet its leadership was conscious that it was too small to defend Germany's borders adequately, and that the only way it could achieve any form of coherent strategy was through the use of maximum mobility. They drew on the lessons of 1914–18 and realised that mechanisation was the solution. Because Versailles prevented them from developing tanks themselves, they formed a clandestine relationship with Russia. In return for providing technical assistance to the establishment of the Soviet defence industry, Reichswehr officers were able to visit Russia to study and experiment with modern weapons. After the departure in 1928 of the Allied Control Commission, which was responsible for enforcing the Versailles terms, the building of experimental tanks was begun in Germany. The foundations of the army that would fight World War II were therefore well in place when Hitler came to power as Chancellor in January 1933.

On 2 February 1933 General Werner von Blomberg, the newly appointed Minister for Defence, hosted a dinner for the freshly elected Chancellor. Present were the Reichswehr's senior commanders. While they did not like Hitler's politics, they welcomed his assurance that he was determined to build a strong army. Indeed, Hitler's dream of recreating Greater Germany, which included union with Austria and the removal of the Versailles-imposed corridor which separated East Prussia from the rest of the country, required strong armed forces. These were to be used in the first instance to persuade neighbouring states to give way to his demands. Should force become necessary, the conflict had to be short – there must be no repeat of the drawn out agony of 1914–18.

The Army became concerned, however, over the increasing influence of the SA and feared, with reason, that it aimed to take over the prime responsibility for defence. To placate Hitler, von Blomberg ordered all members of the Reichswehr to wear the Hoheitsabzeichen (the new national emblem of eagle and swastika) on the right breast pocket of their uniforms as a demonstration of their loyalty. The Reichswehr's position was not confirmed until Hitler turned on the SA in June 1934 – the so-called Night of the Long Knives. But the Army had to pay a price for this. After the death that August of the German President and hero of World War I, Field Marshal Paul von Hindenburg, the Reichswehr was made to swear a new oath of loyalty, not just to the state but also to Hitler himself.

It was in 1935 that Hitler revealed Germany's new and rapidly growing military might to the world at large, demonstrating his contempt for the Treaty of Versailles. He unveiled a new air force, the Luftwaffe, which was to be independent of the other two services. Collectively the armed forces would now be called the Wehrmacht, which would fall under Hitler's direct command, with the Army becoming the Heer. This itself was now undergoing a massive expansion. Hitler had called for a doubling of its existing strength during 1934 and half as much again during the following year, resulting in a twenty-one-division army, its numbers obtained through conscription. This was achieved by hiving off cadres from existing divisions to form others, and then doing the same again. Such was the turbulence caused that the Heer was virtually non-operational when Hitler decided to reoccupy the Rhineland in March 1936. Only three battalions could be spared for the operation, and there were genuine fears that the British and French might react with force. Hitler, however, had judged the situation correctly. Then came the formation of the first Panzer divisions and the re-establishment of the Kriegsakadamie, the traditional forcing house of the General Staff. The Army grew and grew, as did the other two services, and by 1938 Hitler felt confident enough to bring about Anschluss, his longed-for union of Germany with his native country, Austria. This bloodless invasion of March 1938 did reveal serious deficiencies in the Army's training, again brought about by its rapid and continuing expansion. Even so, that autumn Hitler turned to another thorn in his flesh, the predominantly ethnic German Sudetenland province of Czechoslovakia. The Czechs initially displayed a determination to fight, but mediation by Britain and France, as yet not ready for war, enabled Hitler to seize it without conflict. The total dismemberment of Czechoslovakia followed in March 1939.

Hitler's main target was the removal of the Polish Corridor, but the Poles proved intransigent to the threat of what was now the most modern military force in western Europe. The Army itself had now grown to a total of 3.75 million men, a far cry from the 100,000-strong Reichsheer of six years before. The basic building block was the division, and these were recruited from particular areas of the country. At the outbreak of war there were four Panzer divisions, distinguishable by the black uniforms and berets of the tank units which were copied from Britain's Royal Tank Corps, four Light divisions made up of a Panzer battalion and motorised infantry, four motorised divisions, two Jäger (Light Infantry) divisions, three Mountain divisions, one Air-Landing division, and no less than eighty-six straight Infantry divisions. There was also one Horse Cavalry brigade still in existence, whereas there had been three Cavalry divisions in the old Reichsheer. The Air-Landing division was, as its title suggests, designed to be flown into battle, but the new Paratroop arm was part of the Luftwaffe. The Infantry divisions were mobilised as "waves", and in September 1939 Wave 1 consisted of the thirty-five divisions of the Standing Army, Wave 2 represented sixteen divisions formed from Reservists, Wave 3 a further twenty-one divisions of Reservists with limited training and older men, while Wave 4 contained the remainder and were divisions raised from the divisional reinforcement battalions of the Standing Army. This system would remain in operation throughout the war, and by the end of it no less than thirty-three waves had been mobilised.

The early campaigns of World War II confirmed the potential of the German Army. The devastating Blitzkrieg campaigns in Poland, Scandinavia and France astonished the world and more than achieved Hitler's objective of short, sharp campaigns. Indeed, by the end of June 1940 many Germans believed that the war was at an end, and as if to confirm this seventeen Infantry divisions were actually deactivated. Two factors served to show that this was an illusion. Contrary to Hitler's belief, Britain refused to give in and fought on. More significant was Hitler's decision to attack the Soviet Union, and from June 1941 the war on the Eastern Front was to tie down the bulk of the German Army. Indeed, by June 1942 no less than 167 divisions were serving on the Eastern Front and only fifty-one in other theatres (Finland, Norway, France and the Low Countries, the Balkans, and North Africa). But the increasing number of divisions (it rose to 304 by 1945) did not mean a parallel increase in manpower. The Army's strength peaked at 6.55 million in 1943, but thereafter fell away because of casualties. Hitler, however, was often loath to strike divisions off the order of battle after they had been destroyed. Thus, twenty divisions lost at Stalingrad in early 1943 had all been reactivated before the year was out. To overcome the increasing manpower problem the size of a division gradually decreased as the war went on. In 1939 an infantry division could boast a strength of 17,734 men, but this had fallen to 12,700 by 1944. In addition, some 10 per cent of the manpower was made up of Hilfswilliger, or "Hiwis", Russian and other prisoners of war who had been persuaded to change sides.

The supply of weapons and equipment also became an increasing problem. Production could not keep up with losses, and weapons procurement lacked co-ordination and became too diverse. Sometimes the Army had to suffer at the expense of Hitler's own shock troops, the Waffen-SS, who fought alongside the Army and became renowned for their ruthlessness. Its divisions were often given priority when it came to equipment.

An underlying cause of Germany's ever greater dilemma was that Hitler failed to mobilise the country completely for war until 1943, by which time it was too late. In particular, Hitler believed that a woman's place was in the home, and, although female auxiliaries served with the Army from as early as October 1940, they represented only a very small percentage of German womanhood and could have played a larger part in releasing men for more active duties. Likewise, in spite of the widespread use of foreign (including slave) labour in industry, there were still over six million German males in reserved occupations in 1944. Eventually, to tap this manpower the Volksturm was formed that September. This was a part-time home defence force covering all males aged between sixteen and sixty who were not already in uniform. It was, however, a sign of desperation in that by this time Germany's enemies were beginning to threaten its very borders. The Volksturm itself would suffer 175,000 dead and missing during the final battles of the war. Yet, in spite of its growing problems, the German Army largely maintained its cohesion and combat effectiveness right up until the very last weeks.

With the German surrender in May 1945 its armed forces vanished from the scene. Unlike in 1918, the Allies were bent on unconditional surrender and the occupation of the entire country, which was divided into four zones, the Soviet Union being responsible for the eastern zone, and Britain, France and the USA for each of the other three. Berlin was treated as a separate entity and was also divided into four occupation zones. Efforts to treat the country as one soon foundered as it became clear that the Soviet Union was pursuing a different agenda to the western Allies. Indeed, while they soon reduced their military forces to a mere constabulary, a significant part of the Red Army remained in eastern Germany. Even though the Allies had originally agreed to create a new and democratic Germany it soon became clear that the Russians would accept only a Communist government in the east. The Soviets also sealed their zone from the rest of the country. The Cold War now took hold, and in June 1948 the Soviets denied the Western powers access by land to Berlin. The result was the Berlin Airlift, which lasted throughout the following winter as the western Allies kept the inhabitants of West Berlin supplied by air with the essentials of life. This was followed in 1949 by the establishment of the Communist German Democratic Republic (GDR) and the Federal Republic of Germany (FRG), otherwise known as West Germany. In that same year NATO was established and its members recognised that Germany was the most likely battleground of World War III. In 1954 West Germany was allowed to join NATO and in the following year Moscow established the Warsaw Pact, of which East Germany became a member.

It was in this context that two new German Armies came into being. In 1951 West Germany had been allowed to form the Bundesgrenschutz (Federal Border Police), a lightly armed paramilitary organisation for patrolling the border with East Germany. Similarly, the Soviets had organised various police forces in their zone. West Germany's membership of NATO implied that it was expected to assist in the defence of its territory, and to this end the Bundeswehr was formed in summer 1955. The initial volunteers were World War II veterans and many members of the Bundesgrenschutz, and training was overseen by the US Army. The Bundeswehr was initially equipped with a mixture of stockpiled German weaponry and US-supplied armaments. To bring it up to the necessary strength, conscription was introduced. Its uniform was carefully designed to bear no resemblance to the old German Army, although veterans were permitted to wear their World War II decorations and medals, provided these did not bear the swastika. The Bundeswehr was not allowed to serve outside West Germany, but was soon able to play its part in the defence of the NATO Central Region, as the Federal Republic was termed. By the 1970s it was providing three out of the eight army corps in the Central Region, with the Americans (two), Belgians, British and Dutch supplying the others. West Germany also re-established an armaments industry, which became notable for its armoured vehicles, especially the Leopard main battle tank.

The National People's Army (NVA) of East Germany was formed in 1956 and also initially drew its manpower from the various police forces. Like the Bundeswehr, it was initially equipped with German weaponry left over from the war, but this was soon replaced by Soviet-designed weapons. Its uniform did bear a closer resemblance, at least in the early years, to that of World War II, notably the tunic and breeches, although the latter also reflected the Soviet influence, as did the long boot. Ceremonial drill also included the Red Army's high-stepping march, which had a resonance with the old Prussian goose step. A ban on wearing World War II medals was compensated for by the creation of a wide range of orders and decorations, considerably more than were instituted in the Federal Republic. With its smaller population the GDR could not match the FRG in military strength, and the NVA was based on two tank and four motorised rifle divisions. These played very much second fiddle to the Group of Soviet Forces Germany (GSFG) with its ten tank and ten motorised rifle divisions. Indeed, the Soviet Union never really trusted its Warsaw Pact satellite members, and the NVA's role in any attack across the Inner German Border (IGB) was merely as follow-up troops. In the event, while the two armed alliances glowered at one another across the IGB for forty years there was no military clash.

The 10th of November 1989 was a historic day in the history of Germany. The breaking down of the wall that had divided East from West Berlin since August 1961 marked not just the end of the Soviet empire and the Cold War, but also the reunification of Germany. It would, however, be another eleven months before the two Germanys were formally rejoined, and then only after a new democratically elected East German government had negotiated with the USSR, Britain, France, the USA and West Germany. It was agreed that the new Germany would remain a member of NATO, but that none of the Alliance's troops would be stationed in the former GDR. The Bundeswehr now found itself absorbing the former NVA, including its sizeable armoury. Part of the agreement with the former World War II Allies was that Germany's armed forces should be reduced to a maximum strength of 370,000 by the end of 1994. This was successfully achieved, with the former Warsaw Pact weaponry being discarded. At the same time the Bundeswehr, in line with its NATO and European Union commitments and a new policy to assist in global peacekeeping, found itself operating abroad for the very first time. The first deployment was to Cambodia in 1992, when 144 medical staff were sent under United Nations (UN) auspices. More significant was the sending of 2,600 troops to Bosnia as part of the NATO Stabilisation Force (SFOR) in early 1996.

Reunification, however, was causing the country increasing economic problems. At the same time the Bundeswehr's equipment was becoming outdated. During the latter part of the 1990s and into the new century there was a debate over what should be done. The decision was to create slimmer forces and phase out conscription. By 2005 the Army had been reduced to a strength of just under 118,000 men, of which 60 per cent were still conscripts. It had forces deployed in Afghanistan, Bosnia, Serbia and Montenegro, as well as a number of individuals serving with UN observer groups around the world. Much still needs to be done to enable it to face the new challenges that the twenty-first century has brought, especially in terms of equipment, but the German Army is making progress.

In some ways the German Army is now completing a cycle that began in 1919. Its strength is close to that of the Reichsheer and its decision to phase out conscription reflects the all-Regular nature of its Weimar predecessor. But while it still retains responsibility for the defence of the homeland, its roles are otherwise very different to those of the Reichsheer and, in particular, Hitler's army that followed it. While the latter was shaped for conquest, the new German Army is increasingly playing its part in the maintenance of peace. This in itself is a contrast to the situation that faced its immediate predecessors, who for nigh on thirty-five years spent their time preparing for a conflict which would have meant German fighting German.

CHARLES MESSENGER

4

REVOLUTION
AND THE WEIMAR REPUBLIC
(1919–1933)

Above. Revolution! Members of the Volksmarine Division posing with an obsolete Krupp Cannon in the courtyard of the Imperial Palace in Berlin, December 1918. All have removed their national insignia from their caps and are wearing a mixture of Army and Navy uniforms. The revolutionaries are carrying a combination of Gew. 98 and Kar. 98a Rifles

Above. The revolutionaries formed militias called Republikanische Soldatenwehren (Republican Soldiers' Forces) and, when Spartacists took over the movement, formed the Republikanische Schutztruppe (Republican Defense Troops). The Provisional Government wanted to integrate all militias into a single Volunteer People's Force, thereby threatening the control of the Spartacists. On 23 December 1918, members of the Volksmarine and Sparticists stormed and occupied the Reichschancellery and the Berlin Kommandantur. Civil war had begun

Above. Sparticists began taking over government buildings in Berlin. Note the boarding cutlass carried by the sailor and again the mixture of uniforms worn

Above. Due to the total collapse of the German Army after the Armistice and in response to the Communists' uprising, the Provisional Government legalized the loyal militias known as Freikorps on 6 January 1919. Four days later eight Freikorps units occupied the outer districts of Berlin and in the next day stormed the city center. Street fighting was severe. Seen here is one of the Freikorps units that fought in

Berlin. Note the basic uniformity of the troops; nearly all have retained their national and state cockades. A Maxim MG. 08/15 Machine-Gun is defending the barricade made of rolls of unprinted newspaper

Above. Members of the Freikorps unit Lüttwitztruppen occupying the area of Unter den Linden in Berlin during the Kapp-Lüttwitz Putsch, 1920. Note the uniformity amongst the disciplined Freikorps in comparison with the less disciplined revolutionaries. Many Freikorps volunteers were members of elite units such as the Assault Battalions (Sturmtruppen)

WILLY FRITSCH

Above left. This Austrian member of the Heimwehren, an equivalent to the German Freikorps, is wearing various decorations for service, including the Silesian Eagle (Schlesische Adler) Badge and Medal awarded to Freikorps members. He is also wearing the triangular edelweiss pin of the Bund Oberland e.V., the successors of the Freikorps Oberland, which was formed in 1922

Above. An NCO from the Freikorps Brüssow wearing a lightweight *litewka*. Note the small amount of litzen used on his collar

Left. Actor Willy Fritsch wearing the insignia of the Eiserne Division, taken from the busby of the Imperial German 1. Leib-Husaren-Regiment, on his Model 1918 Steel Helmet in this 1930s studio photograph. Though this may be a "Hollywood" use of the insignia, Freikorps members have been known to paint their unit emblems on their steel helmets

Above. Members of the Zeitfreiwilligen-Regiment Leipzig, consisting of volunteers recruited for the duration of a particular emergency. Many Freikorps units began adopting distinctive unit insignia, which they wore on their collars or arms. All appear to be wearing the Model 1915 Field Blouse and Model 1910 Field Caps with national and state cockades. Of particular interest is the overburdened soldier on the far right, who is carrying a Model 1918 Steel Helmet, a Maxim MG .08/15 Machine-Gun, belt of 8mm ammunition, a Model 1917 Stick Grenade, and a Luger Pistol stuck into his tunic

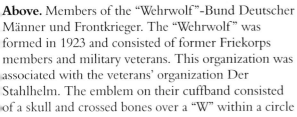

Above. Members of the "Wehrwolf"-Bund Deutscher Männer und Frontkrieger. The "Wehrwolf" was formed in 1923 and consisted of former Friekorps members and military veterans. This organization was associated with the veterans' organization Der Stahlhelm. The emblem on their cuffband consisted of a skull and crossed bones over a "W" within a circle

Right. A Freikorps volunteer with the Deutsche Schutzdivision (31. Infanterie Division). He is wearing World War One surplus Model 1915 Field Blouse and Field Cap

Above. The old and the new army. An officer and NCO of the Provisional Reichswehr pose with cadets dressed in the old uniform of the Kaiser's army. Old Imperial German Army uniforms were issued until supplies were depleted or sufficient stocks of the new uniform were on hand for general issue. Note the twisted-cord shoulder-straps on the new Reichswehr uniforms

Below. Members of the Freikorps von Hülsen and Der Stahlhelm on patrol with German Police

Above. A memorial service being conducted by an Army Chaplain, standing behind the podium, in 1925. The Chaplain's uniform had remained unchanged since the First World War. Amongst the crowd are various former First World War veterans and members of the Reichsheer

Below. A Leutnant with the Selbstschutz-Bataillon Heydebreck. This "self-defence" unit was organized to fight foreign or domestic enemies

Below. A member of the Ostpreussischen Jägerkorps Gerth. His arm badge consisted of a jawless skull with bones behind within a black oval with metal cord edge

Above. Members of the Sächsische-Grenzjäger wearing Modified Model 1915 Field Blouses. Most are wearing the twisted-cord shoulder-strap of the Provisional Reichswehr. The soldier on the far right is wearing the Reichsheer unit badge 112th Infantry Regiment on his left sleeve. Note the new visored service caps and insignia adopted and worn by the seated soldiers

Above. Soldiers of the Provisional Reichsheer wearing various forms of sports and fatigue clothing. The single white bar on the sleeve of the soldier's Model 1915 Field Blouse designated him to be a Gefreiter or Obergefreiter (Infanterie). Of particular interest are the wreathed cockades being worn on the First World War-vintage field caps, and the new general-service, with appropriate *Waffenfarbe*, collar tabs being worn by the soldier on the far right

Above. A NCO from the Freiwilliger Landesjägerkorps (Freikorps Maercker) wearing his unit's insignia over the Guard's-style collar tabs of the Reichsheer. He is wearing one of a few uniform variations of the Reichsheer. This particular version appears to be a Modified Model 1915 Field Blouse with the addition of two breast pockets

Above. Another view of a member of the "Wehrwolf", wearing the distinctive cuffband of the organization and the early Reichsheer tunic

Above right. When the Weimar Republic became stable, many Freikorps units were disbanded, and their men later became members of various veterans' organizations, like these members of Der Stahlhelm. Of particular interest is the arm badge of the II. Marine Brigade Ehrhardt (Freikorps) being worn by the officer on the left

Right. These veterans of Der Stahlhelm and Wehrstahlhelm are all wearing surplus Reichsheer uniforms and headgear. Note the Standard Bearer's Shield being worn by the soldier on the far right

Left. Latecomers to the scene, the stormtroopers of the German National Socialists Worker's Party (NSDAP or Nazi) began making headlines with the Munich "Beerhall" Putsch of 9 November 1923 and street fights with Communists in the following years. Many of its members were disenfranchised former Freikorps and First World War veterans who felt that Germany was stabbed in the back by corrupt government officials during the war. Note the use of the old surplus brown cordoroy trousers of the Schutztruppe by the two members of the Sturmabteilung (SA). Both are armed with Gew. 98 Rifles

Below. A cavalry troop of the Reichsheer, 1922

Left. A Freikorps member wearing the Model 1910 Tunic with Saxon cuffs

Below left. In 1921 twisted-cord shoulder-straps were replaced with rounded-cloth shoulder-straps with *Waffenfarbe* which adopted the universal-pattern grey double *Kapellenlitzen* on dark-green patches. Of interest are the state colors of Bavaria on the left side of the wearer's Model 1918 Steel Helmet

Right. An excellent view of the transitional officer's uniform used by the Provisional Reichswehr (1919–21) with its distinctive green cuffs. However, he has substituted the twisted-cord shoulder-straps and rank rings on his sleeve for the officer's-style shoulder-board of a Leutnant, thereby dating this photo to after 1921, when the new rank insignia and uniforms were introduced

Right. Nazi Stormtroopers during the Munich "Beerhall" Putsch on 9 November 1923, the last act in the military history of the Freikorps. Many are wearing a mixture of First World War ski Troops surplus jackets as well as other types of military uniforms and headgear. The NSDAP armbands are being worn by most of the men

Above. These men are wearing the soft field caps with visors that had been adopted in 1921. All are wearing the universal-pattern grey double *Kapellenlitzen* on dark-green patches

Above. A group shot of an officer and men of the 20th Infantry Regiment wearing the service cap used with the walking-out 1921 Pattern Service Uniform. Note the use of the state cockade over the wreathed national cockade

Above. Members of the Reichswehr wearing the Model 1921 Service Uniform. The six-button tunic consisted of two breast pockets and two slash pockets with flaps on the front skirt

Below. An enlisted man wearing the lightweight twill-cotton version of his Model 1921 Service Uniform. He is using it as a walking-out uniform

Below. A Gefreiter wearing his 1921 Pattern Service Uniform in complete walking-out dress

Left. Another view of the 1921 Pattern Service Uniform being worn by a Feldwebel of an Infantry Regiment

Right. NCOs were granted the right to carry a dress sword which could be worn for formal occassions. A sword knot, known as a Portepee, was usually applied to the hilt of the sword. Note how the sword is worn from leather straps clipped to a snap underneath the tunic

Far right. An Oberleutnant wearing the Model 1921 Officer's Service Tunic. On his right shoulder is the Adjutant's single plaited-cord aiguillette in matte silver

Left. A Feldwebel of an Artillery Regiment in walking-out dress. Note how the NCO tresse or silvered lace goes up around the top of the collar. The insignia consisting of bar and chevron on his left sleeve are are marksmanship qualifications

Right. A clear view of the Weimar-era cockade on a service cap being worn by an Oberst

Below. Soldiers wearing a combination of the field-grey Model 1910 and the 1921 Pattern Field Caps

Above. As denoted by the State Shields on their Model 1918 Steel Helmets, these men are from a Prussian Signals unit. Note the carrier pigeon in the Gefreiter's hand and the courier-dog

Opposite above. The fatigue uniforms had changed little since the time of the Kaiser

Opposite below. New innovations in military technology and tactics since the First World War began to be integrated into the new Reichsheer, such as the concept of motorcycle troops. These soldiers are wearing black leather coats with sleeve and shoulder rank distinctions applied as well as black leather crash helmets. They are armed with Kar. 98a Rifles. The "RW" designation on the license plates of their Victoria-made motorcycles stands for "Reichswehr"

Above. Whenever possible the new Riechsheer commemorated their past military traditions and heritage. The Standard Bearers are displaying the Imperial Regimental standards of the Kaiser's Army

Right. A Cavalry Bugler of the Reichsheer in full campaign rig wearing the distinctive Model 1918 "Cavalry" Helmet

Below. Feldmarschall and President of the Weimar Republic, Paul von Hindenburg, at an army field exercise. Note the Generals' greatcoats with red facings. Note also the Standard Bearer holding the Weimar President's Personal Standard – a tradition carried over from the Kaiser's time

Left and above. A combination of the 1921 Pattern Service and Field Caps being worn. Of particular interest is the extremely rare view of a Reichsheer Standard Bearer's Gorget being worn (see inset for close-up). On closer inspection one can clearly see the Weimar-style eagle in the center of the gorget. In most cases, Reichsheer Standard Bearers used the old Imperial German Gorgets, when available, or none at all

Left. High-ranking officers at a field excercise. Note the Adjutant's aiguillettes and the red facing of the General's greatcoat

Right. A rare view of Hermann Göring in the uniform of a Reichsheer General. Clearly visible is the gold embroidery on the red field of his General's collar tabs. He would later head the German Air Force (Luftwaffe) as Reichsmarschall after the Air Service branch was separated from the Army in 1935

Below. The aging Feldmarschall Paul von Hindenburg continued to wear his First World War regimental rank and collar insignia of the 3. Garde-Regiment zu Füss – a distinction of the *à la suite* commission he had received from the regiment. Note the crossed Field Marshal's batons on his shoulder-boards. Clearly visible are his Grand Cross, Iron Cross and Pour le Mérite

Left. By 1933 the national cockade containing the Weimar eagle was replaced with the Reichskokarde of red, white, and black

COLOR ILLUSTRATIONS

COLOR ILLUSTRATIONS

Above. Following the First World War there was a period of instability during the early years of the Weimar Republic. The Munich "Beerhall" Putsch on 9 November 1923 was the last conflict in the military history of the Freikorps. Seen here is a stockpile of military weapons being collected by the Nazis in preparation of their putsch. Note the Maxim machine-gun on a sled mount. Many are wearing a combination of military, political, and civilian clothing, the armbands being the only item of uniformity

Above. An NCO of the Reichsheer entertaining children. He is wearing the Model 1921 Soft Field Cap and Uniform. Note the Musician's Wings on his shoulders

Above. Reichsheer Mountain Troops preparing to fire a Maxim MG08/15 Machine-Gun. They are wearing the field cap adopted in 1934

Above. A Gebirgsjäger preparing range targets. He has green *Waffenfarbe* on his collar tabs and piping around his shoulder-straps. Below his Obergefreiter chevrons is a series of bars and chevrons on the lower part of his sleeve which are for marksman's qualifications and ranking

Above. In the years following the First World War the Reichswehr experimented with new innovations and concepts such the use of motorized troops. The pink piping around the collar tabs indicated that the motor cyclist was with Armored and Motorized Troops

Above. A field musician adjusting a stack of Gewehr 1898 Rifles. Various types of equipment can be seen

Above. A soldier wearing the Model 1918 Steel Helmet. In 1935 the Hoheitsabzeichen or national emblem, consisting of an eagle grasping a wreathed swastika, was added to the Model 1921 Uniform. Decals with the national colors and the Wehrmacht-style eagle were added to the steel helmets as well

Top left. A Feldwebel and an Obergefreiter from a Signals unit preparing to send off a pigeon. Note the new national insignia of the Third Reich added to the uniforms

Above. Soldiers from a Communications unit working with a field telephone. Note the new gas masks introduced in the 1930s being worn

Top right. A Major wearing the officer's service tunic. Note the white piping for Infantry on his service cap

Right. A Cavalry General wearing the service uniform reviewing his troops marching into Paris, 1940. The very distinctive Army General's broad red stripes are displayed on his trousers

Above. This officer is wearing the Army officer's old-style field-service cap. Note the cloth versions of the national emblem and the wreathed cockade being worn on the field cap. This cap was later replaced by the M38 Field Service Cap

Above. These men are wearing the Model 1936 Tunic with the bottle-green collars. The soldier on the left is wearing a Model 1938 Field Cap. A pair of MG34 Machine-Guns have been placed on an anti-aircraft mount

Above. An armored crew washing their SdKfz 250 Leichter Schutzenpanzerwagen (Light-Armored Personnel Carrier). Hanging from his neck, the soldier on the left has his identification disc in a leather pouch

Above left. This officer is wearing the Model 1943 General Issue Field Cap with officer's silver braid at the crown. On the side of his cap is a distinctive unit insignia attributed to the 290th Infantry Division

Above right. The Infantry officer is wearing a rather worn M38 Field Service Cap that replaced the Army officer's old-style field service cap. Note the officer's braid on the cap. The inverted chevron (soutache) on the field cap eventually disappeared after 1940

Left. The officer's white summer tunic was introduced in 1937. Shoulder-boards, the pin-on national emblem, and buttons were removable

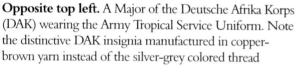

Opposite top left. A Major of the Deutsche Afrika Korps (DAK) wearing the Army Tropical Service Uniform. Note the distinctive DAK insignia manufactured in copper-brown yarn instead of the silver-grey colored thread

Opposite top right. This Oberfeldwebel, decorated with the Knight's Cross with Oakleaves, is wearing the Model 1943 Tunic with straight pocket flaps and pockets without pleats

Opposite left. A column of Panzer with crewmen wearing their distinctive black uniforms. Note most are wearing the Panzer version of the M38 Field Caps

Above. A sentry wearing an all splinter-pattern camouflage uniform, Mountain Troops-style field cap, and helmet. He is armed with a 98k Rifle

Above right. Artillerymen wearing the Model 1940 Tunic with the bottle-green collar removed. A red piped shoulder-strap was worn with the uniform

Right. A German sentry wearing the reed-green denim field-service uniform based on the Model 1940 Tunic. Note the painted camouflage scheme on his helmet

Above. Upon entering the war, Adolf Hitler changed the colors of his double-breasted uniform from the political brown to the military field-grey to signify his position as Commander-in-Chief of Germany's armed forces. The senior ranking generals are wearing their service uniforms with the red piping down the front of the tunics and General's or Field Marshal's collar tabs

Left. A Pioneer, as noted by the black soutache of his M38 Field Cap, with snow camouflage material worn over his greatcoat. The soldier behind has wrapped some white material over his helmet

Opposite above left. Two members of the DAK wearing the Tropical Service Uniform. Note the Tropical version of the Mountain Troops Field Cap

Opposite above right. A Gebirgsjäger wearing the Model 1936 Tunic with "knickerbocker-style" trousers made specially for mountain climbing. Special climbing boots were another distinguishing feature of the Mountain Troops' uniform

Opposite right. An anti-aircraft gun crew wearing camouflaged Model 1935 Steel Helmets

Left. An enlisted East German Paratrooper wearing the walking-out uniform that was introduced by an order on 9 October 1969. The tunic was worn open with a shirt as a walking-out uniform and was closed when on duty. The red beret replaced the field-grey version

Above. From left to right are the Generals and Admirals of the following branches: Police, Air Force, Army, and Navy. The Army General is wearing the distinctive gold embroidered wreath on the red band of his service cap. All are wearing their rank shoulder-boards on their trench coats

Below. The Kampfgruppen der Arbeiterklasse was based on the Landsturm Battalions of the First World War and the Deutscher Volkssturm of the Second World War, in which citizen-soldiers came to the assistance of the Army when there was a national emergency

Above. A parade of soldiers from the Nationalen Volksarmee of the German Democratic Republic. All are wearing the Model 1956 Steel Helmet that was patterned after the wartime 1944 Pattern Experimental Steel Helmet. Since 1956 the East German Army's uniform had been influenced by the uniforms worn by the Wehrmacht during the Second World War

Left. The Kampfgruppen were issued with a distinctive field uniform and were equipped in much the same way as the NVA. Here a "Gehilfe des Stellvertreters des Bataillons-Kommandeurs" stands guard along a parade route in East Berlin. He is armed with a SKS Rifle. Note the East German flag attached to the soldier's bayonet

Below. The Kampfgruppen der Arbeiterklasse worked closely with the Army and interacted frequently. Note the organization's emblem worn on the soldiers' left sleeves. The field caps bear a close resemblance to the Wehrmacht's Mountain Troops Field Cap. The NVA soldiers are wearing parade tunics with the traditional double *Kapellenlitzen* on the collar and cuffs

Above. Members of the Kampfgruppen firing an 82mm Recoilless Gun. Familiarity with weapons used by the NVA was emphasized

Above. An armored crewman stands next to his unit's regimental standard. Note the distinctive Soviet-style padded crash-helmet

Above. An East German soldier, armed with an AKM Assault Rifle, is seen examining a 7.62 x 54 Dragonuv Sniper Rifle that is being handed to him by a Russian soldier

Above. NVA Armeegeneral Hoffmann, center, meeting members of the Grenztruppen (Border Guard Troops). On his right is a Border Guard General. Both Generals are wearing walking-out uniform

Above. New recruits of the NVA give their oath of loyalty upon a regimental standard at the former Sachsenhausen Concentration Camp near Berlin

Above. East German Army NCOs presenting Officer's Honor Daggers to newly graduated officers

Above. Borderguards on the East German frontier wearing camouflage field uniforms

Above. A Bundeswehr Oberfeldwebel working on communication equipment, 2003. His shoulder-patch identifies him as part of the International Security Force sent to maintain the peace in Afghanistan after the overthrow of the Taliban regime in 2001/2002. He is wearing the beret badge of the Dutch-German Corps (I. Deutsche/Nederland Korps)

Above. A West German tank crew wearing their coveralls and distinctive berets over crash-helmets, standing in front of their Kampfpanzer Leopard, 1960s

Above. These crewmen serving on a Leopard 2 A5 Tank (Kampfpanzer Leopard 2 A5) are wearing the "Flecktarn" camouflage field uniforms that were introduced in the late 1980s. Note the padded crash-helmet and field cap being worn by these soldiers

Above. Mules and horses are still used by the Gebirgsjäger troops for carrying supplies through difficult mountain terrain. The 'Flecktarn' camouflage field uniform is standard issue for all branches of the Bundeswehr

Above. The Jagdpanzer Kanone 90mm, later known as Kanonenjagdpanzer, was similiar to the Second World War Jagdpanzer IV. The tanks were deployed in independent battalions or batteries attached to Jäger and Panzergrenadier brigades, or in tank destroyer platoons attached to the 5th Company of a Jäger or Panzergrenadier battalion

Above. The premier unit of the Bundeswehr is the Guards Battalion (Wachtbataillon). All are wearing the green collar tabs and beret of the infantry. Upon the beret is the Guards' badge consisting of a Gothic "W" within an oakleaf wreath. They are standing to attention with their greatcoats and white leather equipment. Note the cuff-title with "Wachbataillon" that is worn on both sleeves of the greatcoat. The shoulder-patch is that of the Armed Forces Central Office

Above. A combination of the past with the present. Members of the Wachtbataillon present arms with Second World War-vintage 98k Rifles. They are dressed in their stone-grey Model 1957 Service Tunics with white leather equipment

Above. Soldiers of the Bundeswehr wearing the new Kevlar Helmet and armed with Heckler & Koch G36 Assault Rifles

Above. A German officer in desert-pattern camouflage field uniform standing to attention with Dutch and German troops. All are wearing the beret insignia of the Dutch-German Corps

Above. A Fallschirmjäger providing security for an Afghan fire-fighting force. He is wearing an antiballistic armor vest over his field uniform

Above. The modern Gebirgsjäger has gone through a lot of changes since the first Ski Battalions were raised during the First World War. This Mountain Trooper is wearing a special snow-camouflage suit over his field uniform

Above. After reunification in 1990, the Bundeswehr began to take on new roles, including serving as peacekeepers. During the Balkan War in 1999 soldiers of the Bundeswehr experienced combat for the first time since the Second World War. Since then, German troops have been deployed to various parts of the world. Here a contingent wearing desert-pattern camouflage field uniforms are being sent to war-torn Afghanistan to serve as a security force

Above. This Second World War veteran Major is wearing his wartime decorations – these were reintroduced in 1957, in a denazified form. The grey backing of his collar tabs and his Bundeswehr qualification badge over his right pocket designate him as belonging to an Army Aviation unit

Above. A West German Generalleutnant wearing the Model 1957 Service Uniform. He has the traditional General's "Alt-Larisch" collar tabs on his lapels. Note the embroidered jump qualification badge on his tunic and the Fallschirmjäger badge on his beret

5

THE THIRD REICH
AND WORLD WAR II
(1933–1945)

Left. New Reichschancellor Adolf Hitler assumed power on 30 January 1933 and immediately began rebuilding the German military structure to its former glory. Hitler's adjutant immediately behind him, recognizable by his aiguillette, is wearing the standard Reichsheer greatcoat

Below. Reichsheer officers and a member of the Allgemeine Schutzstaffel (SS) pose for a photograph during a horsemanship event. The army officers' collar tabs have a yellow base designating them as cavalrymen. The Leutnant on the far right is wearing the distinctive Totenkopf Tradition Unit insignia of Reiter-Regiment 13 on his cap

Above left. This Artilleryman is wearing the newly introduced cap and breast eagles of the Third Reich on his Reichsheer uniform. The cap eagle is the first model because of the short wings. He is still wearing his Reichswehr Belt Buckle consisting of the Weimar eagle within a roundel and the words "Gott mit Uns"

Above right. An Infantry Hauptmann from the 21st Infantry Regiment with the new National Socialist insignia. He is wearing the first-pattern cap eagle

Right. The new insignia, consisting of an eagle with outstretched wings and grasping a wreathed swastika, was introduced to the army in February 1934. The insignia can be seen applied to the soldier's Reichsheer tunics. Behind the MG .08 crew are two soldiers wearing the soft field caps with Reichs cockade. The crew in the foreground are wearing the Model 1918 Steel Helmet

Above. An excellent view of three different model
tunics. The seated Unteroffizier on the left is wearing the
Model 1936 Tunic, the one seated on the right is wearing
the Model 1940 Tunic, and the newly married
Unteroffizier is wearing the Uniform Tunic or
Waffenrock. All are wearing the enlisted service caps with
black leather chinstrap

Right. A Hauptfeldwebel, "Der Spiess", of the
Wachregiment Berlin (Berlin Guard Regiment)
prepares his men for inspection. Note the Gothic "W"
between his ranks pips on his shoulder-strap and those
on the enlisted men's shoulder-straps as well. This
unit later became the Infantry Regiment
Grossdeutschland and was awarded a special cuff-title
bearing that name. All are wearing standard army
Waffenrock. A new Waffenrock was to be proposed for
the regiment to wear from 15 September 1939 on,
based on the standard army model; however, the
elongated *Dopplelitzen* collar patches and
Brandenburg-style cuffs were the distinguishing
features of the uniform. With the outbreak of war,
these tunics were not issued or manufactured –
though prototypes had been made and issued in very
limited numbers

Opposite page right. An infantry Oberschütze
wearing his Waffenrock des Deutschen Heeres für
Mannshaften. The field-grey tunic had a dark
blue-green collar and Swedish cuffs. *Waffenfarbe* piping
was around the collar, cuffs, down the front of the
coat, and on the rear skirt

Opposite page far right. A Gefreiter wearing his
Waffenrock. Note the *Waffenfarbe* piping possibly for
cavalry (gold yellow), signals (lemon yellow), Panzer
(pink), or even motorized reconnaisance (copper
brown). He is wearing the first-pattern Army marksmanship lanyard. Clearly visible is the second and
final eagle cap insignia

Opposite page below. Officers and men wearing
the Waffenrock des Deutschen Heeres introduced on
29 June 1935. The soldiers are also wearing the new
Model 1935 Helmet that eventually replaced the
previous First World War vintage helmets

Above. These two soldiers are wearing Model 1936 Service Uniforms. The collar patches have *Waffenfarbe* on the *Dopplelitzen*. The boots and cap that the Gefreiter on the right is wearing indicate that he is a member of a Mountain Troop or Gebirgsjäger unit

Above. A Hauptfeldwebel/Hauptwachtmeister, "Der Spiess", of a Pioneer unit. The two bands on the sleeves of his Model 1936 Tunic are typical of a senior NCO holding that rank. Note the black piping on his cap and the early pointed shoulder-straps that were eventually replaced with the rounded versions. He is wearing the marksmanship lanyard with the new pattern plaque (consisting of a Wehrmacht-style eagle over a shield with crossed swords). The acorns on his lanyard were added for successive awards

Left. During the Spanish Civil War, 1936–9, Hitler sent men and materials to assist the Spanish Nationalist leader, Generalísimo Francisco Franco, in his fight against the Soviet-supported Republican forces. The German members of the Condor Legion gained valuable combat experience and the opportunity to test out their new weapons. At least 120 PzKw I Ausf. A and B tanks were sent to Spain, the majority being handed over to German-trained Spanish crews when they went into action. These men of a Panzer unit are wearing Spanish Army uniforms with Spanish military ranks above the wearer's left pocket and the black Basque beret

Above. A German field officer oversees his men during a map session. He is wearing a Spanish officer's tunic (some were privately made with some German influence) with his rank in the form of two gold six-pointed stars above his left pocket designating his position as a Major, which was equivalent with the local Spanish rank of Lieutenant-Colonel. The men are wearing Spanish-made dark-brown tanker coveralls. Note the Deathshead, the symbol of the Panzer troops, on the men's berets

Above. A well-known photo of a member of the German volunteer Panzer unit of the Condor Legion. Note the distinctive Panzer Deathshead and the swastika immediately below it. He is wearing the German Army-issue waterproof double-breasted motorcycle coat with a woollen field-grey material-faced collar

Left. Soldiers of the Austrian Presidential Guard upon Germany's annexation of Austria in 1938. Note the application of the German Army-style breast eagle on their Austrian tunics and the addition of German Army decals on their Model 1918 Helmets

Above. As Austrian Army units were being reorganized and incorporated into the German Army, many Austrian soldiers continued wearing their modified uniform for months after the annexation, until supplies from Germany reached their units

Above. An excellent close-up view of the Austrian tunic with the German Army breast eagle

Right. A good view of the back of the Model 1936 Tunic. He is carrying his gas-mask cannister and bread bag with field canteen. Of interest is the canvas cover and the metal muzzle cover for his 98k Rifle. His black leather marching boots have been modified to have side-straps

Above. This Unteroffizier appears already to be a veteran of the campaigns in Poland and in France. He is wearing the Model 1936 Tunic over his reed-green "herringbone twill" denim trousers. He is armed with the Mauser 98k Bolt-Action Rifle. Slighly hidden by his left arm is the butt end of his Walther P-38 Pistol. His M-43 Field Cap is tucked into his belt

Above left. This Obergefreiter's Model 1940 Tunic had been through some hard campaigning, as evidenced by its appearance. He is wearing the Crimea Campaign Shield on his left arm above his rank chevrons

Above right. An enlisted cavalryman wearing the Model 1940 Tunic. It was essentially similiar to the Model 1936 Tunic, although the bottle-green collar was replaced with a field-grey color that matches the rest of the tunic. Note his black leather cavalry boots with spurs

Left. As the war progressed, time and materials were becoming limited. This Obergefreiter fresh from the Russian Front, as denoted by the ribbon sewn to his button hole, is wearing the Model 1943 Tunic and M43 Cap. Note that the pleats on the pockets have been removed and the pocket flaps have been straightened. The shoulder-straps are now field-grey

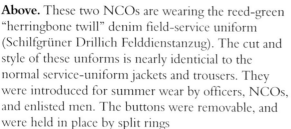

Above. These two NCOs are wearing the reed-green "herringbone twill" denim field-service uniform (Schilfgrüner Drillich Felddienstanzug). The cut and style of these uniforms is nearly identical to the normal service-uniform jackets and trousers. They were introduced for summer wear by officers, NCOs, and enlisted men. The buttons were removable, and were held in place by split rings

Above right. Another view of the Model 1943 Service Tunic. Note the use of the early war bottle-green shoulder-straps. From 1943 on shoulder-straps were made in field-grey cloth for all tunic styles

Right. The Model 1944 Field Blouse was a further modification of the German field-service uniforms and was a complete break with German Army uniform tradition. The style was a radical design due to the collapsing economy and dwindling resources of the Third Reich

Right. The horrors of war in the final days of the Third Reich. Both men are wearing the Model 1944 Field Blouse. One can see the similarity with the British Army Battledress Blouse. Quite noticeable are the waist band that replaces the jacket skirt and the two patch pockets with straight-edged flaps

Below. A postwar scene of German POWs at work. All are wearing surplus M-43 Field caps and Model 1944 Field Blouses, but devoid of rank distinctions and national insignia. Interestingly, the soldier on the far left is wearing officer's-style silver piping on his black Panzer Model 1943 Field Cap. Note the addition of an "X" sewn onto the sleeves of the POWs' blouses

Below. A Hauptmann in the German Army Parade Dress prescribed for officers. The tunic differed slightly from that of the other ranks in quality and rank insignia

Above. An interesting view of the Model 1936 Service Trousers. A small pocket for a fob watch was located in the front as well as two slant pockets. A single pocket was also located in the rear. The man is wearing the Model 1942 Field Cap

Above. Three officers wearing two different styles of service tunic. The officer in the center is wearing the old Reichsheer Officer's Service Tunic (note the distinctive slash-style lower pockets) that continued to be worn by some officers throughout the Second World War. The other two officers are wearing the Army service tunic that was introduced in 1936. A point of interest is that the officer on the right has tucked some documents into the barrel cuffs of his tunic – a common practice by both officers and men

Above left. A Major in complete parade dress. Besides the full-sized medals and aiguillettes, he is wearing the prescribed Army officer's parade belt in silver and dark-green braiding. In addition, he would be carrying a pair of white or grey gloves, sword, and highly polished black leather boots or shoes (worn with long trousers)

Above right. This Leutnant is wearing the Officer's Piped Field Service Tunic that was a mixture of the service tunic and the uniform or parade tunic. Note the *Waffenfarbe* piping for infantry on his collar, cuffs, and down the front of his coat. The officer collar tabs are of the style usually found on the parade tunic

Left. The Oberleutnant wearing the Officer's Service Tunic which can be worn as an undress uniform without belt and decorations (with the exception of ribbon bars). A veteran of the Great War of 1914–18, he is wearing the First World War Wound Badge Second Class and his ribbon-bar of Imperial German decorations. Clearly visible is his Army Officer's Dagger

Right. A very rare photograph of an Officer's Service Tunic modified to resemble the Model 1944 Field Blouse. Another variation of a modified Officer's Model 1944 Field Blouse can be seen in a photo of Generaleutnant Graf von Schwerin, Commanding Officer of the 76th Panzer Corps, who had been photographed wearing a modified blouse with a fly front and two breast-patch pockets having box pleats and curved-edged pocket flaps. Appropriate officer ranks and insignia were then applied to the modified blouse

Below right. General der Infanterie wearing the service uniform for Generals. This uniform was like that of the officers, but was of higher quality and finish than the issue tunics. Noticeable is the red piping down the front of the coat and the deep barrel cuffs. His trousers or riding breeches display the distinctive Army General's "broad red stripe"

Below. A Generalmajor wearing the sleeve insignia of the Jäger Divisions and Jäger Battalions that was issued on 2 October 1942. A similiar version for Ski-Jäger was also issued bearing the same oakleaves but with crossed skis. Both badges had a corresponding metal insignia that was worn on the field caps

Above. All recruits upon entering the army were issued an off-white denim fatigue uniform. The material was of "herring-bone twill", and was used extensively for work details, training on the parade ground and in the field, weapons-cleaning, vehicle maintenance, and fatigue duty

Left. Field Marshal Keitel is seen wearing the uniform or parade dress for Generals as an undress uniform. Clearly visible are the General's "red-striped" trousers

Below. An Oberinspektor serving as an Army Clothing Official. The official's *Waffenfarbe* color was rose or rose-pink

Above. An excellent close-up view of the Panzer Wrap Tunic. Note the pink *Waffenfarbe* piping around the shoulder-straps, the collar tabs, and the collar. The machine-woven national eagle and oakleaf wreath with cockade are clearly visible. By 1940 the beret was discontinued, and eventually replaced with the black Model 1938 Field Cap

Below. Members of a Reconnaissance unit are seen wearing the distinctive black Panzer Uniform. The black Panzer Beret or Schutzmütze covered a crash-helmet that was used as a means of protection for the armored crews

Above. An Oberfeldwebel wearing the white summer tunic that was introduced on 9 July 1937. Instead of just wearing his shoulder rank, he has added collar tabs and sewn on an Army breast eagle. The tunic was meant to be worn from 1 April to 30 September of each year and to be used as a walking-out uniform

Above. By 1942 the pink piping around the collar had been discontinued. The Feldwebel is wearing the black Panzer Model 1938 Field Cap with the pink *Waffenfarbe* over the national cockade. He is also wearing the Tank Combat Badge (Panzerkampfabzeichen) that was established on 20 December 1939

Above. This Gefreiter is wearing the special field-grey uniform for Tank Destroyer and Self-Propelled Assault Gun units. The insignia on his sleeve makes him an artillery-gun layer. The bronze badge he is wearing is the German Horseman's Badge (Das Deutsche Reiterabzeichen)

Left. Panzer crew members of the Grossdeutschland Division wearing the reed-green two-piece Panzer Denim Suits. Visible are the large patch pockets with flaps on the crewmen's jackets. These uniforms were intended for the summer months and in warm climates

Above. Another view of the Panzerjäger Special Field-Grey Uniform worn by an Obergefreiter. The Army-style collar tabs gradually replaced the Totenkopf by the end of the war

Left. A Hauptmann wearing the Tropical Field Service Uniform issued to the DAK. He is wearing the subdued officer's buckle with a canvas web belt

Above. Members of the DAK driving through a Tunisian town. All are wearing the German Army Tropical Field-Service Uniform and specially made Tropical Helmets for the DAK. Note the large camouflaged duffle bag in the splinter pattern at the rear of the side car

Above. DAK members with Italian soldiers. The two Germans are wearing the canvas and leather lace-up Tropical Boots

Left. The German Tropical Sun Helmet displayed two embossed metal helmet plates. The helmet was short-lived, and was eventually replaced with the soft tan field cap (Feldmütze) that was similiar to those worn by Mountain Troops. The weapon is an Italian Breda 6.5mm Model 30 Machine-Gun

Above. The black inverted chevron or soutache of 'Russia Braid' on the Tropical Field Cap makes this soldier a Pioneer. He is wearing the Qualified Helmsman for Engineer Assault Boats Badge (Steuermann) on his left sleeve

Left. An enlisted man in the DAK. Note the absence of any rank insignia on his Tropical Shirt. It was similiar to the field-grey Army shirt but of cotton twill. Special rank bars were intended for this shirt

Above. The breast Army eagle is unique to the DAK uniform in that the insignia was made in copper-brown yarn instead of the silver-grey thread. The "Africakorps" cuff-title was instituted on 18 July 1941 and was worn on the right sleeve of the field-service, uniform, and service tunics, as well as the greatcoat

Above right. A captured Oberst, a recipient of the Knight's Cross and the German Cross in Silver, of the DAK is wearing the Tropical Field Service Uniform. He is seen with officers of the United States Navy and the United States Coast Guard

Right. During the mid-1930s the Army, as well as the new Luftwaffe, began experimenting with the concept of Parachute Troops. Both Army and Luftwaffe wore similiar jumpsuits and equipment, however, the soldiers would wear their respective service field uniforms under their jump smocks. The Army's Fallschirm-Infanterie-Bataillon was absorbed into the Luftwaffe on 1 January 1939

Above left. Female members of the Army Staff Auxiliaries, which was formed in February 1942. This branch began receiving uniforms by October 1943 from surplus Signals Auxiliaries stocks. A difference between the two branches was the addition of a cuff-title bearing the words "Stabshelferin des Heeres", as evidenced in this photograph. Other cuff-titles worn with this unform were "NH des Heeres", "Stab HSNH", and "Wirtschaftshelferin des Heeres"

Above right. A member of the Army Nachrichtenhelferin (Corps of Female Signals Auxiliaries). This unit, formed on 1 October 1940, was the forerunner of a number of other female branches in the various arms of the Wehrmacht. These auxiliaries were combined into a single corps of Female Auxiliaries or Wehrmachthelferinnen on 29 November 1944. Note the Army-style national emblem on her cap and pocket flap, the brooch, and the piping in the front part of her field cap

Below. In the early campaigns of the war, many former Army paratroopers still mixed their Army equipment with those of the Luftwaffe, as evidenced by the soldier on the far left. One can clearly see the Army breast eagle on his jump smock and his Army enlisted man's belt buckle. The soldiers are wearing the Fallschirmjäger Model 1938 Steel Helmet

Left top. The female auxiliaries were issued with greatcoats, although they were inadequate in extremely cold climates, as is evidenced in this photograph. These women are wearing men's Model 1940 Service Tunics without insignia, including the collar tabs, and the men's Model 1938 Field Cap with insignia. All are wearing the felt overboots that were issued to German troops during the sub-zero temperatures in the winter months on the eastern front. Of particular interest is the one who refused to wear men's pants and continued wearing her Army uniform skirt

Left centre. The Gefreiter on the far left is a member of the Grossdeutschland Infantry Regiment. His cuff-title bearing the words "Grossdeutschland" in script replaced two earlier versions in 1940. On his shoulder-straps are the embroidered letters "GD"

Left bottom. On 6 December 1944 Generalfeldmarschall August von Mackensen (1849–1945) was presented with a special honor, a cuff-title bearing the name "Feld-Marschall von Mackensen". The cuff-title was to be worn by all ranks of the 5. Kavallerie-Regiment

Right. An Unterfeldwebel being awarded the Knight's Cross. This highly decorated soldier is wearing two cuff-titles (see inset). The top one is a campaign cuff-title bearing the word "Afrika" with palms that was introduced on 15 January 1943. The bottom cuff-title, "Kriegsberichter", denotes his duties as a war correspondent. Amongst the many awards noticeable on his Model 1943 Tunic are the German Cross, Close Combat Badge in Silver, War Merit Cross, Iron Cross 1st Class, Luftwaffe Ground Combat Badge, Wound Badge in Silver and three Tank Kills Badges slightly visible on his right sleeve

Johannes M. Dörscheid

Above. An enlisted man wearing the cuff-title "Feldherrnhalle" in German script. This was originally awarded to the men of Infanterie-Regiment 271 on 4 September 1942. The title was in the brown cloth of the Sturmabteilung (SA) with edging in silver-grey cotton thread and the script in silver machine-woven thread

Above left. This member of the Feldgendarmerie is seen wearing the cuff-title embroidered with "Deutsche Wehrmacht". In the first months of the war, members of the Civil Police were placed with Army units to assist in keeping order behind the lines and in occupied territories, in directing traffic and guarding prisoners. He is seen wearing the Police-issue tunic with brown cuffs and orange piping on his collar and tabs, shoulder-straps, cuffs and down the front of his tunic

Left. When a branch of Field Police was created in the Army in 1939, many policemen serving with the Wehrmacht were transferred to this new service. This Unteroffizier is wearing the standard Army Model 1936 Tunic with the green Police eagle insignia and cuff-title bearing the words "Feldgendarmerie" on the wearer's left sleeve. The *Waffenfarbe* color was orange for Field Police

Above. Some Army personnel were selected to act as a para-Police force and serve as advisers to military personnel at railway stations. These soldiers were to maintain order and discipline amongst the troops and civilians traveling through these stations. They were to wear a gorget when on duty

Above right. With the addition of the cuff-title and Police-style arm insignia, the Field Police would be issued with a gorget that gave these military policemen the derisive nickname "Chained Dogs" by the servicemen. Both the Army-style eagle and the script ribbon bearing the words "Feldgendarmerie" would glow in the dark for night duties. Another gorget adopted later was for the Feldjägerkorps. It was nearly identical, but with the substitution of "Feldjägerkorps" instead of "Feldgendarmerie" on the ribbon

Right. The gorget bore the words "Bahnhofswache" on the ribbon with two Wehrmacht-style eagles at each end. Those detachments of troops providing security for railway trains moving through hostile territory wore a similiar gorget with "Zugwachabteilung" on the ribbon. Another identical gorget had "Kommandantur" on the ribbon and was worn by those appointed by a military district commander to conduct street patrols within their areas of command. Like the Gendarmerie Gorget, these too glowed in the dark for night duties. Above the ribbons were positioned the detachment numbers

Above. Army NCOs who were appointed to serve as Color Bearers of the unit's regimental standard wore a special gorget. During the early years of the Third Reich a combination of Imperial and Weimar-era Standard Bearer's Gorgets were used; however, a new Army-pattern gorget bearing the Wehrmacht-style eagle was introduced on 4 August 1936

Above. The first arm shield for Standard Bearers was introduced into units of the Imperial German Army in 1898 and used up to 1919. It was reintroduced on 4 August 1936. The crossed regimental flags were faced in the colors of the service branch

Left. Recruits swearing an oath of loyalty to Adolf Hitler upon the regimental standard of their Infantry unit. Note the Standard Bearer's Gorget being worn by the NCO

Above. A Cavalry Standard Bearer passing review. The gorget could be worn not only with the field-service and uniform tunics but with the greatcoat as well

Below. Generalmajor Emilio Esteban Infantes, Commander of the Spanish Blue Division, confers with a German Division Commander. He and his Spanish volunteers wore the standard German uniforms, insignia, and rank distinctions, although they wore the Spanish Foreign Volunteer Arm Shield on their right arm to distinguish them from other German and foreign volunteer soldiers. Along with their German awards, many Spaniards continued wearing their Spanish decorations earned from the Spanish Civil War

Above. An interesting image of a Standard Bearer of a Panzer unit with his arm shield on his left arm. His Spanish Cross with Swords in Silver and his Legion Condor Tank Crew Badge indicate that he is a veteran of the Spanish Civil War

Above right. A ceremony in the Spanish Embassy in Berlin. Amongst the NSDAP dignitaries and Spanish Falange Party members are two uniformed NCOs from the Blue Division

Right. A Finnish soldier displaying the German Army breast eagle on his Finnish Army-issue summer tunic

Above. The Spanish Blue Division frequently made the news in German periodicals, including the magazine *Signal*. The distinctive blue shirts of the Spanish Falange Party were often worn underneath the German tunics while out in the field. Upon their return and off-duty, the tunics were removed and Falangists proudly wore their blue shirts displaying Spanish rank insignias and awards. These Falangists have applied German Army breast eagles and the Spanish Foreign Volunteer Arm Shield on their blue shirts

Above. Members of the Free India Legion (Legion Freies Indien), formed by captured Indian soldiers serving with the British Army in North Africa. Note the variety of headgear. Of particular interest is the regimental standard of the legion

Left. An excellent photo of an Unteroffizier of the Free India Legion wearing the German Army-issue Tropical Field-Service Uniform and Field Cap. Note his Foreign Volunteer Arm Shield displaying the Indian colors of saffron, white, and green with a rampant tiger superimposed

Right. Generalfeldmarschall Erwin Rommel reviewing members of the Free India Legion along the French coast, 1944. All are wearing various models of the heavier woollen German tunics that were more appropriate for the European climate. Of interest are the various forms of headgear, including the turban worn by the Sikh

Above. An Unteroffizier of the 369th Croatian Reinforced Infantry Regiment wearing his Croatian Foreign Volunteer Arm Shield on his right sleeve. Instead of the German Army cap eagle and cockade he is wearing a gold oval badge with the letters "NDH" (standing for 'Independent State of Croatia') on his M43 Field Cap

Right. The largest number of volunteers and variety thereof were from the many republics that made up the Soviet Union. Because of the large number of ethnic minorities joining the Wehrmacht, a great deal of variety in uniform and insignia existed within these foreign volunteer formations

Above. A Leutnant from the Russian Liberation Army. He is wearing the German-issue Model 1943 Tunic. Note the absence of an Army breast eagle, expressly forbidden by Hitler to be worn by Slavs. Note also the distinctive collar tabs, "POA" Foreign Volunteer Arm Shield, and the various bravery and merit awards for soldiers of the eastern nations

Above. A Cossack Gefreiter wearing the collar tabs for non-commissioned ranks adopted in May 1943. Notice the Russian-style shoulder-straps and the wearing of the German Army breast eagle

Left. German prisoners of war from the Normandy front being brought to English shores by the United States Coast Guard. Amongst the prisoners are two Russian volunteers (located fourth and fifth from the left row facing the camera). The two Gefreiters, as designated by their shoulder-straps, are wearing the appropriate "half" *litzen* that did not go past the collar tabs. The fifth soldier is wearing the correct collar tab reserved for Asiatics and Caucasians, while the other, looking at the camera, substituted his for the German-style tabs (possibly due to supply problems in getting the correct style)

Above. This soldier is wearing the Reichsheer Model 1934 Field Cap. Note the soutache with *Waffenfarbe* around the national cockade

Above. The Model 1942 Field Cap. Basically, the readoption of the old Reichswehr Field Cap without soutache

Above. The Model 1938 Field Cap with soutache

Above. The Model 1938 Field Cap without soutache

Above. The Gebirgsjägers or Mountain Troops readopted their field cap or Bergmütze of First World War fame. Note the distinctive edelweiss worn on the side of the cap

Above. Another view of the enlisted man's Bergmütze

Above. The M43 General Issue Field Cap was widely distributed amongst the troops and proved to be quite popular. Clearly visible above his Obergefreiter chevrons is the Crimean Campaign Shield

Above. On 11 June 1943 the popular Bergmütze was adopted for general issue, known as the M43 General Issue Field Cap (1943 Einheitsfeldmütze). Note the appropriate officer's silver piping around the crown of the cap

Above. Mountain Troop officers usually wore a higher quality Bergmütze with or without the officer's-grade piping around the crown

Above. A camouflaged version of the M43 Field Cap in Army-green splinter pattern

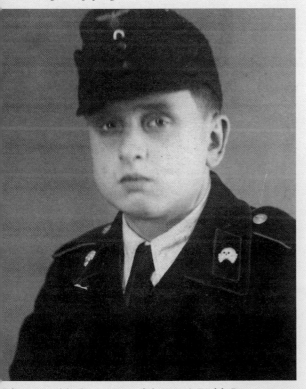

Above. A black version of the M43 Field Cap was adopted for use by the Panzer troops

Above. Another version of the M43 Field Cap, made from Italian camouflage material

Above. The 1st Brandenburg Dragoon Regiment Nr. 2 originally wore the Dragoon Eagle or Schwedter Adler. The Tradition Badge was introduced in 1921 and then worn by the regimental staff and 2nd Squadron of 6. Reiter-Regiment. In 1926 the 4th Squadron received the honor of wearing the badge, and finally in 1937 the Kradschützen Bataillon 3 was granted permission to wear it

Above. The Brunswick Infantry Regiment 92 originally wore the Totenkopf Tradition Badge. In 1921 the badge was passed on to the 1st and 4th Companies of 17. Infanterie-Regiment. Later, in 1939, the Regimental Staff, the 1st and 2nd Battalions, and the 13th and 14th Companies of the 17. Infanterie-Regiment were granted permission to wear the Tradition Badge. Another Tradition Badge, Totenkopf with bones behind the skull, that was similiar to those used by Panzer troops, was worn by selected squadrons of the 5th Cavalry Regiment and by all units, with the exception of the 41st Cavalry Regiment, of the 4th Cavalry Division

Left. German Army Chaplains (Heeresgeistliche) wore officer-quality field-service uniforms without rank insignia or shoulder-straps. A violet armband similar to those used in the First World War was worn. A cross, either Protestant or Catholic, was hung from the neck, and the Gothic Cross worn by Army Chaplains (Heerespfarrer) and Field Bishops (Feldbschöfe) was worn between the national eagle insignia and the Reichs cockade on the visored cap (Schirmmütze). In addition, a special field-grey frock coat was worn that was single-breasted and went down to the knees. It was intended for occasions not requiring service dress

Above. The official Army cap emblem consisting of an edelweiss for Mountain Troops worn on the visored cap or Schirmmütze

Above. The edelweiss emblem for Mountain Troops being worn on the Bergmütze. Both devices for the Bergmütze and Schirmmütze were introduced on 2 May 1939

Left. The Model 1918 Cavalry Steel Helmet, like its sister helmet, continued service in one form or another after the adoption of later models. Toward the end of the war both helmets were widely issued to civilian auxiliary organizations, foreign units, and the Deutscher Volkssturm

Far left. The Model 1916/1918 Steel Helmet continued to see limited service throughout the Third Reich era. The helmet was relegated to standby equipment when the new pattern helmets were introduced after 1935

Left. The Model 1935 Steel Helmet was introduced on 1 July 1935 and was a much smaller and lighter redesigned version of the Model 1916/1918 Steel Helmet. In 1940 another variation, the Model 1940, came out that eliminated the separate ventilation rivets, the air vents being embossed into the sides of the helmet. The helmet decals were gradually phased out by 1943

Right. An excellent view of German helmets worn during the last days of the Third Reich. Various helmet models were introduced during the war, including the Model 1942 Steel Helmet. This helmet was simplified, and was stamped without the edges being "rolled" inward. This gives the helmet a noticeable rim around the back, as seen in this photograph. Note the Fallschirmjäger Steel Helmet among the prisoners

Below. "Der Spiess" wearing the Sanitätsunterpersonal or Medical Personnel Specialist Badge on his right sleeve

Right. Enlisted medical personnel attending to an injured bicyclist. Both are wearing the Red Cross armband. Amongst the equipment being worn is the Medical leather box containing medicine and bandages as well as the large medical canteen that was double the size of the field canteen

Below right. A captured Medical Officer examining fellow prisoners of war at an American field aid station. He would have the Medical Staff and Serpent Device on his shoulder-boards and his piping color would have been cornflower-blue. Note the Wehrmacht-issue Red Cross armband

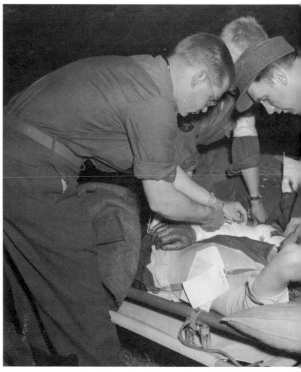

Above. Various styles of winter headgear were used by troops during the war. Seen here is a common-style fur-covered cap (Pelzmützen) used by soldiers serving on the Russian front. Note the use of an Army breast eagle being used as a cap insignia

Above. A variety of greatcoats were issued to the German Army throughout the Second World War. Seen here are most of the styles, beginning with the early pre-war bottle-green collar, the subsequent coat with field-grey collar, and the final version with the large field-grey collar. This last style, adopted in 1943, was inferior in quality for reasons of economy

Above. A carry-over from the First World War was
the use of a heavy sheepskin greatcoat for those on
guard duty in extremely cold climates, and was usually
referred to as the "Watch Coat". The other two
soldiers are wearing the pre-war standard field-grey
greatcoats with the bottle-green collar. Note that the
guard is wearing the old Model 1918 Steel Helmet

Above. The Motorcyclist Waterproof Coat was usually
issued to motorcycle units and individual motorcyclists.
The loose-fitting coat could be buttoned around the
wearer's legs in order that he operate his motorcycle
safely. Field equipment could be worn over the coat

Above. A nice image of an Oberfeldwebel wearing the early-pattern pointed shoulder-strap. The collar tabs had *Waffenfarbe* designating branch of service, such as Infantry with this NCO. The use of collar tabs with *Waffenfarbe* declined after 1943, and a generic style was used for all branches

Below. Later, rounded shoulder-straps were introduced, as seen with this Feldwebel. Note the peculiar style of silver-embroidered collar tabs being worn

Above. The reversible winter uniform being worn on the Russian front. These uniforms were made large enough to be worn over the field-service uniform. The side being shown here is the mouse-grey, which when reversed would show the Army-green splinter-pattern camouflage. Of interest is the various equipment being worn, such as the 98k Bayonet, mess kit, breadbags, and canteens

Left. The Tropical Shirt worn by a Hauptmann serving with the Deutsche Afrika Korps. His rank is designated by a special system of green oakleaves and bars on a black field. Apart from on the Tropical Shirts, this system of ranking was also used with camouflage smocks, winter uniforms, and other special combat clothing. Interestingly, it was also adopted by the Waffen-SS for use with their uniforms, but with the appropriate rank terminology used by that organization

Above. Some units bore special elite-unit distinctions on their shoulder-straps such as this member of the Grossdeutschland Infantry Regiment. Some of the following elite units used distinctive insignia on their shoulder-straps: Grenadier-Regiment 134, Panzer Grenadier Regiment 60, Feldherrnhalle Infantry Regiment, Führer-Grenadier-Regiment, 5th Cavalry Regiment, and Wachregiment Berlin

Above right. An Army Sonderführer wearing the officer's service tunic. Note the distinctive collar tabs and the *Waffenfarbe*, which would have been grey-blue, on his shoulder-boards

Right. This Sonderführer is wearing the collar tab for officials with NCO rank. The single bar of braid barely visible on his shoulder-strap indicates that he was an aspiring NCO (Unteroffizieranwärter)

Above. Two Army Administration Officials (Heeresbeamte) holding High-Grade Career (Höherer Dienst) positions that were equivalent to field-officer ranks. The official on the right is either an Oberintendanturrat or another similar title which corresponded to a Lieutenant-Colonel, while the one on the left is an Intendanturrat or similiar title which corresponded to a Major. In 1934 the officials were designated as Armed Forces Officials and were regarded members of the Army as much as soldiers

Below. Army Musicians wore a special removable device on their shoulders called "Musician's Wings" or "Swallow's Nest". Three groups of musicians were entitled to wear the Musician's Wings: Drum and Fife Musicians, Battalion Buglers, and Regimental Bandsmen and Trumpeters. These were worn by all branches of the German Army

Above. German Army Administration Official

Above. Generalfeldmarschall List wearing the regulation collar tabs for his rank that were introduced in 1942 and worn up to 1945

Right. An excellent detailed shot of the crossed batons of a Field Marshal's shoulder-boards worn by Generalfeldmarschal Reichenau. The distinctive shoulder-board was introduced in 1940. Of interest is that he is still wearing the collar tabs prescribed for Generalmajor up to Generaloberst. Prior to the introduction of the Field Marshal's collar tabs in 1942, the collar tabs for Generaloberst were still in use with the Field Marshal's shoulder-boards

Left top. Generaloberst von Falkenhorst in service uniform. As Generaloberst he wears the appropriate collar tab and the three-star pips on his gold-and-silver entwined shoulder-boards

Left middle. A rare picture of the German Army chemical suit and gas mask in use. The suits were neatly folded into a pouch and worn from the strap of or attached to the gas-mask cannister

Left bottom. Barracks room being inspected by a Duty NCO of the Day with an enlisted assistant. Note the armbands "GvD" (Gehilfe vom Dienst) and "UvD" (Unteroffizier vom Dienst) being worn. The letters on the armbands were white on a red field

Above. An excellent study of various equipment in use. Note the binoculars, map case, cartidge pouches, mess kits, trench flashlights, shovel, and headgear

Right above. An enlisted man armed with a MP 38 (Machinenpistole 38) submachine-gun, commonly referred to as the "Schmeisser". On his left hip is a magazine pouch that carried three magazines for the gun, each magazine carrying thirty-two rounds of 9mm Parabellum ammunition

Right below. Various cloth helmet-covers were made especially for camouflage purposes. These men are wearing the Army-green splinter-pattern camouflage helmet-covers

Below. This Knight's Cross recipient has a net of woven string over his helmet and is wearing the late-war rain-pattern lightweight camouflage smock

Above. Waiting for the Soviet onslaught in Germany, 1945. This member of the Volksgrenadier is armed with the Sturmgewehr 44, a K43 Semi-Automatic Rifle, and a Panzerfaust. He is wearing a Model 1942 Steel Helmet and a camouflage smock

Above. German Pioneers placing Teller Mines. All are wearing the reversible winter uniform with the Army-green splinter-pattern camouflage side showing. They are armed with the 98k Rifle

Above. The German Army-issue shelter-half-tent or Zeltbahn had a multitude of uses other than providing shelter. It was also used as a waterproof cape. Note the Army-green splinter-pattern on the Zeltbahn

Above. Der Deutscher Volkssturm was raised in the final months of the war, to be headed by Reichsführer-SS Heinrich Himmler but trained, armed, and uniformed by the Army. Every effort was made in uniforming the Volkssturm, including the use of obsolete Army uniforms and various surplus NSDAP organizational uniforms. A Leutnant of the Grossdeutschland Infantry Regiment is giving tactical information to various high-ranking Volkssturm leaders. Most appear to be uniformed in Army Officer's Service Tunics without army insignia or rank shoulder-boards, while others are wearing a combination of Reichsarbeitdienst (RAD) or various NSDAP organizational uniforms. All are wearing the Volkssturm armbands designating them as part of the German armed forces. Note the use of the Diplomatic Service eagle on the wearer's left arm by some of the Volkssturm Generals (Bataillonführer)

Above. Members of the Standschützen Battalions or Austrian Volkssturm passing in review in Innsbruck. Most are wearing the Model 1943 tunic with SA/SS style collar tabs. The Battalion number and district (Gau) were placed on the wearer's right collar tab, while his rank was displayed on his left tab. Most are wearing the NSDAP political eagle on their M43 Field Caps. Most appeared to be armed with Austrian Model 1895 Steyr-Mannlicher Rifles

Above. The wartime caption to this picture read "A Volkssturm General commits suicide when US Troops entered Leipzig, 1945". Note the use of the armband as a cuff-title, a common practice. The Volkssturm adopted their own rank system and displayed a series of rank pips of aluminium color on black SS-style collar tabs. The rank tabs were worn in pairs or as a single on the wearer's left collar (while the right tab would be plain or with unit designation). The following ranks were used by the Deutscher Volkssturm: Volkssturmman (private), plain black collar patches; Gruppenführer (corporal), single pip on black patches; Zügführer (sergeant), two pips arranged diagonally on black collar patches; Kompanieführer (captain), three pips arranged diagonally on black collar patches, Bataillonsführer (Lieutenant-Colonel), four pips on black collar patches

Above. Contrary to current popular imagination, every effort was made to provide some form of uniform to the Volkssturm so that they would be treated as members of the German armed forces rather than as guerillas or insurgents who could be summarily executed. This Volkssturmmann is wearing the Army-issue greatcoat with large collar and an M43 Field Cap

Above. The debris of war

6

NATIONALEN
VOLKSARMEE
(1946–1991)

Above. The East German Army was initially made up of German POWs that the Russians had captured and persuaded to participate in the fight against Nazism. Here, a POW working for the Russians is reading propaganda literature over the airwaves. This POW's uniform is devoid of any military insignia, although he is wearing an armband inscribed with the words "Freies Deutschland"

Above. Immediately upon securing the eastern sector of Germany, the Soviet authorities began looking at ways of clandestinely re-establishing an armed German force to meet Soviet needs without alarming the western Allies. As permitted in the treaty with the Allies, the Soviets began creating a police force for maintaining security within Eastern Germany's borders. Thus, the Kasernierten Volkspolizei (KVP) or Barracked People's Police came into existence. Seen here is a member of the Barracked Police armed with a Sturmgewehr 44 Assault Rifle. Note the distinctive M43-style Field Cap with the KVP insignia

Right. The uniform was a combination of German and Russian influence. Much of the early equipment issued to this police units were captured German stocks – such as the case with this obsolete Maxim MG .08 Machine-Gun

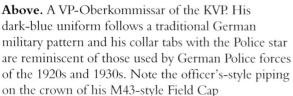

Above. A VP-Oberkommissar of the KVP. His dark-blue uniform follows a traditional German military pattern and his collar tabs with the Police star are reminiscent of those used by German Police forces of the 1920s and 1930s. Note the officer's-style piping on the crown of his M43-style Field Cap

Above right. Members of the KVP wearing the M43-style Field Cap and the Service Cap. Note the difference between the two tunics, definitely of German influence. The tunic on the left bears a resemblance to the Model 1915 Field Blouse and is probably a reworked Luftwaffe Fliegerbluse from leftover wartime stocks. The belt buckles bore a tricolor shield of black, red, and yellow in the center of the Police-style starburst within the roundel. Note the adoption of the German police style shoulder-boards for the VP-Hauptwachtmeister (left) and VP-Oberwachtmeister (right)

Above. A close-up showing the KVP collar tabs. The color base of the tabs designated the branch of service for the KVP and State Security Forces. The following *Waffenfarben* were used: (1) KVP: Generals – red, Infantry – maroon, Artillery – black, Panzer – cobalt blue, Signals – black, Pioneers – black, Chemical Troops – black, Motorized Troops – black, Railway Troops – black, Administration, Medical, Judicial Service – dark green; (2) VP-Luft – light blue; (3) VP-See – dark blue, Administrative Service – silver-grey, Coastal Service – wine red; (4) Ministry of State Security/State-Secretary – red, Border Service – light green

Left. The Soviets and East German authorities began creating youth organizations in order to prepare them for military service. Seen here are young women of the Freie Deutsche Jugend (FDJ) marching with .22 caliber training rifles in 1952

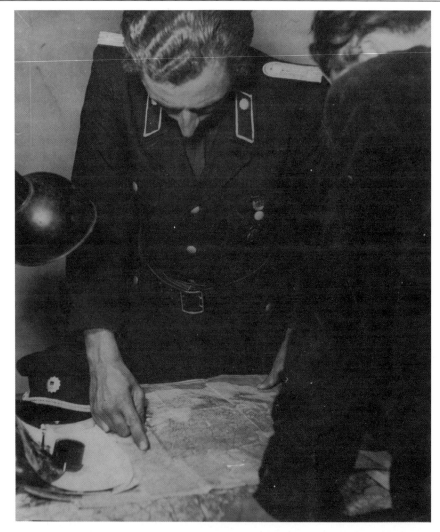

Above. A female KVP member with the rank of VP-Wachtmeister, 1950–2

Left. A VP-Oberkommissar in service uniform, 1950–2

Above. Senior KVP officers wearing the motorcyclist's waterproof coat or Kradmantel with woollen collar and officer's shoulder-boards

Left. KVP women wearing blue sportsuits for athletics. Note the one with the Volkspolizei emblem over her breast pockets

Above. Female members of the Kasernierten Volkspolizei (KVP) wearing their dark-blue service uniform as walking-out dress. The tunics, caps, and belts with buckles appear to be the same as those issued to the men, with the skirts being the only female item specially tailored

Right top. Male and female KVP members wearing the dark-blue service greatcoat, 1950–2. The pattern is similiar to those used by the army before the Second World War

Right middle. Another group photograph. Note the use of trousers by the KVP women

Right bottom. KVP members posing for a photograph, 1950–2. Note the various headgears worn and the slight difference between the men's and women's uniforms

Right. Men of the KVP representing the three services: Kasernierten Volkspolizei (KVP), Volkspolizei-Luft, and Volkspolizei-See. They are wearing the appropriate service uniforms for each of the services. The KVP soldier on the far right is wearing a Soviet-influenced uniform and collar tabs. His maroon collar tabs indicate that he serves in the Infantry, and he is armed with a Russian PPSh 41 Submachine-Gun. Note the new-style field cap worn by the KVP soldier and airman

Below. Between 1952 and 1956 the Kasernierten Volkspolizei (KVP) took on a more military appearance. The khaki field-service uniforms were heavily influenced by the Soviets and in most cases were supplied by them. Soviet-style collar patches with branch colors, mentioned previously, are worn on the service uniforms and greatcoats. A national cockade bearing the colors of black, red, and yellow is worn on the front of the Russian-style service cap. The black leather belt and boots appear to be the only things that are of German origin

Left. The Nationalen Volksarmee (NVA) came into existence on 19 January 1956 and adopted a whole new appearance. Their most distinctive item was the Model 1956 Steel Helmet that was based on the wartime experimental Model 1944 Steel Helmet of the Wehrmacht. The Gefreiter is wearing the new grey greatcoat with German-style army shoulder-boards. In addition, the NVA returned to the traditional German *Waffenfarbe* system of identifying branch of service: therefore, white was again for Infantry, red for Artillery, pink for Panzer, black for Pioneers, etc. Note the Russian-style ammunition pouches for the Mosian-Nagant Rifle

Below left. An Unteroffizier of the NVA wearing the new grey service uniform adopted in 1956. The uniform bears a very strong resemblance to those worn by the German Army during the Second World War. The double *Kappellenlizten* collar tabs with *Waffenfarbe* are worn on the charcoal-grey collar. Note the helmet decal bearing the East German colors

Below. A 1956 press-release photo showing the introduction of new uniforms for the branches of the NVA: Landstreitkräfte (Army), Seestreitkräfte (Navy), and Luftstreitkräfte (Air Force)

Opposite above. First public display of the new parade uniforms being worn by newly trained NCOs of the Nationalen Volksarmee, May 1956

Opposite below. In the distance an Army band is passing a formation of sailors. Note the return of the Musician's Wings being worn by the bandsmen

Above. NCOs and other men wearing the Model 1956 Parade Uniform. Note the double *Kappellenlitzen* on the cuffs. They are carrying Russian PPSh 41 Submachine-Guns, DP Light Machine-Guns, and a Rocket Propelled Grenade (RPG)

Right. A NVA color guard in parade uniform standing to attention with their regimental standard. The officers have white piping around the collar while the NCO has the traditional silver lace around his collar

Above. During the period of transition in standardizing the NVA, there were times when KVP and NVA uniform items were mixed. The Oberfeldwebel is wearing his Model 1956 Service Tunic with the old KVP Field Cap with the new oakleaf-wreathed cockade of the German Democratic Republic (Deutsche Demokratische Republik – DDR). Note the short-lived use of the helmet decal on the Model 1956 Steel Helmet

Below. The East German tank crew of a Russian T-34 Tank. They are wearing the tanker's coveralls with Russian-style tanker's crash-helmets

Above. NVA soldiers in a mixture of field uniforms, 1950s. The two dark quilted-pattern suits are former KVP issue while the motorcyclist is wearing the newer NVA-issue field jacket

Below. Ski troops dressed in white snowsuits and firing their Russian Mosin-Nagant Model 1944 Carbines

Above. An excellent view of the camouflage combat suit and overseas cap being worn by this soldier

Below. The lightweight drill uniform being worn by three NVA-enlisted men. Note the absence of bottom pockets on the front skirts of the drill jackets. All are wearing the grey painted buckles depicting the hammer-and-compass emblem of the DDR, and grey web belts

Above. An NVA handing a Russian DP Light Machine-Gun and a PPSh 41 Submachine-Gun to a fellow soldier. Both are "splotch-pattern" camouflage combat suits. Note the Second World War-style canteen

Above. As part of socialist ideology, women were permitted in various branches of the armed forces of the German Democratic Republic. Seen here is a female Unterfeldwebel serving in a Signals unit in the early 1980s

Left above. East German Paratroops (Fallschirmjäger) on parade, 1960s. All are wearing the "splotch-pattern" camouflage jackets and dark-grey berets

Left below. A scene that didn't change much in the twenty years that followed, NVA soldiers in parade uniform marching with AK-47 (later AK-74 and AKM) Assault Rifles, 1968

Right. An NVA General awarding the Scharnhorst-Orden to the regimental standard of a Kampfgruppen der Arbeiterklasse unit, 1977. This organization was based on the Landsturm and later Deutscher Volkssturm, whereby these Home-Guardsmen would provide assistance to the NVA in times of emergency. Controlled by the East German Communist Party (Sozialistische Einheitspartei Deutschlands – SED), these units were trained, supplied, and led by the NVA

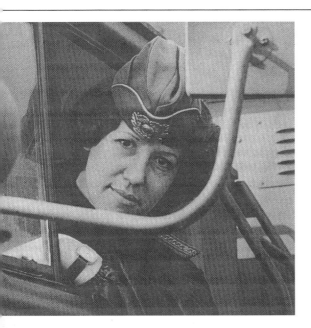

Above. A Female Fähnrich or Warrant Officer wearing the black coveralls usually worn by Panzer and/or vehicle-maintenance personnel. Note the distinctive Overseas Cap or Schiffchen worn by female NVA soldiers

Above right. These women are wearing the rain-pattern camouflage field uniforms adopted in 1965. Note the general-issue berets being worn by these women. All are carrying their gas-mask and chemical-suit bags

Above. The field uniform used by the Kampfgruppen der Arbeiterklasse differed from those used by the NVA and doubled also as a walking-out and parade uniform. Note the organization's emblem, consisting of an arm grasping a red-flagged rifle, on the Schiffchen. The emblem is also used as a sleeve insignia

Below. The two red bars on the officer's field jacket identify him as either a Hundertschaftskommandeur or Batteriekommandeur. Note the Kampfgruppen der Arbeiterklasse emblem worn by the soldier being decorated

Below. A young girl from the FDJ presenting flowers to a Standard Bearer of a Kampfgruppen der Arbeiterklasse unit. His rank, consisting of a thick over a thin red bar, indicates that he is a Stellvertreter des Hundertschaftkommandeur or Stellvertreter des Batteriekommandeur

Above. An enlisted man in the NVA Parade Uniform

Above right. An excellent view of the service cap. The chinstrap and visor of the cap were manufactured out of black plastic

Right. A Major in parade uniform reviewing troops, 1968. He is grasping his Officer's Honor Dagger or Ehrendolch der Offiziere that was introduced in 1961

Above. In the photo we can clearly see the Officer's Honor Dagger being worn from the brocade parade belt. The dagger was to be worn with the parade and walking-out uniform on State holidays, on the anniversary of the NVA, and on special order of the commanders and the garrison superior

Right. An NVA Officer marching at the head of his troops with a Parade Sword. The langet of the sword's hilt bore the arms of the DDR

Above. Armeegeneral H. Hoffmann, head of the
NVA, is wearing the double-breasted Social Uniform
for Generals, 1968. Note the East German Admiral's
uniform on the far right

Right. Armeegeneral H. Hoffmann, 1975

Below. An excellent study of the General's Service
Cap worn by Armeegeneral Hoffmann

Above. Hoffmann wearing the officer's summer trench coat, 1968

Below. NVA officers wearing the short summer staff-service jacket, 1975. Note the similarities between the Czechoslovakian and East German uniforms, both of which were influenced by those used in the Soviet Army. The jackets were meant to be worn as a walking-out uniform

Above left. An Unteroffizier wearing a parade tunic with NVA decorations. Of interest is the Marksmanship Lanyard for Infantry, DDR Sports Badge, General Qualification Badge, and Best Soldier Badge

Above. By 1986 the dark charcoal-grey collar was gone and the enlisted man's tunic was worn collar open with a shirt and tie showing underneath. It was to be worn as a walking-out and parade uniform. The sentry standing guard over General von Clausewitz's Grave is armed with an East German-manufactured AKM Assault Rifle

Left. This Stabsfähnrich of a Panzer unit is instructing NCOs in the mechanisms of an armored vehicle. Clearly visible is his arm shield and shoulder-boards identifying his rank. He is permitted to wear officer-quality uniform, headgear, and insignia, including the collar tabs seen here

Above. A recently commissioned Unterleutnant with family members, 1988. He is wearing the open-collar officer's parade tunic with Schiffchen. Note the white piping around the collar and cuffs. The false embroidered officer's collar tabs are made of stamped metal with the correct *Waffenfarbe* of twisted cord running through the *Kappellenlitzen* and then pinned through the grey-cloth-covered cardboard backing

Below. A field version of the Schiffchen can be worn with the field-service uniform. Most of the equipment's grey webbing, including the belt, made from synthetic materials. The Feldwebel leading his men has a brown leather map case strapped to his side

Above. NVA soldiers in field-service uniforms, 1980s. The camouflage uniform introduced in 1965 was nicknamed by the troops "One-Streak-No-Streak-Outfit" because of the camouflage scheme consisting of brown streaks on the green field. Most of the soldiers are armed with the MPiKMS-72 Assault Rifle

below. Armeegeneral Hoffman wearing the white social dress uniform with officers wearing the officer's summer social dress uniform, 1980s. Note the broad General's stripes, which are red, on the trousers

Above. An NVA tank crew aboard a T-72 Tank. Note the Soviet-style Tanker's Helmet being worn by the crewmen

Below. A close-up on the beret being worn by this female NCO, 1980s. Although the metal version of the wreathed cockade was usually applied to service caps, it has been applied to various other headgear as well

Above. East German Paratroopers preparing for a jump. Note the MPiKMS-72 Assault Rifle next to the soldier in the front row. They are wearing the winter-camouflage field-service uniforms

Below left. Like the Kampfgruppen der Arbeiterklasse, the Gesellschaft für Sport und Technik (GST) was an organization affiliated with the Army and a source of future young and experienced soldiers for the NVA. The GST consisted of older teenage members from the FDJ. Note the organization's emblem on the unique field cap, which is brown with red piping

Below right. GST members wore basically the same field uniforms as the Kampfgruppen der Arbeiterklasse, though with different insignia and field cap. Military training and fitness was strongly instilled in the GST

Above. As part of the Warsaw Pact, East Germany collaborated with various Communist nations. Here an East German Oberstleutnant is conferring with a Soviet Army officer. Note the difference between the winter "fur" pile caps worn by the soldiers. The holstered weapon that the NVA officer is carrying is possibly an East German copy of the Russian Makarov Pistol

Left top. The enduring legacy that the German Democratic Republic left for history after its collapse in 1990 was a wall that was designed not to keep enemies out but to prevent its own population from escaping. Seen here are two members of the Grenztruppen on the "deathstrip" along the Berlin Wall. On 9 November 1989 East Germany opened its borders and peoples of East and West celebrated on the breached wall in front of the Brandenburg Gate seen in the distance

Left middle. NVA Military Police with their Soviet counterparts. A distinctive feature of their uniforms besides the winter coats with fur collar they are wearing is the white leather "Sam Browne" Belts. Note the white band around the Model 1956 Steel Helmet with the "KD" within a diamond on the front. The Kommandantendienst (KD) perform traffic-control and law-enforcement duties as well as courier services

Left bottom. Members of the Grenztruppen were considered to be a part of the NVA but, in fact, fell under the Ministry of State Security. They wore the same uniforms and used the same equipment as their Army counterparts; however, they were distinguished by their green *Waffenfarbe*. Note the cuff-titles bearing the words "Grenztruppen der DDR" worn by the two soldiers. The army also used cuff-titles such as "Wachregiment Friederich Engels", "Militärmusikschüler", "NVA-Wachregiment", and "Erich-Weinert-Ensemble"

7

DER BUNDESHEER (1946–2013)

Above. The various greatcoats worn by members of the West German Bundeswehr. The grey winter greatcoat and raincoat were also adopted in 1955 for all ranks' use

Below. A new recruit passes two NCOs dressed in the winter greatcoat. Note the use of the visor cap and mountain cap

Above. The uniforms for the Army of the new Bundeswehr were introduced on 12 November 1955. The uniforms adopted had no connection whatsoever with traditional German military dress

Below. All ranks in the West German Army wore grey service and walking-out uniforms, olive-green field uniforms and a camouflage battledress

Above. NCOs dressed in olive-drab field uniforms marching in new recruits for the Bundeswehr. One can see a heavy American influence on the design of the field uniforms and the chevrons being worn by the NCOs. The only thing distinctly German in influence was the olive-green mountain cap

Right.
Hauptgefreiter in the olive-drab field uniform, 1955. An olive-green mountain cap was worn with the field uniform and the helmet with battledress. He is carrying a pair of 98k Rifles of Second World War vintage

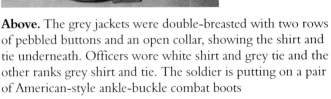

Above. The grey jackets were double-breasted with two rows of pebbled buttons and an open collar, showing the shirt and tie underneath. Officers wore white shirt and grey tie and the other ranks grey shirt and tie. The soldier is putting on a pair of American-style ankle-buckle combat boots

Above. An Unteroffizier standing in formation with his men. The mountain caps bear the national cockade of yellow, red, and black over a pair of crossed sabers – the new insignia of the West German Army

Above. The early Bundesheer was equipped with American weapons until West German manufacturers were able to rebuild their armament industry. The soldiers are armed with a Model 1918A2 Browning Automatic Rifle and M1 Carbines. Note the use of the *Zeltbahn* as ponchos by some of the soldiers

Above. An Unteroffizier (rear rank) and Stabsunteroffizier (front rank) with their men presenting arms in their grey double-breasted service uniforms. All are armed with 98k Rifles. Note the use of American-style M1A1 Steel Helmets and Pistol Belts

Above. A West German tank crew of an American M-48 Tank with a Master Sergeant of the United States Army. Miltary advisers from the Allied occupation forces in western Germany assisted in the training of the new German Army

Above. Firing an American bazooka

Below. Review of the new Bundesheer by West German President Konrad Adenauer, 1955. All ranks are wearing the grey greatcoats

Above. West German troops in camouflage uniforms crossing a pontoon bridge. The camouflage pattern bears a close resemblance to the Second World War splinter-pattern. One soldier is equipped with a sniper model M1 Garand Rifle while the others are armed with M1 Carbines

Above. The creation of the Bundeswehr also created a new industry for re-arming and equipping the military. Seen here are the first vehicles of German design pressed into service

Left. An Unteroffizier in combat dress clowning around with new recruits

Opposite top left. Soldiers sighting in their M1 Carbines during marksmanship training. Note the cargo-style pockets on the trousers.

Opposite top right. Examining the first shipment of weapons, in this case Model 1918A2 Browning Automatic Rifles, from the United States, 1955

Opposite below left. Training with the 98k Rifle. Note the use of the Second World War-style two-buckle canvas leggings that were originally intended to be worn with ankle boots in 1943

Opposite below right. In the early days of the Bundeswehr the Army's field dress resembled strongly that of the United States Army, from the boots up to the helmet. The only difference was the insignia applied to the uniforms that identified them as Bundesheer

Above. A Feldwebel sighting in his equipment. Service insignia was pinned to the collar of the uniform, in this case the crossed rifles for Infantry

Above. The rank of Hauptfeldwebel was adopted on 26 July 1957. Note the Signal Service insignia pinned to his collar

Above. West German Military Police (Feldjägertruppe) with their motorcycles. Their collar service insignia consisted of a Gilt Imperial Guard-style star. Note the use of white equipment and the band around their helmets

Above. After 1957, the Bundeswehr went through several changes in equipment and uniforms. More traditional uniforms and equipment began to creep back into offical use, such as the black marching boots, the Second World War-style splinter-pattern camouflage uniforms, and the leather map case being carried by one of the soldiers

Below. Army Musicians wearing the Bandsmen Service insignia, in the form of a lyre, on their collars

Below. Members of the Bundesheer clowning around in the early 1960s. The soldier in the center is wearing the German-made plastic helmet distinguishable by the liner pins around the sides. The plastic helmet was worn for parades, sentry duty, and maneuvers. In September 1958 a one-piece model FJ 60 Steel Helmet was introduced, followed by another similiar model in May 1960

Above. A machine-gun crew with an MG3 Machine-Gun. The MG3 was adopted in 1958 and was basically the Second World War MG42 chambered for the 7.62 NATO instead of 7.92mm. Note use of the Second World War-style gas-mask cannister

Above. West German Infantry watching American-made M48 Tanks roll by during the early 1960s. The Infantrymen are armed with FN 7.62 NATO Light Rifle (7.62 FN Schnellfeuergewehr)

Above. Assault troops boarding a rubber raft. Of interest is the steerman wearing a Second World War-vintage German steel helmet, while the others are wearing American-style helmets

Above. The Army once again reintroduced the Paratroopers or Fallschirmjäger as part of one of its services. Along with the return of the Parachute Troops was the return of the distinctive and unique Second World War-vintage Fallschirmjäger Model 1938 Steel Helmet

Opposite right. From 1957, the pointed shoulder-strap was used until replaced by rounded shoulder-straps in 1962. Seen here are the older and newer shoulder-straps being used concurrently. Note the unit emblems of the 6th Armored Grenadier Division worn on the Model 1957 Service Tunic

Left. A Feldwebel wearing the Panzer Beret over a crash-helmet. Note his rank insignia on the sleeve of his tanker coveralls

Below. The new service-dress uniform for the Bundesheer was adopted in 1957 and remains in use to this day. The stone-grey service tunic bears a close resemblance to the style used by the German Army during the Second World War

Right. This West German Colonel, a Second World War veteran and Knight's Cross recipient, is wearing the Model 1957 Service Uniform as formal or parade dress. He is holding the older dark-grey service cap with senior officer's braid on the visor. Note the 1957 reissued but modified versions of wartime decorations awarded during the Third Reich. The offending swastika of the National Socialists was removed from all decorations. He is wearing the rampant-lion sleeve insignia of the 10th Armored Infantry Division

Above. In addition to returning to a more traditional uniform, the West German Army also adopted a variation of the double *Kapellenlitzen* with branch-of-service-colored collar tabs. Note the new service cap with junior-grade officer's braid on the visor being worn by the two 1st Leutnants

Above left. Along with the reintroduction of the traditional collar tabs, the familiar General's gold embroidered-on red field-collar tabs made a comeback as well. The stone-grey service cap with General's-quality braid on his visor can be clearly seen. He is wearing his 1957 wartime reissue decorations in ribbon form

Above right. A Mountain Troop officer with his men in formation. Note the contrast between the charcoal-grey trousers and the stone-grey Mountain Troops' short service tunic

Left. A distinctive form of service dress was adopted by the Mountain Troops (Gebirgsjäger) consisting of a short tunic. The Mountain Troops' short service jacket bears a faint resemblance to the Model 1944 Tunic. Note the reuse of the traditional edelweiss, first introduced in 1939, on the side of the mountain caps, and *Waffenfarbe* on the collar tabs. All are wearing the shoulder-patch of the 1st Mountain Division. The Hauptfeldwebel in the center is a Second World War veteran, as denoted by his wartime ribbons. The traditional German military enlisted man's belt buckle bearing the eagle of the German Federal Republic with the motto "Einigkeit, Recht, Freiheit" was introduced in 1962

Above. A Leutnant-Colonel of the 1st Mountain Division wearing the distinctive Mountain Troops' short service tunic. His officer's mountain cap would have the silver piping around the crown

Right above. This 1st Leutnant is wearing the Parachutist's Wings that were introduced in 1965. Bearing a close similiarity with the Second World War close-combat clasp, the silver embroidered badge is issued in three classes, represented respectively by a gold, silver, or bronze wreath

Right middle. Presentation of a regimental standard to an Anti-Tank (Panzerjäger) unit, mid-1960s. Note the wearing of the black beret by the soldiers. The first troops issued with berets were the Panzer and Reconnaissance Troops. Since 1971 all Rifle units (Jäger) have ben issued with green berets and airborne troops with Bordeaux-red berets, and from 17 November 1978 all services of the Bundesheer replaced the service cap and sidecap with the beret

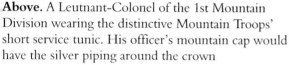

Right below. "Slip-on" pointed shoulder-boards being worn on the service shirts. They were eventually replaced by a more "rounded" version

Left. A Fallschirmjäger Color Guard passing in review, 1970s. Note the change from the Fallschirmjäger Model 1938 Steel Helmet to the US-style Paratrooper helmet as denoted by the chinstraps

Below. A Gebirgsjäger marching band with a soldier bearing a Schnellenbaum or "Jingling-Johnny", 1970s. The return of traditional German dress and fanfare was necessary in order to instill pride and a sense of a continuing heritage of the past with the present-day servicemen of the Bundeswehr

Opposite above. A military tattoo being conducted by a Musikmeister or Bandleader, 1970s. While some traditions returned, the distinctive Musician's Wings did not

Opposite below. Mixed personnel from various units wearing the red beret, 1970s. The beret badges identified the wearer's service branch, as can be seen with these members of the Artillery, Anti-Aircraft Artillery, Chemical, Communications, Maintenance, and Supply Troops

Above. The Bundesgrenzschutz, formed in 1951, is considered a part of the Bundeswehr and kept many wartime influences in the style of the uniforms, rank insignia, and even the Model 35 Steel Helmet. The rank insignia was identical to those used by the Schutzpolizei of the Third Reich period. This organization is home of the famous anti-terrorist unit, GSG 9, formed in 1972. In time of armed conflict the Border Guard Troops would come under the command of the military, and, though classed as combatants, would continue with their law-enforcement duties

Right. Medical personnel in field uniforms. Note the use of Red Cross armbands. The Stabsunteroffizier on the far right has a camouflage cover and netting over his helmet

Above. The basic West German soldier's locker contained everything he needed. Seen here is a soldier's service, field, and athletic uniforms, including his field equipment and winter clothing

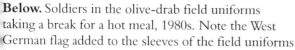

Above. Winter parka and snow-white camouflage smocks being worn by Artillerymen

Below. Soldiers in the olive-drab field uniforms taking a break for a hot meal, 1980s. Note the West German flag added to the sleeves of the field uniforms

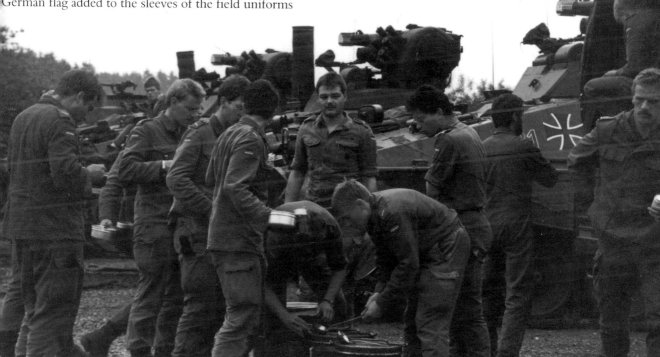

Left. Members of a Jäger unit firing off a MG42/MG3 Machine-Gun. Rheinmetall GmbH is one of the manufacturers of the popular .308 NATO version of the Second World War Machine-Gun, and other countries, such as Spain, have manufactured versions of the weapon as well

Opposite above. West German and American Paratroopers prepare for a jump. The American soldier is distinguishable by the woodland-pattern camouflage helmet cover, early 1980s

Opposite below. Men of a Jägertruppe wearing the green beret and armed with a wide assortment of weapons, such as the H&K G3 Assault Rifle, H&K HK13 Machine-Gun, the MP2 (Uzi) Sub-Machine Gun, the MG42/MG3 Machine-Gun, and a leichte (light) Panzerfaust (lePzf)

Below. A column of West German Leopard Tanks rolls by, 1970s

Above. This American-built M7 B2 Self-Propelled Gun was constructed upon a Sherman Tank chassis and armed with a 105mm field cannon. Upon the tank is the unit emblem of the 145th Artillery Regiment. The M7 B2 was in the service of the Bundeswehr from 1956 to 1962. The Artillerymen are wearing red berets and field uniforms

Below. A West German Waffenträger (Weapons Carrier) Wiesel 1 MK20/TOW commonly used by Parachute Units, 1990s. Manufactured by Rheinmetall Landsysteme, the Wiesel 1 was first used by the Bundeswehr in 1990 in two versions, the TOW and the MK20

Above. A West German Jagdpanzer without its 90mm Cannon, 1980s. The Kanonenjagdpanzer is a modern variation of the Second World War Jagdpanzer 38 Hetzer (Baiter) Tank that was introduced late in the war. Introduced in the mid-1960s, these tank destroyers had a variety of other uses as well, such as with Pioneer Troops as the Pioneerpanzer 2 Dachs and with Maintenance Troops as the Bergepanzer 2 auf Fahrgestell Leopard 1. Many of these armored vehicles were scrapped after Germany's reunification. Note the Panzer coveralls being worn by one of the crew members, which are in field-green

Right. The "Flecktarn" camouflage uniforms began appearing in the late 1980s and remain to this day the standard-issue field uniform. The olive-drab field uniforms were completely replaced with the camouflage uniforms. Note the special padded crash-helmet for armored crews

Above. Until 1995 all Bundeswehr troops were equipped with the new spot "Flecktarn" camouflage uniform. In addition, a new helmet made of Kevlar, similiar to those in use by the US armed forces, was introduced to the Bundeswehr. This Obergefreiter is armed with an H&K G3 Assault Rifle

Right. Bundesheer soldiers in winter uniforms. They are armed with H&K G3 Assault Rifles. The one in the center is wearing the new camouflage winter pile cap while the others are wearing knitted caps

Left. A Fahnenjunker, as indicated by the strip of cord across the Unteroffizier sleeve rank of his "Flecktarn" camouflage parka, is giving instruction in the use of the MG3 Machine-Gun

Above. Women soldiers of the Bundesheer wearing the "Flecktarn" camouflage field caps and uniforms, 1990s. There are two types of camouflage field caps in use: one is the traditional mountain cap, while the other bears more of a resemblance to a sports cap

Below. A female soldier sighting in her H&K G3K or HK33K Assault Rifle without a magazine. The rifle is a compact version of the G3 and HK33 (Foreign Export Model) series of assault rifles. Of particular interest is the camouflage helmet cover being worn

Above. A range officer supervising a recruit firing his rifle

Below. A soldier sighting in his H&K G36. Note the unique feature of a rifle scope built into the carrying handle of the rifle. German troops and the new rifle saw their first combat since the Second World War during the Balkan War of 1999

Above. An Obergreiter disassembling his G3 Machine-Gun

Left. An excellent study of field equipment being used in the present-day Bundesheer

Above right. The 5.56mm H&K G36 features a folding stock, dual-function sighting equipment, ambidextrous S-E-F fire-control group, and a magazine release that facilitates ambidextrous operation

Right. The Wachregiment on duty at the Neue Wach in Berlin. He is wearing the distinctive Gothic "W" beret badge and is armed with the Second World War vintage 98k Rifle. In addition he would wear a cuff-title bearing the word "Wachbataillon"

Above. German Military Police or Feldjäger wearing white covered service caps, white equipment, and an armband identifying their branch of service. In addition, the Feldjäger wore a red beret bearing an oakleaf-wreathed Guard Star Badge

Below. This soldier is wearing the beret badge of the Supply Troops (Nachschubtruppe)

Above. A soldier wearing the "GvD" (Gehilfe vom Dienst) armband: his duty was is assist the NCO on duty

Above. A soldier wearing the new Kevlar Helmet about to fire a Panzerfaust 3 (Pzf 3)

Right. Members of the Dutch-German Corps (I. Deutsche/Nederland Korps) firing the German MG3 and an American M16 Assault Rifle. The Corps' shoulder insignia consists of a pair of hands, each with the national colors of Germany and the Netherlands, grasping a sword on a green field. The Corps is one of a series of alliances with the armies of other European nations. Other similiar formations are the Eurokorps and the Deutsch-Französische Brigade (German-French Brigade). In some cases a beret badge based on the shoulder patch is worn by these special formations

Above. A Field Medic of the Sanitation Troops is wearing the "Flecktarn" camouflage combat/field uniform and the new Kevlar Helmet. His shoulder-patch identifies him as a member of the Peacekeeping Force of the United Nations serving in Bosnia, a former province of Yugoslavia. In the background is a Spürpanzer Fuchs that was used by the Sanitation Troops and by the Chemical Warfare Troops

Below. An Oberstleutnant of a Fallschirmjäger unit confers with a foriegn officer serving with the International Security Forces in Afghanistan, 2004

Above. German soldiers in the desert-pattern camouflage uniform being sent to Afghanistan as Peacekeepers in 2002

Below. An Artillery Observer wearing the insignia of the Peacekeeping Forces serving in Kosovo, 2004. Since the creation of the German Empire in 1870, the German Army has gone through a series of birth, death, and rebirth, each time reinventing itself while still managing to retain its proud and rich military heritage in an ever-changing and uncertain future

Above. Bundeswehr Generalmajor Markus Kneip addressing a crowd of Afghan, American, German, and other Coalition forces in Afghanistan. Upon his promotion to Generalmajor, he assumed command of 1 Panzerdivision in Hannover in 2008. The division was tasked with the lead function for all German land forces operations in 2011. In his current assignment, Generalmajor Kneip will command Regional Command North in Mazar-e Sharif, Northern Afghanistan for one year, including all multinational forces deployed in the nine provinces of Regional Command North. He will also act as senior national commander of all German troops operating in Afghanistan and Uzbekistan

Below. The MG42 continues serving the Bundeswehr as the MG3, as seen being used by this crewmember of a Leopard tank

Above. The Wachregiment continues to perform its duties as a ceremonial unit to this day (2013) and as part of their traditional equipment continue to use the Second World War-vintage 98k Bolt Action Rifle

Below. Another view of a MG3 in use in Afghanistan, 2010. This soldier of the Bundeswehr's Task Force Kunduz (Stellung Polizei HQ ASB) is seen wearing his "Typ SK" protective vest manufactured by Mehler Vario

Above. This member of an armored vehicle crew is seen manning a MG3 in Afghanistan, 2011. Of interest is his Velcro-backed patch specifying his blood type in case of a medical emergency

Above. The German troops serving in Afghanistan have begun adopting unofficial as well as official unit patches. These are fast becoming collectors' items in themselves, along with those worn by American and other Coalition troops

Above. After serving in Afghanistan for over ten years the German troops built a memorial in their base in Kunduz, reminiscent of those memorials built by their forefathers during the First and Second World Wars

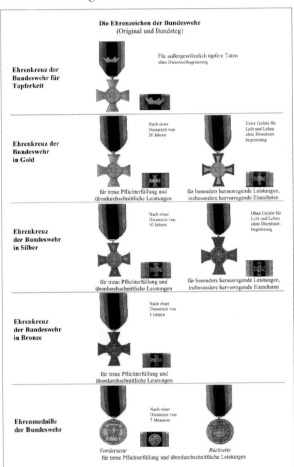

Above. The Ehrenzeichen der Bundeswehr (Badge of Honor of the German Armed Forces) was introduced in 1980 on the occasion of the 25th anniversary of the Bundeswehr's formation. It comes in various classes and is the closest equivalent to the old Iron Cross

Left. Another view of the NATO-OTAN Coalition troops' patch

Above. In May 2010 fourteen US MEDEVAC crewmen were awarded the German Gold Cross for risking their lives to come to the rescue of German soldiers during a firefight in Kunduz, Afghanistan. Germany's Gold Cross of Honor is one of the nation's highest awards for valor and this was the first time in history foreigners had ever received it

Above. A Brigadegeneral presenting a Gold Badge of Honor of the German Armed Forces to an Oberstleutnant. Note the gold pebbled buttons and embroidery on the general's greatcoat and the silver buttons and embroidery on the colonel's

Above. Generalmajor Markus Kneip is seen presenting one of the Badges of Honor of the German Armed Forces to an American soldier serving in Afghanistan

Above. German Chancellor Angela Merkel is seen examining a Heckler & Koch MP7 during a visit to Afghanistan

Above. Bundeswehr soldiers qualifying with M4 carbines based on the famous line of Armalite Rifles such as the M16 and AR15. The HK416 (5.56mm) was developed for US special operations forces as a major product improvement of M4/M16-type carbines and rifles. Using the HK-proprietary gas piston system found on the G36, the HK416 does not introduce propellant gases and carbon fouling back into the weapon. The HK416 has been combat-proven in Southwest Asia and has also gained the attention of military, law enforcement, and security users outside of the US. The HK416 was selected as the new Norwegian Army rifle in April 2007

Above. This German sapper's sidearm is an H&K P8. In 1995 the 9mm USP pistol was adopted by the Bundeswehr as its new service pistol, under the designation P8

Above. As of 2013 the H&K G36 has proven to be a reliable veteran while serving in Afghanistan and in other theaters

Above. Two well-proven veterans, the Rheinmetall MG3 (MG42) and the H&K G36, which span over seventy years of German firearms development

Above. The Shemagh headscarf has been widely used by Coalition troops serving in Afghanistan as seen here being worn by an American soldier on the left while his German sniper companion is wearing a headscarf with a "Flecktarn" camouflage scheme

Above. The H&K MG4 has been selected to replace the 7.62 mm MG3 General-Purpose Machine Gun at the squad support level; it will complement the MG3 in other roles. The machine gun was initially known as the MG43 prior to its adoption by the Bundeswehr

Above. The H&K G3 comes in various combinations – each with its own specific military designation. The modified versions are still used by snipers and special operations groups

Below. This German soldier is armed with a modified H&K G3. Note the use of a desert-colored Shemagh as part of his equipment – a common adaptation for forces serving in Southwest Asia

Above. The green foliage "Flecktarn" camouflage pattern that was first adopted in the early 1990s is still worn, but mainly in Europe and other similar climates. The soldier is seen about to fire a MILAN missile, which is launched at an upward angle so the missile guides itself to strike the less well-protected roof of the target vehicle

Below. German troops permitting an American infantryman to fire one of their MG3s in Afghanistan. Note the position for firing the weapon from the shoulder

Fallschirmjäger in training. Note the use of the Multiple Integrated Laser Engagement System (MILES) gear. Individual soldiers carry small laser receivers scattered over their bodies, which detect when the soldier has been illuminated by a firearm's laser. Each laser transmitter is set to mimic the effective range of the weapon on which it is used. When a person is "hit", a medic can use the digital readout to determine what level of first aid is required

A German dog handler quickly pulls his working dog off a simulated criminal during a K-9 demonstration by the German Army at Mubarak Military City in Egypt, 16 October 2001. BRIGHT STAR 01-02 was a multinational exercise involving more than 74,000 troops from forty-four countries that was designed to enhance regional stability and military-to-military cooperation among the US, key allies, and regional partners. It prepared US Central Command to rapidly deploy and employ the armed forces to deter aggressors and, if necessary, fight and win side-by-side with their allies and regional partners. Of particular interest is how the canine is "uniformed"

Above. Bundeswehr soldiers rush into the "Viper Pit" during Combat Lifesaver training in Wiesbaden, Germany, 12 May 2012. The Viper Pit is a room designed to inflict stress on trainees by bombarding them with loud commands, sirens, smoke, sounds of gunfire, simulated injuries, and fake blood. They are carrying non-firing plastic training models of the M16A2 during this exercise

Above. Markus Kneip at the time when he was a Brigadegeneral (single gold pip within a wreath) is wearing his desert "Flecktarn" camouflage uniform

Above. Amazingly the Bundeswehr still uses mules to carry supplies in difficult terrain much as their forefathers in the First and Second World Wars did

Above. In 1993 Germany began trials of a desert camouflage pattern based on the style of its standard issue "Flecktarn". Initially unofficially nicknamed "Tropentarn" ("tropical camouflage"), this desert pattern would remain in the trial stages until 1998–9, when the first official version was introduced. The design consisted of sparse dark olive & reddish-brown spots on a sandy background. It became officially known as "drei Farben Tarndruck der Bundeswehr" (three-color camouflage of the Bundeswehr), or as "Wüstentarn" (desert camouflage or desert "Flecktarn" pattern)

Above. Another pattern, as seen being worn by the Hauptfeldwebel on the right, was introduced in 2004 and is known as "Wüstentarndruck der Bundeswehr" (desert camouflage of the Bundeswehr). The new pattern has been primarily issued to German special operations units (although it is available commercially and has been worn in Afghanistan by individuals purchasing uniforms privately). The new Bundeswehr desert camouflage consists of clusters of pinkish-grey and brown spots on a light tan background. The design is intended to perform in very dry regions with virtually no vegetation

Above. Members of the German-French Brigade taking their oath on the regimental flag. Note the distinctive entwined German and French colors on their beret badges

Above. Women are continuing to play a role in the modern Bundeswehr as evidenced by this soldier of a signals unit while on maneuvers

Above. A German soldier looks through the scope mounted to his G3 while aboard a UH-60L Blackhawk helicopter during an aircraft familiarization demonstration at Mazar-e-Sharif, Afghanistan, 13 June 2011. The soldier is assigned to the International Security Assistance Force (ISAF)

Above. An excellent view of the ZF 3x4° dual combat sighting system as used on German G36A1 Assault Rifles

Above. A Bundeswehr general is seen addressing members of the Heeresfliegertruppe (Army Aviation Troops) as distinguished by the winged sword emblems on their berets. The officer on the right has his emblem in silver embroidery while the other ranks wear a metal version of the badge

Above. Combat gloves began to gain prominence in the world's military in the 1990s. After 2001 these gloves became part of the soldier's standard kit. These tough "Flecktarn" pattern cordura-mix gloves are made with a Goretex membrane and waterproof when new as well as a grey leather abrasion-resistant palm

Above. The standard fare found in a German soldier's messkit has not changed fundamentally since the First and Second World War. It usually consists of the following elements: bread, a starchy main course (in this case Ramen noodles with vegetables), dessert (fruit yogurt), and coffee

Below. A regular sight in Afghanistan is the ATF Dingo, a heavily-armored infantry mobility vehicle based on a Unimog chassis with a V-shaped hull design, produced by Krauss-Maffei Wegmann (KMW). It is designed to withstand land mines, small-arms fire, artillery fragments and NBC threats. ATF stands for Allschutz-Transport-Fahrzeug, meaning all-protected transport vehicle in German. The Dingo's standard armament is a remote-controlled Rheinmetall MG3 machine gun turret. The 7.62mm MG can be replaced with a 12.7mm MG or a HK 40mm GMG Automatic Grenade Launcher

Right. Pioneers of the 5. Kompanie des Gebirgspionierbataillons 8 (5./GebPiBtl8) from Ingolstadt with their messkits at the ready. Their "Flecktarn" field caps and aluminum messkits are styled after those used during the Second World War (Bundeswehr)

Above. A combined German and American exercise in Germany. Both are wearing Kevlar helmets. The Germans have designated their helmets as the M826 Kevlar ballistic helmet, which are still currently in use

Below. In addition, since the German entry into the Afghan theater of operations that Bundeswehr troops began adopting certain equipment from their American counterparts such as the Modular Integrated Communications Helmet (MICH) seen here

Above. Soldiers of the Gebirgslogistikbataillon 8 are seen wearing their mountain troops' cap normally worn with their service dress instead of the "Flecktarn" field caps worn with the combat uniform. The edelweiss emblem seen on the side of their caps still designate these men as mountain troops – a tradition since the First World War. They are seen taking part in an annual event, "Gebirgsmarsch 2007", with their Austrian counterparts

Right above. A German Gebirgsjäger sniper using a 12.7mm G82 (a variant of the Barrett M107 with a Zeiss 6-24x72 telescopic sight)

Right middle. German mountain troops wearing their snow camouflage suits, but the "Flecktarn" tactical vests do not completely blend with the snow scheme, 2006. These troopers are armed with the G36 Assault Rifle and the MG4 Squad Automatic Weapon

Right below. A comparison between snow camouflage uniforms worn by the Austrian officer on the left and the German officer on the right, 2006

Above. During Operation "Restore Hope" in Somalia, German Army soldiers are seen onboard an armored personnel carrier (APC) on hand for the dedication of a well which they dug for the Somalis on 18 December 1993. Germany's Defense Minister dedicated the well as part of his nation's contribution to the relief effort. Of interest is the unit emblem of the Fallschirmjägerbataillon 261 (261st Airborne Battalion)

Below. German Gebirgsjäger (mountain troops) manning a 12cm Mörser (mortar)

Above left. German Feldjäger (Military Police) wearing riot gear during a ceremony for the swearing-in of recruits. Note the protective neck guard and face shield attached to their Kevlar helmets

Above right. Another excellent study of the MICH helmet in use by members of the Bundeswehr. Of interest is the old Prussian motto "Gott mit Uns" on the right side of the soldier's helmet

Below. A fitting final tribute to those members of the Bundeswehr who gave their lives in creating a stable Afghan government through "peace-keeping" duties with the ISAF. As of 10 June 2011, fifty-three German soldiers and three policemen died in Afghanistan, raising the death toll to fifty-six. Among them are the first German reservists to fall in actions and the first German policemen to die in a deployment abroad. In addition to these fatalities, 245 German soldiers and four police officers suffered injuries of varying degrees caused by hostile activity. The number of fatalities has caused a stir in Germany since it is the highest suffered in all German army deployments abroad since 1945

A

UNIFORM PLATES
OF THE
IMPERIAL GERMAN ARMY

Illustrations from p. 335 to p. 340 are from *Die Deutsche Armee vor dem Weltkriege*.
Leipzig: Verlag von Moritz Ruhl, 1926

Illustrations from p. 341 to p. 342 are from *Das Kleine Buch vom Deutschen Heere*.
Kiel & Leipzig: Verlag von Lipsius & Tischer, 1901

Above. Prussia: Garde du Corps (infantry and cavalry)

Below. Prussia: infantry

Above. Prussia: Cuirassiers (Heavy Cavalry), Dragoons, and Jäger zu Pferde (Mounted Rifles)

Below. Prussia: Hussars and Uhlans (Lancers)

Above. Prussia: artillery, Pioneers, train and transport troops

Below. Prussia: Gendarmerie (Military Police), staff orderlies, cadets, military school administration staff

Above. Prussia: medical doctors, military administration officials, etc.

Below. Mecklenburg – Oldenburg – Braunschweig

Above. Baden – Hessen

Below. Bavaria

Above. Saxony

Below. Württemberg

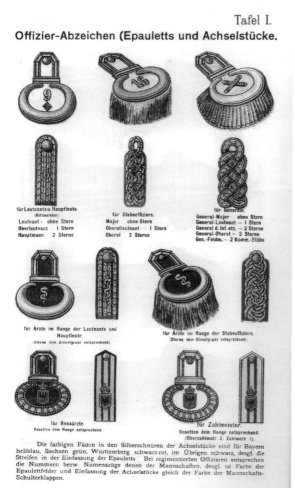

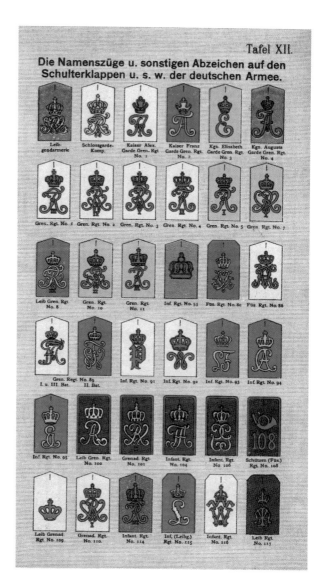

Above. Officers' insignia (epaulettes and shoulder-boards)

Above. Distinctive regimental emblems on shoulder-straps of the German Army

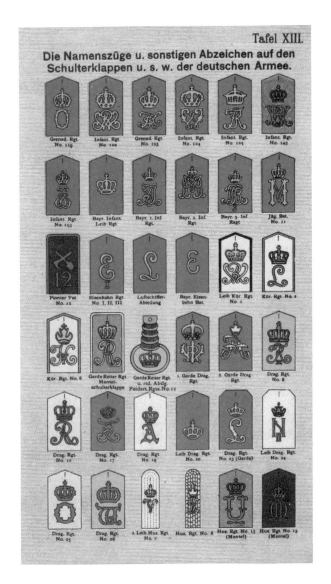

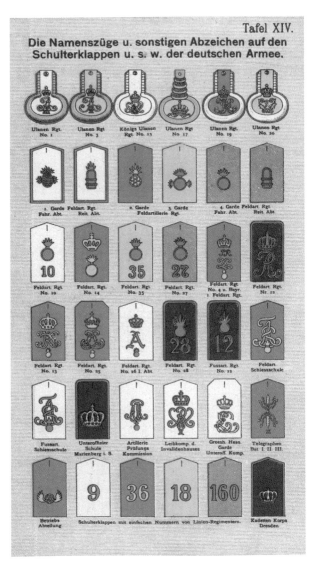

Above and above right. Distinctive regimental emblems on shoulder-straps of the German Army

UNIFORM PLATES
OF THE
IMPERIAL GERMAN
COLONIAL TROOPS

Illustrations from p. 345 to the top of page p. 348 are from *Die Ehemaligen Kaiserlich Deutschen Schutztruppen*. Leipzig: Verlag von Moritz Ruhl, 1910

Schutztruppe für Südwestafrika.

Offiziere.
im Mantel. Parade-Anzug. Kl Dienst-Anzug. Feld-Anzug.

Soldat.
Dienst-Anzug.

Hornist.
Ausgeh-Anzug.

Unter-Büchsenmacher.
Ordonnanz-Anzug.

Above and below. *Schutztruppe* for German Southwest Africa

Schutztruppe für Südwestafrika.

Arzt.
Kl Dienst-Anzug.

Lazarethgehilfen.
im Mantel. Ordonn-Anzug. Ausgeh-Anzug.

Unteroffizier.
Parade-Anzug.

Rossarzt.
Dienst-Anzug.

Zahlmeister.
Kl.Dienst-Anzug.

Feldwebel.
Ausgeh-Anzug.

Schutztruppe für Ostafrika.

Zahlmeister.	Offiziere.	Kleiner Dienst-Anzug.	Aerzte.	Lazarethgehilfe	Sergeant.
Dienst-Anzug.	Parade-Anzug.		im Mantel.	Ordonnanz-Anzug.	

Above and below. *Schutztruppe* for German East Africa

Schutztruppe für Ostafrika.

Feldwebel.	Zahlmeister-Aspirant.	Ober-Feuerwerker.	Ober-Büchsenmacher.	Unter-Büchsenmacher.	Unteroffiziere.	Sudanese.
Ordonnanz-Anzug.	Ausgeh-Anzug.		Ordonn.-Anzug.	Ausgeh-Anzug.	im Mantel. Ordonnanz-Anzug	

Schutztruppe für Kamerun und Togo.

Zahlmeister.	Zahlmeister-Aspirant.	Ober-Feuerwerker.	Arzt.	Offiziere.	Unteroffizier Gefreiter.
Kl Dienst-Anzug.	Ausgeh-Anzug.		Dienst-Anzug.	Dienst-Anzug. Kl Dienst-Anzug.	Ausgeh-Anzug.

Above. *Schutztruppe* for German Cameroon and Togo   **Below.** Rank and other insignia

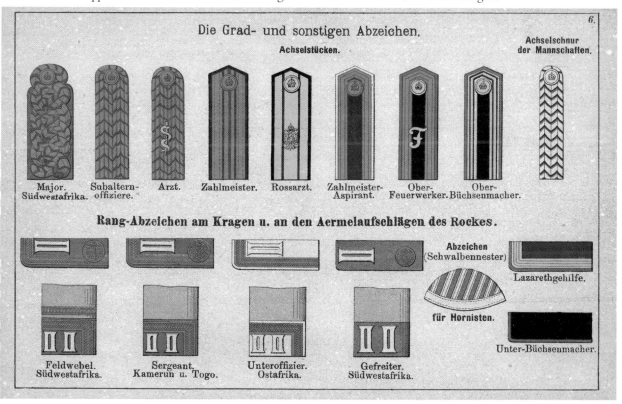

Die Grad- und sonstigen Abzeichen.

Achselstücke.

Achselschnur der Mannschaften.

| Major. Südwestafrika. | Subaltern-offiziere. | Arzt. | Zahlmeister. | Rossarzt. | Zahlmeister-Aspirant. | Ober-Feuerwerker. | Ober-Büchsenmacher. |

Rang-Abzeichen am Kragen u. an den Aermelaufschlägen des Rockes.

Abzeichen (Schwalbennester)

Lazarethgehilfe.

für Hornisten.

Unter-Büchsenmacher.

| Feldwebel. Südwestafrika. | Sergeant. Kamerun u. Togo. | Unteroffizier. Ostafrika. | Gefreiter. Südwestafrika. |

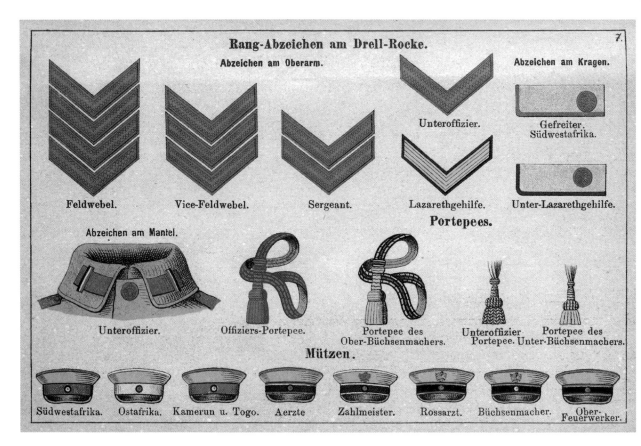

Above. Rank insignia, portepees and caps

Below. A turn-of-the-nineteenth-century illustration showing uniforms of the Naval Sea Battalion and colonial troops in German East Africa

APPENDIX

UNIFORM PLATES
OF THE
IMPERIAL GERMAN ARMY
DURING WORLD WAR I

Illustrations are from *Die Graue Felduniform der Deutschen Armee*.
Leipzig: Verlag von Moritz Ruhl, 1910

Die graue Felduniform der Offiziere.

General.   Oberst vom   Garde-Infant.-   Infanterie-Offizier.   Jäger-Offizier.   Garde-Pionier-   Pionier-   1. G.-Maschinengew.-Abt.
   Generalstabe.   Offizier.   21. Armeekorps.   Offizier.   Offizier.   Offizier.

Die graue Felduniform der Offiziere.

R. Gardes du Corps.   Kürassier-   Dragoner-   Husaren-   Feldartillerie-   Jäger z. Pferde.   Garde-Train   Garde-Ulanen-
   Offizier.   Offizier.   Offizier.   Offizier.   Offizier.   Offizier   Offizier.   Offizier.
      7. Kür.-R.   12. Drag.-R   16. Hus.-R   v. 2. R. Jäg. z. Pf.

Die graue Felduniform der Offiziere.

| Bayer. Inf.-Leib-R. Offizier. | Bayer. Jäger-Offizier. | Bayer. Ulanen-Offizier. | Chevauleger-Offizier 4. Chevaul.-R. | Sächs. Leib-Gren.-R. 100 Offizier. | Sächs. Schützen-Reg. 108 Offizier. | Sächs. Fussartillerie. Offizier. | Sächs. G.-Reiter-R. Offizier. |

Die graue Felduniform der Sanitätsoffiziere u. s. w., sowie der Militärbeamten.

| Zahlmeister. | Feuerwerks-Offizier. | Sanitäts-Offizier. | Veterinär-Offizier. | Festungsbau-Offizier. | Proviantverwltgs-Beamter. | Kriegsgerichtsrat. | Intendantur-Beamter. Wirkl. Geh. Kriegsrat. |

Die graue Felduniform der Mannschaften.

II.   1.

5. Garde-Gren.-R.   3. Garde-Feldart.-R.   Garde-Pionier-Bat.   Garde-Schützen-Bat.

4. Garde-Reg. z. Fuss.   Garde-Train-Bat.   Garde-Jäger-Bat.   2. Garde-Maschinengew.
   Sergeant   Abteilung.

Die graue Felduniform der Mannschaften.

II.   2.

Infanterie IV. A.-K.   Infanterie VIII. A.-K.   10. Jäger-Bat.   Infant.-R. 114.

Infanterie II. A.-K.   Hornist   Infanterie V. A.-K.   7. Maschinengew.-Abt.   Krankenträger. Unteroffizier
Gren.-R. 2.   I.-R. 26.   Feldwebel I.-R. 58.

II.   8.

Die graue Felduniform der Mannschaften.

Feldart.i.A.-K.   5. Kür.-R.   13.Hus.-R.   13. Pion.-Bat.
Gefreiter
Gardes du Corps.   Leib-Garde-Hus.-R.   6.Hus.-R.   7. Fussart.-R.

II.   4.

Die graue Felduniform der Mannschaften.

3. Garde-Ul.-R.   5. Ul.-R.   1. G.-Drag.-R.   15. Drag.-R.   16. Ul.-R.   6. Drag.-R.   9. Train-Bat.   4. R. Jäger z. Pf.

Die graue Felduniform der Mannschaften-Sächsische Truppenteile.

Infanterie XIX.-A.-K.
12. Jäger-Bat. Unteroffizier Schützen-R. 108.
Infanterie XII. A.-K.
Leibgr.-R. 100. Karab.-R.
21. Ul.-R.
Train.
Fussartillerie.
18. Hus.-R.
Pionier.
Feldart. XII. A.-K.
Gefreiter

Die graue Felduniform der Mannschaften-Bayerische Truppenteile.

Infanterie-Leib-R.
Jäger
Infanterie
II. A.-K.   III. A.-K.
1. Ul.-R.
3. Chevauleger-R.
Fussartillerie.
Train.
Pionier.   1. schw. Reiter-R.
Feldart. III. A.-K.

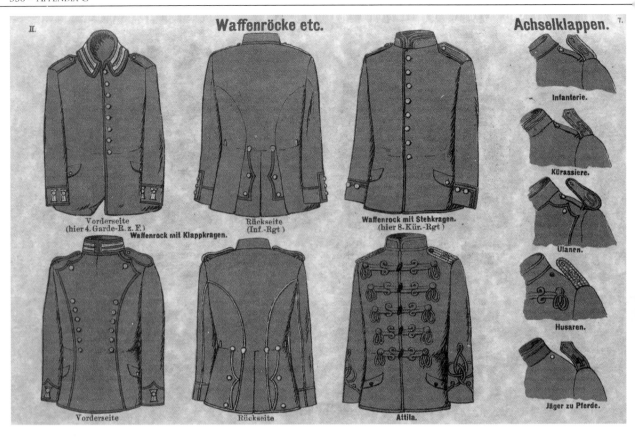

II. **Waffenröcke etc.** **Achselklappen.** 7.

Vorderseite
(hier 4. Garde-R. z. F.)

Waffenrock mit Klappkragen.

Rückseite
(Inf.-Rgt.)

Waffenrock mit Stehkragen.
(hier 8. Kür.-Rgt.)

Infanterie.

Kürassiere.

Ulanen.

Husaren.

Jäger zu Pferde.

Vorderseite

Rückseite

Attila.

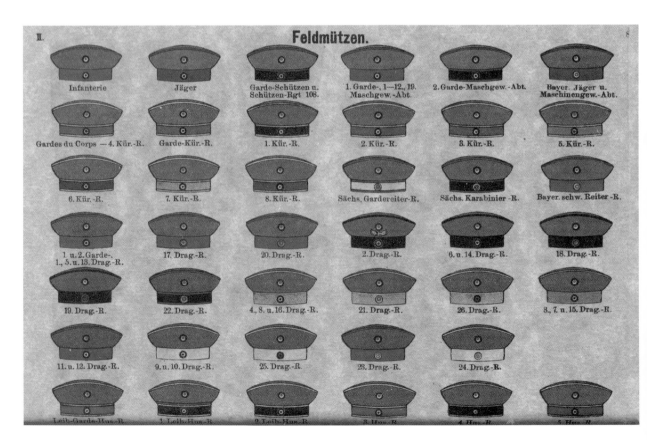

II. **Feldmützen.** 8.

Infanterie	Jäger	Garde-Schützen u. Schützen-Rgt 108.	1. Garde-, 1—12., 19. Maschgew.-Abt.	2. Garde-Maschgew.-Abt.	Bayer. Jäger u. Maschinengew.-Abt.
Gardes du Corps — 4. Kür.-R.	Garde-Kür.-R.	1. Kür.-R.	2. Kür.-R.	3. Kür.-R.	5. Kür.-R.
6. Kür.-R.	7. Kür.-R.	8. Kür.-R.	Sächs. Gardereiter-R.	Sächs. Karabinier-R.	Bayer. schw. Reiter-R.
1 u. 2. Garde-, 1., 5. u. 13. Drag.-R.	17. Drag.-R.	20. Drag.-R.	2. Drag.-R.	6. u. 14. Drag.-R.	18. Drag.-R.
19. Drag.-R.	22. Drag.-R.	4., 8. u. 16. Drag.-R.	21. Drag.-R.	26. Drag.-R.	3., 7. u. 15. Drag.-R.
11. u. 12. Drag.-R.	9. u. 10. Drag.-R.	25. Drag.-R.	23. Drag.-R.	24. Drag.-R.	
Leib-Garde-Hus.-R.	1. Leib-Hus.-R.	2. Leib-Hus.-R.	3. Hus.-R.	4. Hus.-R.	5. Hus.-R.

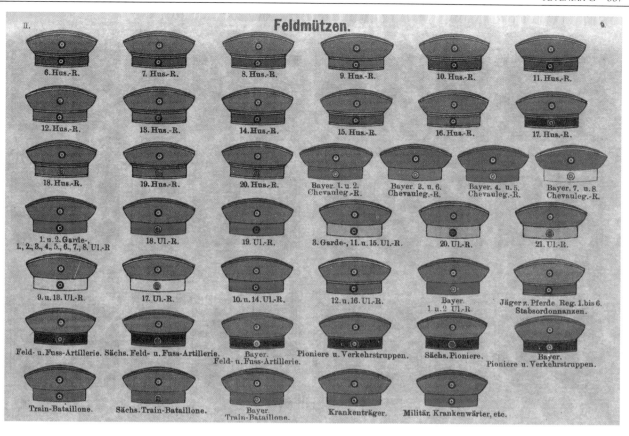

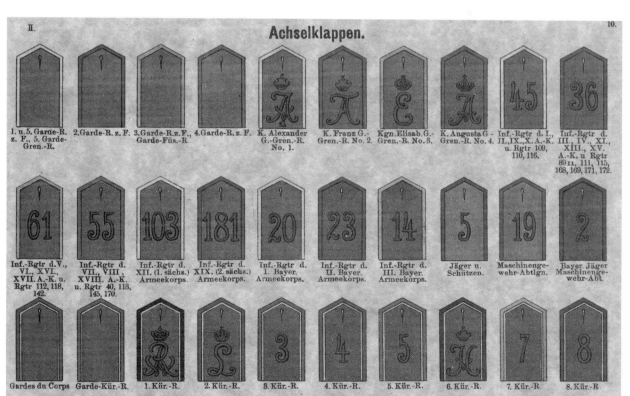

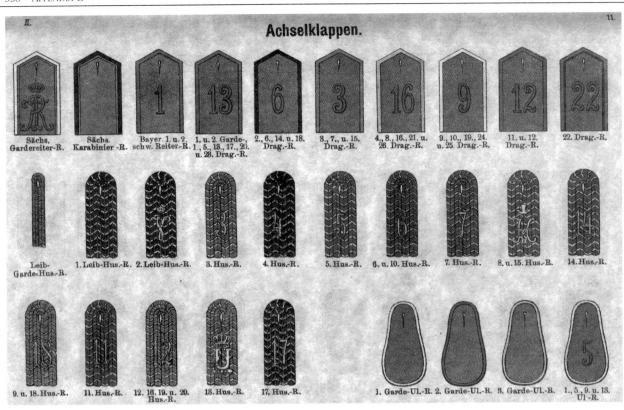

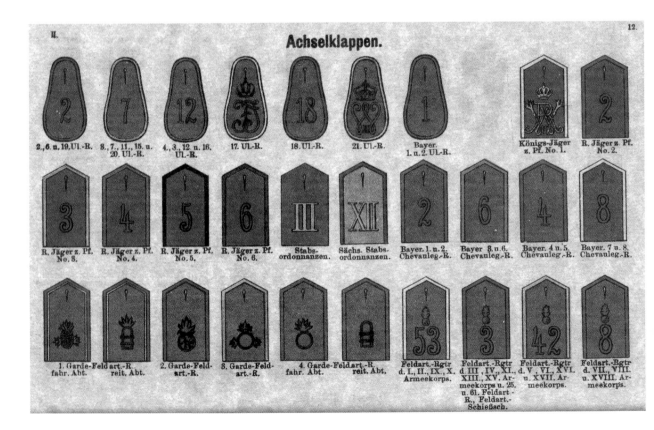

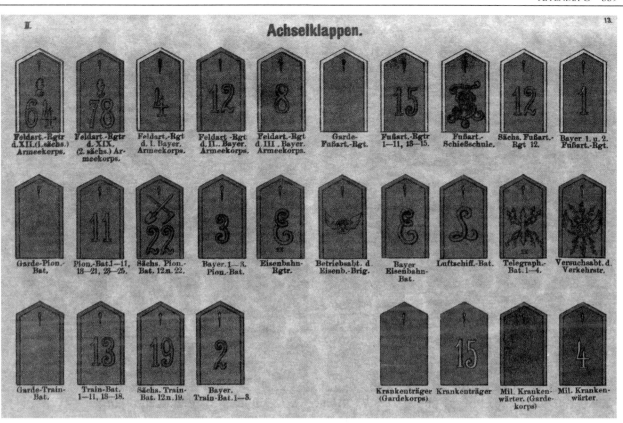

II. 13.

Achselklappen.

Feldart.-Rgtr d.XII.(1.sächs.) Armeekorps.
Feldart.-Rgtr d. XIX. (2. sächs.) Armeekorps.
Feldart.-Rgt d. I. Bayer. Armeekorps.
Feldart.-Rgt d. II. Bayer. Armeekorps.
Feldart.-Rgt d. III . Bayer. Armeekorps.
Garde-Fußart.-Rgt.
Fußart.-Rgtr 1—11, 13—15.
Fußart.-Schießschule.
Sächs. Fußart.-Rgt 12.
Bayer 1. u. 2. Fußart.-Rgt.

Garde-Pion.-Bat.
Pion.-Bat.1—11, 13—21, 23—25.
Sächs. Pion.-Bat. 12 u. 22.
Bayer.1—3. Pion.-Bat.
Eisenbahn-Rgtr.
Betriebsabt. d. Eisenb.-Brig.
Bayer Eisenbahn-Bat.
Luftschiff.-Bat.
Telegraph.-Bat. 1—4.
Versuchsabt. d. Verkehrstr.

Garde-Train-Bat.
Train-Bat. 1—11, 13—18.
Sächs. Train-Bat. 12 u. 19.
Bayer. Train-Bat. 1—3.
Krankenträger (Gardekorps)
Krankenträger
Mil. Kranken-wärter. (Gardekorps)
Mil. Kranken-wärter.

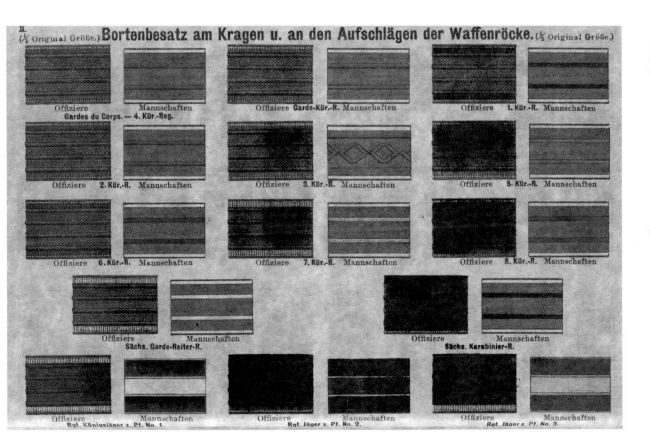

II. (⅕ Original Größe.) **Bortenbesatz am Kragen u. an den Aufschlägen der Waffenröcke.** (⅕ Original Größe.)

Offiziere | Mannschaften
Gardes du Corps. — 4. Kür.-Reg.
Offiziere Garde-Kür.-R. Mannschaften
Offiziere 1. Kür.-R. Mannschaften

Offiziere 2. Kür.-R. Mannschaften
Offiziere 3. Kür.-R. Mannschaften
Offiziere 5. Kür.-R. Mannschaften

Offiziere 6. Kür.-R. Mannschaften
Offiziere 7. Kür.-R. Mannschaften
Offiziere 8. Kür.-R. Mannschaften

Offiziere | Mannschaften
Sächs. Garde-Reiter-R.
Offiziere | Mannschaften
Sächs. Karabinier-R.

Offiziere | Mannschaften
Rgt. Königsjäger z. Pf. No. 1.
Offiziere | Mannschaften
Rgt. Jäger z. Pf. No. 2.
Offiziere | Mannschaften
Rgt. Jäger z. Pf. No. 3.

II. (⅓ Original Größe.) **Bortenbesatz am Kragen u. an den Aufschlägen der Waffenröcke.** (⅓ Original Größe.) 15

Offiziere — Mannschaften
Rgt. Jäger z. Pf. No. 4.

Offiziere — Mannschaften
Rgt. Jäger z. Pf. No 5.

Offiziere — Mannschaften
Rgt. Jäger z. Pf No 6.

Kragen und Ärmelaufschläge nebst Rangabzeichen für Unteroffiziere.

Klappkragen mit Sergeant-Abzeichen
(Garde-Infanterie)

Stehkragen mit Unteroffizier-Abzeichen
(Dragoner)

Stehkragen mit Gefreiten-Abzeichen
(2. Garde-Ulanen)

(Brandenburgische) mit Abzeichen eines etatsmäß. Feldwebels. (Infanterie)

(Schwedische) mit Unteroffiziers-Abzeichen (Garde-Feldart.)

Aermelaufschlag b. 5. Garde-Gren.-Reg.

Aermelaufschlag b. Garde-Schützen-Bat.

Aermelaufschlag b. Kürassieren.

Aermelaufschlag an der Ulanka.

Schwalbennester der Spielleute.

bei Fußtruppen.

bei Garde-Fußtruppen.

bei berittenen Truppen, außer den Rgtr Jäger zu Pferde.

bei berittenen Garde-Truppen.

bei Jägern zu Pferde.

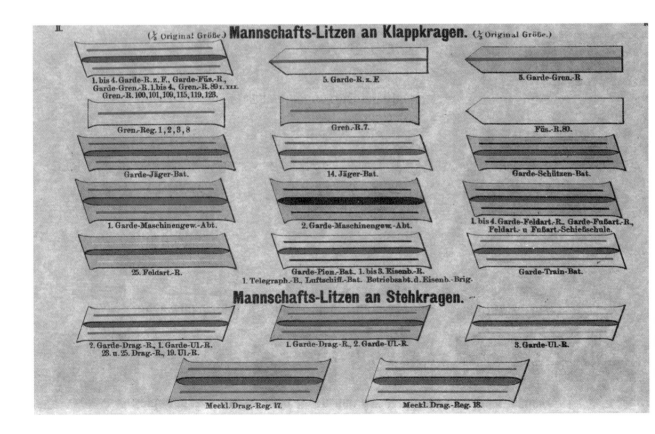

II. (⅓ Original Größe.) **Mannschafts-Litzen an Klappkragen.** (⅓ Original Größe.)

1. bis 4. Garde-R. z. F., Garde-Füs.-R., Garde-Gren.-R. 1 bis 4., Gren.-R. 89 I., XIII. Gren.-R. 100, 101, 109, 115, 119, 123.

5. Garde-R. z. F.

5. Garde-Gren.-R.

Gren.-Reg. 1, 2, 3, 8

Gren.-R. 7.

Füs.-R. 80.

Garde-Jäger-Bat.

14. Jäger-Bat.

Garde-Schützen-Bat.

1. Garde-Maschinengew.-Abt.

2. Garde-Maschinengew.-Abt.

1. bis 4. Garde-Feldart.-R., Garde-Fußart.-R., Feldart.- u Fußart.-Schießschule.

25. Feldart.-R.

Garde-Pion.-Bat., 1. bis 3. Eisenb.-R.
1. Telegraph.-B., Luftschiff.-Bat. Betriebsabt. d. Eisenb.-Brig.

Garde-Train-Bat.

Mannschafts-Litzen an Stehkragen.

2. Garde-Drag.-R., 1. Garde-Ul.-R. 23. u. 25. Drag.-R., 19. Ul.-R.

1. Garde-Drag.-R., 2. Garde-Ul.-R.

3. Garde-Ul.-R.

Meckl. Drag.-Reg. 17.

Meckl. Drag.-Reg. 18.

APPENDIX

THE PRUSSIANIZATION
OF THE AMERICAS:
A BRIEF OVERVIEW

With the victory of Germany over France in 1871, many countries began to emulate the uniform styles, tactics and equipment of the Kaiser's armies. The element most frequently and obviously copied was the distinctive *Pickelhaube*. Many countries either copied directly or made variations on the German spiked helmet. Sweden (1845), Norway (1845), Russia (1846), Romanian Moldau (1847), Denmark (1851) and Spain (1855) adopted the spiked helmet prior to the Franco-Prussian War. The many countries which followed suit included the United States of America (1872), England (1878), Portugal (1885), Brazil (1889), Chile (1890), Argentina (1900) and Mexico (1910). To this day, the *Pickelhaube* is still worn in Sweden, Spain and a few Latin American countries.

Latin America was eager to obtain anything German, from military training to uniforms, and eventually became the main client for German arms manufacturers. In 1886 German military advisers, under the leadership of Captain Emil Körner, were asked to organize and train the Chilean Army. The Chileans embraced the Prussianization of their armed forces. Once the Chilean Army had mastered German military drills and even adopted Prussian military customs, it began to spread its new-found identity to other Latin American nations by sending over its own military advisers!

Almost every Latin American country adopted a variation on the Gewehr 1893 and 1898 Bolt Action Rifles manufactured by Mauser and Deutsche Waffen-und-Munition (DWM). Even the United States adopted the M1903 Springfield Rifle that was based on the Mauser. During the Chaco War (1932–5) thirty thousand Bolivian soldiers, trained by German General Hans von Kundt, attacked Paraguay. Even with the aid of Krupp Cannons and Aircraft the Bolivians were driven back by the Paraguayans. The German influence on uniforms of the Bolivian Army was so strong that after the departure of General Kundt military missions from Spain and Czechoslovakia failed to make any impact. However, the Bolivians did influence a German military adviser, Ernst Röhm, in the design of an insignia for the head of Hitler's Brownshirts or Sturmabteilung (SA), consisting of a star-shaped emblem based on the collar tabs worn by Bolivian generals.

With the defeat of imperial Germany in World War I, the influence of the Prussians in Latin America began to wane through the 1920s and 1930s. Interestingly, Argentina and Chile nonetheless adopted the German Model 1935 Steel Helmet when war broke out in 1939. Supplies became harder, and the

South American nations began manufacturing fiber versions of the helmet in order to continue its use for parades. A few Latin American countries quietly supported Germany during World War II, such as Juan Perón's Argentina, only to give tacit support to the Allies when Germany's fortunes began to turn for the worse. Despite Germany's defeat in the two World Wars, the Chilean Armed Forces still display a strong Prussian militaristic influence that is more prevalent than in any other Latin American country.

"On national holidays and important ceremonial occasions the famous old Paradeschritt (The Prussian 'Goose-Step') pounds rhythmically on the paving stones of squares and avenidas. Even the military marches have kept their original Prussian character, though Spanish words have been substituted for German."[‡] Today, cadets of the military academies of Chile, Colombia and Ecuador still wear the *Pickelhaube*, as well as the nineteenth-century Prussian-style uniforms. To this day, many *Pickelhauben*, shakos, parade and field helmets, uniforms, gorgets, insignia and edged weapons used for special occasions are still being made to order by a limited number of craftsmen in Germany for these proud Latin American soldiers who uphold the traditional belief that "Made in Germany" means quality.

Above. While the Germans were a very strong influence in the Americas, they did have some slight influence in the uniforms, equipment and weapons of other armies elsewhere in the world, especially in China. The Chinese had been loyal clients of the German small-arms industry since the turn of the nineteenth century. At the outbreak of World War II the Chinese were armed with German or locally manufactured small arms such as the Model 98k Rifle, Maxim Machine Gun and the Model C96 "Broomhandle" Mauser Pistol. These Chinese soldiers are wearing the German Model 1935 Steel Helmets; the Chinese Army also adopted a cap based on the German mountain cap

[‡]D'Ami, *World Uniforms in Colour*

Above. An Argentinian cadet with the *Pickelhaube* adopted in 1900. Note the distinctive Prussian-style epaulettes

Above. Well into the 1930s and through the 1950s the Argentinian Army wore a uniform similar to that worn by the Reichsheer of the 1920s and early 1930s. Of interest is the adoption of the Guard-style double *Kapellenlitzen* on the collar with appropriate *Waffenfarbe* or branch-of-service color

Right. An Argentinian Color Guard wearing the Model 1935 German Helmet. In some cases the standard bearer wore a German-style gorget bearing the Argentinian coat of arms, although it was discontinued in the years following the War. Note the decals bearing Argentinian colors worn on the sides of the helmets

Above. In 1910 Mexico adopted the *Pickelhaube*, continuing to use it until 1920. Seen here is the Color Guard of the 29th Infantry Battalion, armed with Mauser Mexican Model 1910 Rifles, during the rule of Porfirio Díaz at the time of the outbreak of the Mexican Revolution

Above. Some nations were not influenced by German military doctrine, even if they adopted particular uniform styles, equipment and/or weapons. These Finnish soldiers are wearing German Model 1916/18 Steel Helmets. Other armies that adopted German helmets were from young countries born after the Great War, which bought up the abundant German war surplus at bargain prices. Among the countries using these helmets were the Baltic states, Hungary and Ireland. Interestingly, the Irish Army wore these helmets with British-style uniforms and equipment, and when supplies were growing scarcer, new versions were remanufactured in England!

Above. The uniform and cap worn by this senior Mexican officer shows strong German influences

Above. Even in 1939 the Chilean Army still maintained a strong Prussian influence in its bearing as well as its uniforms. Note the strongly German-influenced shoulder-boards worn by this Chilean officer. The Chilean Army has retained much of its German influence well into the twenty-first century

Above. General Juan Vicente Gómez, Venezuela's constitutional president from 1908 to 1935. This photograph, taken prior to the advent of World War I, shows his uniform and insignia, and in particular his strongly Prussian-influenced sword, which had been left to him by German and Chilean military missions that helped to form the Venezuelan Army into an efficient force from 1892 to 1910. The sword is typical of the infantry officer's models made available for export by Solingen edged weapons manufacturers like WKC, Carl Kaiser, E. & F. Hörster and Carl Eickhorn

Above. This Californian militiaman from San Francisco is wearing imported German *Pickelhaube*, *c.*1880. Note the distinctive Prussian-style American Eagle helmet plate. The US Model 1872 Uniform is of the style adopted by the United States Army and state militias in the mid-1870s, and display a strong German influence in such elements as the Brandenburg-style cuffs on the tunic, branch-of-service colors (*Waffenfarbe*) on the cuffs and collar, and the epaulettes. The edged weapon is a Model 1860 Line and Staff Officers' Sword. The star-shaped medal identifies him as a Civil War veteran and a member of the Grand Army of the Republic (GAR). The *Pickelhaube* appears to be of the 1867 style with the rounded front visor. Interestingly, various models from 1842 to 1887 are known to have been used by American militia units between the Civil and Spanish-American Wars. (*Courtesy Mark Kasal*)

A P P E N D I X

UNIFORM PLATES
OF THE
PROVISIONAL REICHSWEHR
(1919–1921)

Illustrations from p. 369 to p. 372 (top) are from
Die Deutsche Reichswehr. Leipzig: Verlag von Moritz Ruhl, 1919

FREIKORPS

Illustrations from p. 372 (bottom) to p. 373 are from *Die Neue Deutsche Reichswehr,*
Die Freiwilligen-Verbände und ihre Characteristischen Abzeichen. Leipzig: Verlag von Moritz-Ruhl, 1919

THE REICHSWEHR
(1921–1933)

Illustrations from p. 374 to p. 376 are from *Die Deutsche Reichswehr*. Leipzig: Verlag von Moritz Ruhl, 1921

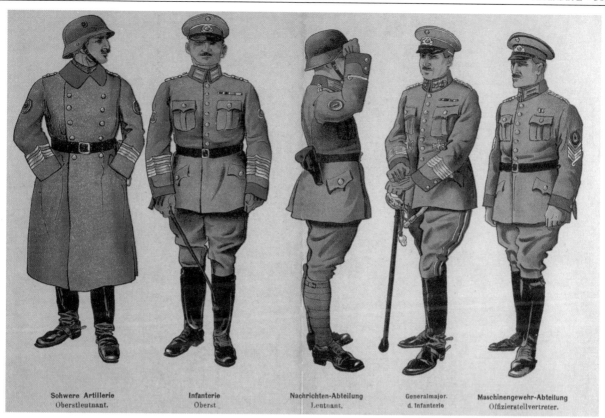

| Sohwere Artillerie | Infanterie | Nachrichten-Abteilung | Generalmajor. | Maschinengewehr-Abteilung |
| Oberstleutnant. | Oberst | Leutnant. | d. Infanterie | Offizierstellvertreter. |

| Schützen. | Sanitätsoffizier | Jäger | Kavallerie | Generalstab |
| Feldwebel | mit Leutnantsrang. | Oberleutnant. | Major. | Hauptmann. |

Infanterie	Kavallerie	Leichte Artillerie	Train	Pionier
Soldat	Gefreiter	Unteroffizier.	Sergeant.	Vizefeldwebel.

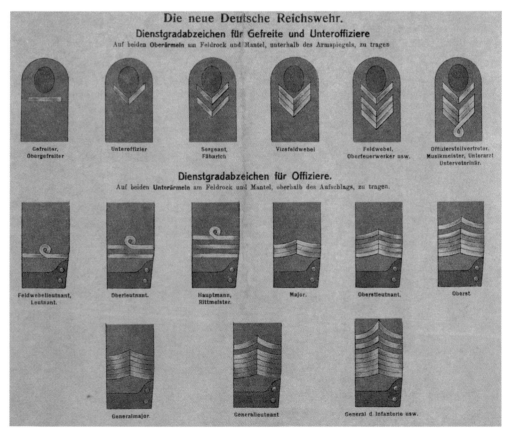

Die neue Deutsche Reichswehr.

Dienstgradabzeichen für Gefreite und Unteroffiziere

Auf beiden Oberärmeln am Feldrock und Mantel, unterhalb des Armspiegels, zu tragen

Gefreiter, Obergefreiter	Unteroffizier	Sergeant, Fähnrich	Vizefeldwebel	Feldwebel, Oberfeuerwerker usw.	Offizierstellvertreter, Musikmeister, Unterarzt Unterveterinär.

Dienstgradabzeichen für Offiziere.

Auf beiden Unterärmeln am Feldrock und Mantel, oberhalb des Aufschlags, zu tragen.

Feldwebelleutnant, Leutnant.	Oberleutnant.	Hauptmann, Rittmeister.	Major.	Oberstleutnant.	Oberst.

Generalmajor.	Generalleutnant	General d. Infanterie usw.

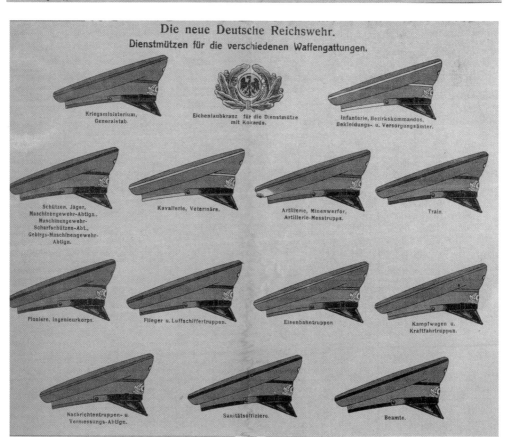

Die neue Deutsche Reichswehr.
Armspiegel zur Kennzeichnung der Waffengattung und des Truppenteils.
Auf beiden Oberarmen am Feldrock und am Mantel anzulegen.

Infanterie	Schützen	Jäger	Maschinengewehr-Abtign.	Maschinengewehr-Scharfschützen-Abtign.	Gebirgs-Maschinengewehr-Abtign.
Kavallerie.	Leichte Artillerie.	Schwere Artillerie.	Flakformationen.	Gebirgsartillerie.	Minenwerfer.
Artillerie-Messtrupps.	Artillerie-Parks.	Train.	Traindepots.	Pioniere.	Ingenieurkorps.
Fliegertruppen.	Luftschiffertruppen.	Eisenbahntruppen.	Kampfwagentruppen	Kraftfahrtruppen.	Nachrichtentruppen

Die neue Deutsche Reichswehr.
Dienstmützen für die verschiedenen Waffengattungen.

Kriegsministerium, Generalstab.

Eichenlaubkranz für die Dienstmütze mit Kokarde.

Infanterie, Bezirkskommandos, Bekleidungs- u. Versorgungsämter.

Schützen, Jäger, Maschinengewehr-Abtign., Maschinengewehr-Scharfschützen-Abt., Gebirgs-Maschinengewehr-Abtign.

Kavallerie, Veterinäre.

Artillerie, Minenwerfer, Artillerie-Messtrupps.

Train.

Pioniere, Ingenieurkorps.

Flieger u. Luftschiffertruppen.

Eisenbahntruppen.

Kampfwagen u. Kraftfahrtruppen.

Nachrichtentruppen- u. Vermessungs-Abtign.

Sanitätsoffiziere.

Beamte.

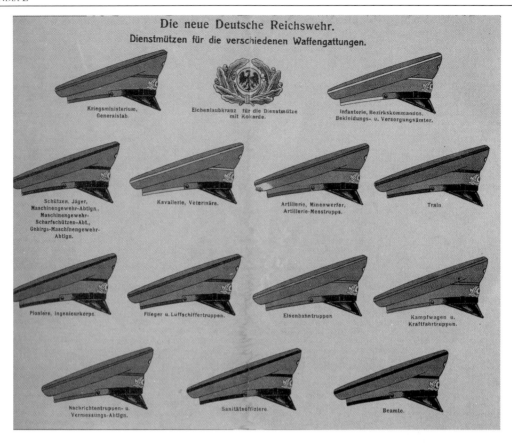

Die neue Deutsche Reichswehr.
Dienstmützen für die verschiedenen Waffengattungen.

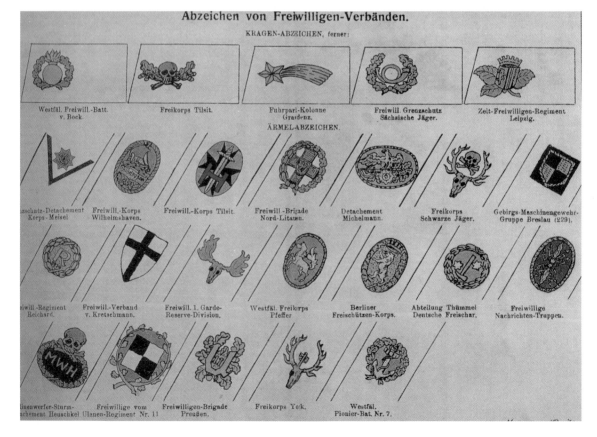

Abzeichen von Freiwilligen-Verbänden.

Abzeichen von Freiwilligen-Verbänden.

KRAGEN-ABZEICHEN, ferner:

Freiwill.-Verbände Anhalt. Inf.-Regt. Nr. 93.	Freiwill. Inf.-Bat. Bremen.	Badisches Sturm-Bat. Ober-Ost.	Freikorps Severin. (Minden.)	Freikorps Dohna.
Westfäl. Jäger-Freikorps.	Freiwillige Grenadiere Nr. 2.	Freiwillige Grenadiere Nr. 9.	Freikorps Schleswig-Holstein.	Hessisch-Thüringisches Freikorps.
Freiwill.-Detachement Tüllmann.	Freikorps Breslau.	Freikorps Düsseldorf.	Grenzschutz-Batterie v. Medem.	Freiwill.-Abteilung Osterroth.
Detachement Grothe.	Freiwill.-Bataillon v. Klüfer.	Grenzschutz-Kommando Suwalki.	Reg. Schutztruppe Bremen.	Freiwill. Hannoversche Jäger.

Abzeichen von Freiwilligen-Verbänden.

Das Weitertragen dieser Abzeichen ist denjenigen Verbänden, die als solche in die Reichswehr aufgenommen sind, gestattet.

KRAGEN-ABZEICHEN.

Freikorps Feldmarschall Hindenburg.	Generalkommando Lüttwitz.	Garde-Kavallerie-Schützen-Division.	Landesjäger.	Landesschützen.
Freischützenkorps.	Freiwill. Detachement Leib-Garde-Husaren.	Detachement Neufville.	Freikorps Lützow.	Maschinengewehr-Scharfschützen-Abtlg Preis.
Freikorps Eulenburg.	Grenzschutz Ost. (XVII. Armeekorps.)	Ostpreußisches Freikorps.	Eiserne Eskadron. (Garde-Kavallerie-Schützen-Korps.)	12. Infanterie-Division.
Freikorps Brüssow.	31. Infanterie-Division.	Freiwillige Luftschiffer (III). Grenzschutz Ost.	Freiwill.-Bataillon Altenburg.	Wachtregiment Halle.

Nachrichten-Abteilung
Offizier mit Stahlhelm

Generalmajor der Infanterie

Kavallerie-Offizier
im Mantel mit Stahlhelm

Truppen-Generalstab
Offizier

Infanterie
Stabsoffizier

Artillerie-Offizier
Adjutant

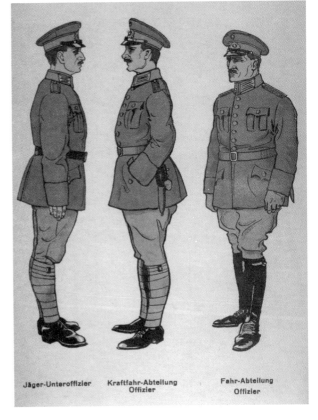

Jäger-Unteroffizier

Kraftfahr-Abteilung
Offizier

Fahr-Abteilung
Offizier

Infanterist
Soldat im Mantel mit Stahlhelm

Kavallerie-Gefreiter

Artillerist im Mantel

Pionier mit Stahlhelm

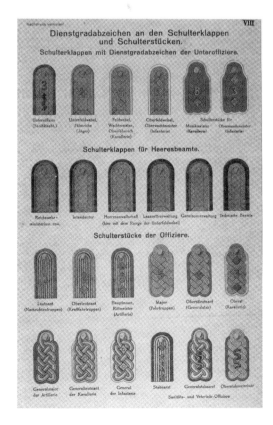

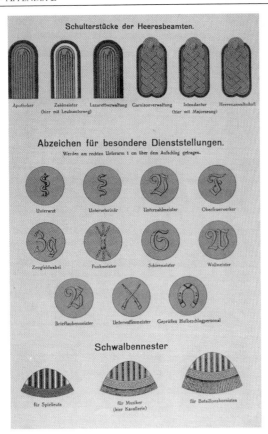

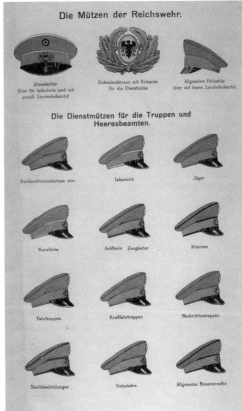

APPENDIX F

UNIFORMS OF THE GERMAN ARMY DURING THE THIRD REICH (1933–1945)

Illustrations are from
Reibert, W., Major (Heer). *Der Dienst-Unterricht im Heere: Ausgabe für den Schützen der Schützenkompanie.*
Berlin: E. S. Mittler & Sohn, 1938

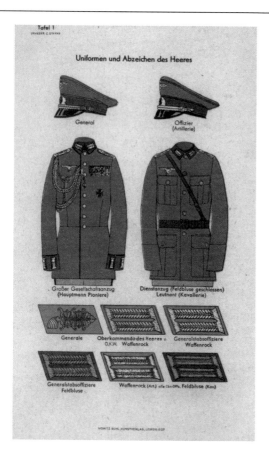

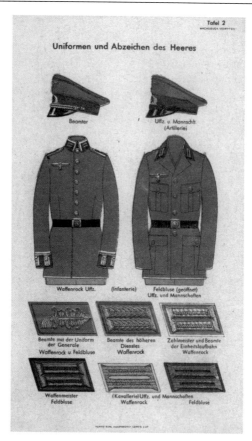

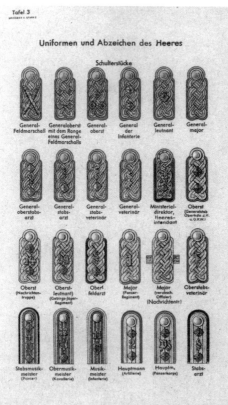

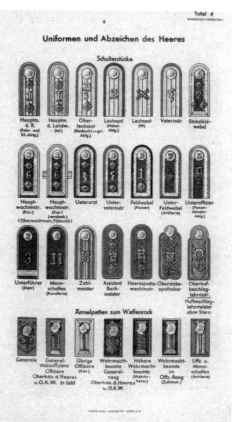

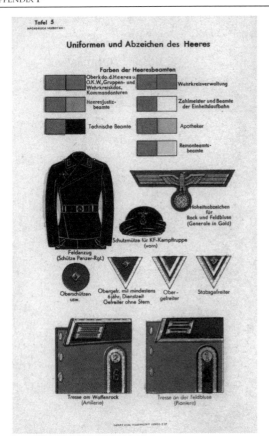

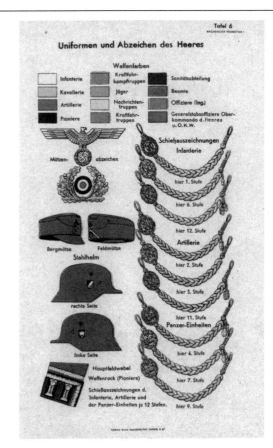

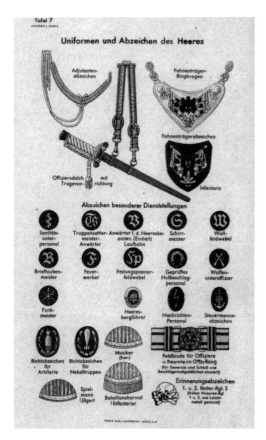

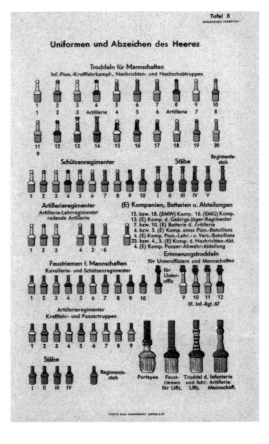

UNIFORMS OF THE NATIONALEN VOLKSARMEE OF THE DDR

Illustrations on p. 383 are from *Unsere NVA, Ausgabe 1989*.
Berlin: Militärverlag der DDR, 1988

Illustrations from p. 384 to p. 390 are from *Handbuch Militärisches Grundwissen, NVA-Ausgabe*.
Berlin: Militärverlag der DDR, 1988

Uniformen der Landstreitkräfte (Auswahl)

Uniformart: Felddienstuniform, Sommer
Funktion: Fallschirmjäger
Dienstverhältnis: Soldat auf Zeit
Waffengattung: Luftlandetruppen

Uniformart: Paradeuniform, Sommer
Funktion: Zugführer
Dienstverhältnis: Berufsoffizier
Waffengattung: mot. Schützentruppen

Uniformart: Felddienstuniform, Sommer
Funktion: Geschützführer
Dienstverhältnis: Unteroffizier auf Zeit
Waffengattung: Raketentruppen und Artillerie

Dienstgradabzeichen der NVA

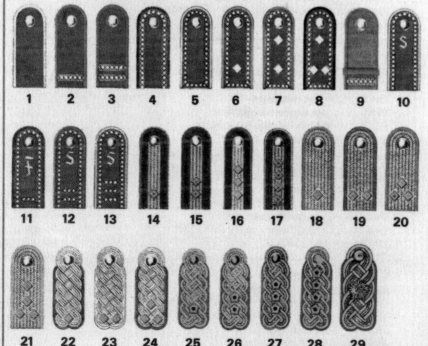

1 Soldat (mot. Schützen)
2 Gefreiter (Panzer)
3 Stabsgefreiter (Fallschirmjäger)
4 Unteroffizier (rückw. Dienste)
5 Unterfeldwebel (mot. Schützen)
6 Feldwebel (Nachrichten)
7 Oberfeldwebel (Luftstreitkräfte)
8 Stabsfeldwebel (Pioniere und techn. Dienste)
9 Gefreiter in der Uffz.-Ausbildung (Panzer)
10 Offiziersschüler, Hochschulreifeausbildung (mot. Schützen)
11 Fähnrichschüler 1. Studienjahr (rückw. Dienste)
12 Offz.-Schüler 2. Studienjahr (Raketentr. und Artillerie)
13 Offz.-Schüler 3. Studienjahr (mot. Schützen)
14 Fähnrich (Luftstreitkräfte)
15 Oberfähnrich (rückw. Dienste)
16 Stabsfähnrich (Panzer)
17 Stabsoberfähnrich (mot. Schützen)
18 Unterleutnant (Luftstreitkräfte)
19 Leutnant (Luftverteidigung)
20 Oberleutnant (Panzer)
21 Hauptmann (Nachrichten)
22 Major (rückw. Dienste)
23 Oberstleutnant (mot. Schützen)
24 Oberst (Raketentruppen und Artillerie)
25 Generalmajor (Landstreitkräfte)
26 Generalleutnant (Landstreitkräfte)
27 Generaloberst (Luftstreitkräfte)
28 Armeegeneral (Landstreitkräfte)
29 Marschall der DDR

Deutsche Demokratische Republik

Nationale Volksarmee und Grenztruppen der DDR
Dienstgradabzeichen LaSK, LSK/LV, GT der DDR

Soldat
(mot. Schützen)

Gefreiter
(Raketentruppen
und Artillerie)

Stabsgefreiter
(Luftstreitkräfte)

Unteroffizier
(Grenztruppen
der DDR)

Unterfeldwebel
(Luftverteidigung)

Feldwebel
(Nachrichten)

Oberfeldwebel
(Pioniere und techn. Truppen)

Stabsfeldwebel

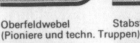

Uffz.-Schüler
(Panzer)

Fähnrichschüler
(1. Studienjahr,
Grenztruppen der DDR)

Offiziersschüler in
Hochschulreifeausbildung

Offz.-Schüler
(3. Studienjahr,
Artillerie)

Postenführer
(Grenztruppen der DDR)

Ärmelstreifen
für Hauptfeldwebel
(getragen auf beiden
Unterärmeln)

Ärmelwinkel für
Soldaten auf Zeit und
Unteroffiziere auf Zeit
(Volksmarine goldfarben)

Ärmelabzeichen
für Fähnriche

Fähnrich
(Raketentruppen
und Artillerie)

Oberfähnrich
(Luftstreitkräfte)

Stabsfähnrich
(Nachrichten)

Stabsoberfähnrich
(Panzer)

Unterleutnant
(Luftstreitkräfte)

Leutnant
(Fallschirmjäger)

Oberleutnant
(Panzer)

Hauptmann
(Nachrichten)

Major
(rückw. Dienste)

Oberstleutnant
(Panzer)

Oberst
(mot.
Schützen)

Kokarde

Generalmajor
(Grenztruppen der DDR)

Generalleutnant
(Luftstreitkräfte)

Generaloberst
(Landstreitkräfte)

Armeegeneral

Marschall
der DDR

F 3 — Deutsche Demokratische Republik

Nationale Volksarmee und Grenztruppen der DDR
Dienstgradabzeichen und Dienstlaufbahnabzeichen

Dienstgradabzeichen an Flieger- und Technikeranzügen

Soldat

Gefreiter

Stabsgefreiter

Unteroffizier

Unterfeldwebel

Feldwebel

Oberfeldwebel

Stabsfeldwebel

Uffz.-Schüler

Fähnrichschüler
1. Studienjahr
(2 Striche –
2. Studienjahr)

Offz.-Schüler
1. Studienjahr

Offz.-Schüler
4. Studienjahr

Fähnrich

Oberfähnrich

Stabsfähnrich

Stabsober-
fähnrich

Unterleutnant

Leutnant

Oberleutnant

Hauptmann

Major

Oberstleutnant

Oberst

Gilt analog
für die
Dienstgrade
der
Volksmarine

Generalmajor

Generalleutnant

Generaloberst

Dienstlaufbahnabzeichen

Militärjustizorgane
Soldaten und   Fähnriche und
Unteroffiziere   Offiziere

medizinischer
Dienst
Fähnriche

Militärmusiker
Fähnriche

Deutsche Demokratische Republik

Nationale Volksarmee und Grenztruppen der DDR
Ehrentitel, Orden, Preise, Medaillen

Held
der Deutschen
Demokratischen
Republik

Verdienter
Angehöriger der
Nationalen Volksarmee

Verdienter
Angehöriger der
Grenztruppen der DDR

Verdienter
Militärflieger
der DDR

Scharnhorst-Orden

Kampforden
für Verdienste um
Volk und Vaterland
(drei Stufen)

Friedrich-Engels-Preis
(drei Klassen)

Theodor-Körner-Preis
(eine Klasse)

Verdienstmedaille
der NVA
(drei Stufen)

Medaille der
Waffenbrüderschaft
(drei Stufen)

Medaille für
vorbildlichen
Grenzdienst

Medaille für
treue Dienste
in der NVA
(vier Stufen)

Deutsche Demokratische Republik

Absolventenabzeichen – vergeben nach Abschluß

der Ausbildung zum Berufsoffizier mit Diplom

der militärakademischen Ausbildung

der Ausbildung mit Diplom an Berufsoffiziere

Militärische und zivile Hochschuleinrichtungen

Militärakademie „Friedrich Engels"

Militärpolitische Hochschule „Wilhelm Pieck"

Militärische und zivile Hochschuleinrichtungen

Akademie des Generalstabs der Sowjetarmee

Militärakademien der sowjetischen Streitkräfte

Leistungsabzeichen der NVA

Leistungsabzeichen der Grenztruppen der DDR

Symbole der Schützenschnüre

Turmbewaffnung Panzer

Turmbewaffnung SPz/SPW

Bestenabzeichen

Nationale Volksarmee

Grenztruppen der DDR

(bei wiederholter Verleihung mit wechselbarer Zahl)

Artillerie

Grenztruppen der DDR

Schützenschnur mit Symbol für allgemeine Schützenschnur

(Volksmarine blaue Kordel, Symbole goldfarben)

Abzeichen für große Fahrt

Fallschirmsprungabzeichen der NVA mit Anhänger (hier für 50 Sprünge)

Deutsche Demokratische Republik

Nationale Volksarmee und Grenztruppen der DDR
Abzeichen

Klassifizierungsabzeichen (3 Leistungsklassen)

Panzer, Ketten-,
Panzertechnik

Flugzeugführer/
Hubschrauberführer

Seemännisches
Personal

Symbole für Klassifizierungsabzeichen

Mot. Schützen

Raketentruppen/
Fla-Raketentruppen,
Truppenluftabwehr

Artillerie, Sperrwaffen

Pionierwesen,
Chemische Dienste

Nachrichten; Funkmeß-,
Waffenleit-, Führungstech-
nik; Technik Funkelektroni-
scher Kampf

Rückwärtige Dienste

Kfz-Dienst

Raketen-
und Waffentechnischer
Dienst

Fliegeringenieurdienst

Schiffsmaschinenpersonal

Allgemeines Klassifizie-
rungsabzeichen
Nationale Volksarmee

Allgemeines Klassifizie-
rungsabzeichen
Grenztruppen der DDR

Deutsche Demokratische Republik

Deutsche Volkspolizei
Dienstgradabzeichen

F 9

Anwärter der VP

Unterwachtmeister
der VP

Wachtmeister der VP

Oberwachtmeister
der VP

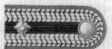

Hauptwachtmeister
der VP

Meister der VP

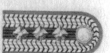

Obermeister der VP

Offz.-Schüler der VP
(1. Studienjahr)

Ärmelabzeichen
Schutzpolizei

Ärmelabzeichen
Abschnittsbevollmächtigter

Kokarde

Armwinkel
ab 5 Dienstjahre

ab 10 Dienstjahre

ab 15 Dienstjahre

ab 20 Dienstjahre

Unterleutnant der VP

Leutnant der VP

Oberleutnant der VP

Hauptmann der VP

Major der VP

Oberstleutnant der VP

Oberst der VP

Generalmajor

Generalleutnant

Generaloberst

Armeegeneral

F 11 — Deutsche Demokratische Republik

Kampfgruppen der Arbeiterklasse und Zivilverteidigung
Dienststellungsabzeichen

Kampfgruppen der Arbeiterklasse

Truppführer, Gruppen-führer, Geschützführer, Werferführer

Zugführer

Stellvertreter des Kommandeurs des selbständigen Zuges

Kommandeur des selbständigen Zuges

Stellv. des Hundert-schaftskom , Stellv. des Batteriekom.

Hundertschafts-kommandeur, Batte-riekommandeur

Gehilfe des Stellvertreters des Bataillons-kommandeurs, Propagandist, Fahrlehrer

Stellvertreter des Stabschefs, Bataillonsarzt

Stellvertreter des Bataillonskomman-deurs, Parteisekretär

Bataillons-kommandeur

Innendienstleiter

Emblem

Zivilverteidigung

Truppführer und Gleichgestellte

Gruppenführer und Gleichgestellte

Stellvertretender Zugführer

Zugführer, Leiter einer Einrichtung der Spezial-behandlung

Stellvertreter des Kommandeurs einer Abteilung, Kommandeur einer Brigade medizinische Hilfe

Kommandeur einer Abteilung, Stellvertreter des Stabschefs für Operativ einer Bereitschaft bzw. eines Stabes der Einsatzkräfte

Mitarbeiter und Gehilfen der Führungsorgane der Einsatzkräfte

Stellvertreter des Kommandeurs einer Bereitschaft, Stellvertreter des Kommandeurs eines Stabes der Einsatzkräfte

Kommandeur einer Bereitschaft, Kommandeur eines Stabes der Einsatzkräfte

Emblem der Zivilverteidigung

APPENDIX H

UNIFORMS
OF THE
BUNDESHEER
(1955–2005)

Illustrations from p. 393 to p. 394 (bottom left) are from
Uniformen und Abzeichen der deutschen Bundeswehr, 1956

Illustrations from p. 394 (bottom right) to p. 397 are from *Bundeswehr Heute: Uniformen*.
Bonn, Germany: Das Bundesministerium der Verteidigung, 1993.

Illustrations from p. 398 to p. 403 show Bundeswehr uniforms as of 2004.
Courtesy of the Ministry of Defence, German Federal Republic

Heer und Luftwaffe

Dienstanzug   Luftwaffe   Ausgehanzug Sommer

Luftwaffe keine
Truppengattungsabzeichen

Luftwaffen-
Ärmelband
auf beiden Ärmeln

Leutnant

Heer und Luftwaffe
Ausgehanzug

Offiziere und gehobene Unteroffiziere   einfache Unteroffiziere und Mannschaften

Luftwaffe

Luftwaffe keine
Truppengattungsabzeichen

Luftwaffen-Ärmelband
auf beiden Ärmeln

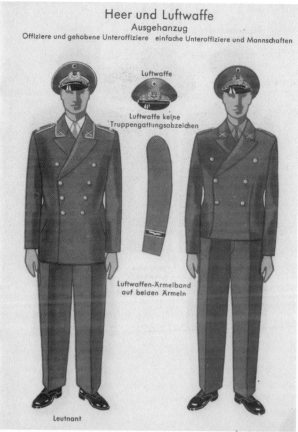

Leutnant

Heer und Luftwaffe

Regenmantel   Tuchmantel
(hier mit Ausgehanzug)   (hier mit Dienstanzug)

Luftwaffe

Luftwaffen-
Ärmelband
auf beiden Ärmeln
(nur auf Tuchmantel)

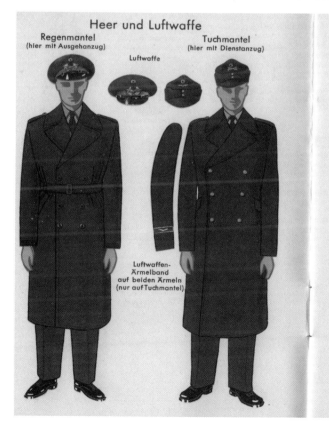

Heer und Luftwaffe
Arbeitsanzug

Luftwaffe

Luftwaffe keine
Truppengattungsabzeichen

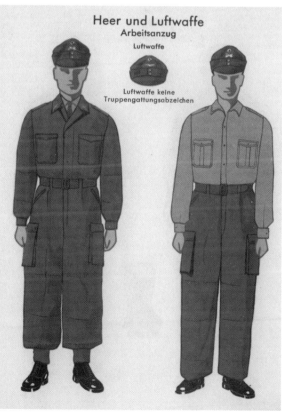

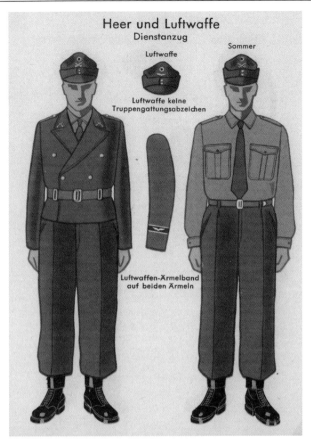

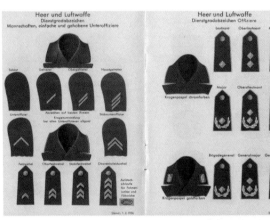

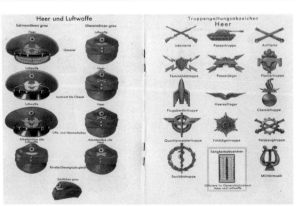

DAS HEER
DIENSTGRADABZEICHEN

HAUPTFELDWEBEL DER INFANTERIE
IM NÄSSESCHUTZANZUG MIT MÜTZE

MAJOR | OBERSTLEUTNANT | OBERST

BRIGADEGENERAL | GENERALMAJOR

GENERALLEUTNANT | GENERAL

ARZT
IM RANGE EINES
OBERSTABSARZTES | ZAHNARZT
IM RANGE EINES
OBERSTABSARZTES | APOTHEKER
IM RANGE EINES
OBERSTABSAPOTHEKERS | VETERINÄR
IM RANGE EINES
OBERSTABSARZTES

KRAGENSPIEGEL

 INFANTERIE
 PANZER-/PANZERJÄGER-TRUPPE
 PANZER-AUFKLÄRUNGS-TRUPPE
 ARTILLERIETRUPPE

 HEERESFLUG-ABWEHRTRUPPE
 PIONIERTRUPPE
 FERNMELDETRUPPE

 ABC-ABWEHR-TRUPPE
 HEERESFLIEGER-TRUPPE
 TECHNISCHE TRUPPE

 MILITÄRMUSIK-DIENST
 FELDJÄGERTRUPPE
 SANITÄTSTRUPPE

 OFFIZIERE IM GENERALSTABSDIENST
 GENERALE

HAUPTMANN IM DIENSTANZUG
MIT BLOUSON

DAS HEER
BARETT-ABZEICHEN

 PANZERGRENADIERTRUPPE
 JÄGERTRUPPE

HAUPTMANN DER FERNMELDETRUPPE
IM DIENSTANZUG MIT PULLOVER

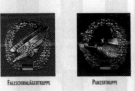
FALLSCHIRMJÄGERTRUPPE | PANZERTRUPPE

PANZERJÄGERTRUPPE | PANZERAUFKLÄRUNGSTRUPPE
FRONTNACHRICHTENTRUPPE

 OPERATIVE INFORMATION

LEUTNANT DER ARTILLERIE
IM DIENSTANZUG

 FERNSPÄHTRUPPE

 ARTILLERIETRUPPE
 TOPOGRAPHIETRUPPE

 HEERESFLUGABWEHRTRUPPE
 HEERESFLIEGERTRUPPE
 PIONIERTRUPPE

 ABC-ABWEHRTRUPPE
 FERNMELDETRUPPE

 FELDJÄGERTRUPPE

DAS HEER

DAS HEER
BARETT-ABZEICHEN

NACHSCHUBTRUPPE

INSTANDSETZUNGSTRUPPE

SANITÄTSTRUPPE

MUSIKKORPS

WACHBATAILLON

DEUTSCH-FRANZÖSISCHE BRIGADE

STABSÄRZTIN IM DIENSTANZUG

OBERFELDARZT IM DIENSTANZUG

DAS HEER
VERBANDSABZEICHEN

BUNDES-MINISTERIUM DER VERTEIDIGUNG

ZENTRALE MILITÄRISCHE BUNDESWEHR-DIENSTSTELLEN

WEHRBEREICHS-KOMMANDO II–VIII (HIER: WEHRBEREICHS-KOMMANDO VI)

TERRITORIAL-KOMMANDO NORD

TERRITORIAL-KOMMANDO SÜD

KORPS U. TERRITORIAL-KOMMANDO OST

TERRITORIAL-KOMMANDO SCHLESWIG-HOLSTEIN

I.- III. KORPS (HIER: III. KORPS)

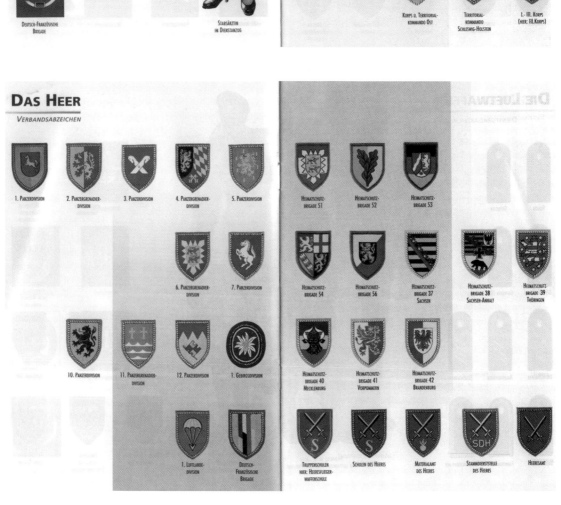

DAS HEER
VERBANDSABZEICHEN

1. PANZERDIVISION

2. PANZERGRENADIER-DIVISION

3. PANZERDIVISION

4. PANZERGRENADIER-DIVISION

5. PANZERDIVISION

6. PANZERGRENADIER-DIVISION

7. PANZERDIVISION

10. PANZERDIVISION

11. PANZERGRENADIER-DIVISION

12. PANZERDIVISION

1. GEBIRGSDIVISION

1. LUFTLANDE-DIVISION

DEUTSCH-FRANZÖSISCHE BRIGADE

HEIMATSCHUTZ-BRIGADE 51

HEIMATSCHUTZ-BRIGADE 52

HEIMATSCHUTZ-BRIGADE 53

HEIMATSCHUTZ-BRIGADE 54

HEIMATSCHUTZ-BRIGADE 56

HEIMATSCHUTZ-BRIGADE 37 SACHSEN

HEIMATSCHUTZ-BRIGADE 38 SACHSEN-ANHALT

HEIMATSCHUTZ-BRIGADE 39 THÜRINGEN

HEIMATSCHUTZ-BRIGADE 40 MECKLENBURG

HEIMATSCHUTZ-BRIGADE 41 VORPOMMERN

HEIMATSCHUTZ-BRIGADE 42 BRANDENBURG

TRUPPENSCHULEN HIER: HEERESFLIEGER-WAFFENSCHULE

SCHULEN DES HEERES

MATERIALAMT DES HEERES

STAMMDIENSTSTELLE DES HEERES

HEERESAMT

TÄTIGKEITSABZEICHEN

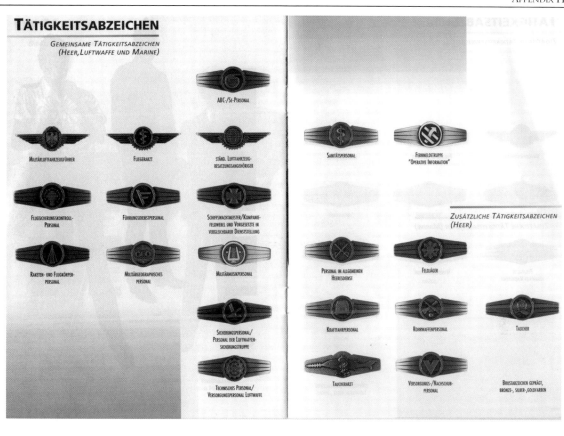

GEMEINSAME TÄTIGKEITSABZEICHEN
(HEER, LUFTWAFFE UND MARINE)

ABC-/SE-PERSONAL

MILITÄRLUFTFAHRZEUGFÜHRER

FLIEGERARZT

STÄND. LUFTFAHRZEUG-
BESATZUNGSANGEHÖRIGER

FLUGSICHERUNGSKONTROLL-
PERSONAL

FÜHRUNGSDIENSTPERSONAL

SCHIFFSWACHTMEISTER/KOMPANIE-
FELDWEBEL UND VORGESETZTE IN
VERGLEICHBARER DIENSTSTELLUNG

RAKETEN- UND FLUGKÖRPER-
PERSONAL

MILITÄRGEOGRAPHISCHES
PERSONAL

MILITÄRMUSIKPERSONAL

SICHERUNGSPERSONAL/
PERSONAL DER LUFTWAFFEN-
SICHERUNGSTRUPPE

TECHNISCHES PERSONAL/
VERSORGUNGSPERSONAL LUFTWAFFE

SANITÄTSPERSONAL

FERNMELDETRUPPE
"OPERATIVE INFORMATION"

ZUSÄTZLICHE TÄTIGKEITSABZEICHEN
(HEER)

PERSONAL IM ALLGEMEINEN
HEERESDIENST

FELDJÄGER

KRAFTFAHRPERSONAL

ROHRWAFFENPERSONAL

TAUCHER

TAUCHERARZT

VERSORGUNGS-/NACHSCHUB-
PERSONAL

BRUSTABZEICHEN GEPRÄGT,
BRONZE-, SILBER-, GOLDFARBEN

SONDERABZEICHEN

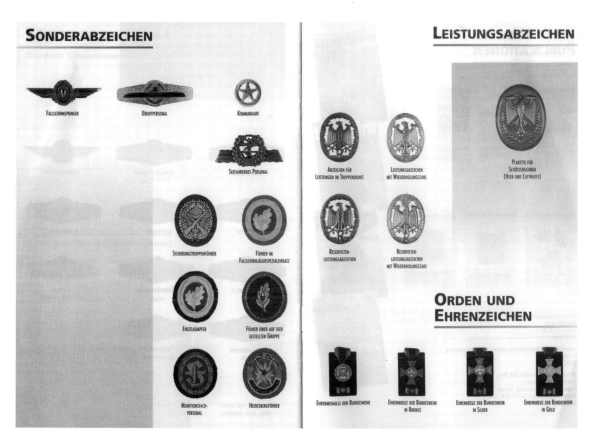

FALLSCHIRMSPRINGER

UBOOTPERSONAL

KOMMANDANT

SEEFAHRENDES PERSONAL

SICHERUNGSTRUPPENFÜHRER

FÜHRER IM
FALLSCHIRMJÄGERSPEZIALEINSATZ

EINZELKÄMPFER

FÜHRER EINER AUF SICH
GESTELLTEN GRUPPE

MUNITIONSFACH-
PERSONAL

HEERESBERGFÜHRER

LEISTUNGSABZEICHEN

ABZEICHEN FÜR
LEISTUNGEN IM TRUPPENDIENST

LEISTUNGSABZEICHEN
MIT WIEDERHOLUNGSZAHL

RESERVISTEN-
LEISTUNGSABZEICHEN

RESERVISTEN-
LEISTUNGSABZEICHEN
MIT WIEDERHOLUNGSZAHL

PLAKETTE FÜR
SCHÜTZENSCHNUR
(HEER UND LUFTWAFFE)

ORDEN UND
EHRENZEICHEN

EHRENMEDAILLE DER BUNDESWEHR

EHRENKREUZ DER BUNDESWEHR
IN BRONZE

EHRENKREUZ DER BUNDESWEHR
IN SILBER

EHRENKREUZ DER BUNDESWEHR
IN GOLD

DAS HEER Dienstgradabzeichen

Dienstgradabzeichen
für den Dienstzug

Soldat

Gefreiter

Gefreiter
Unteroffizieranwärter

Gefreiter
Feldwebelanwärter

Gefreiter
Offizieranwärter

Obergefreiter

Hauptgefreiter

Stabsgefreiter

Dienstgradabzeichen
für den Feldanzug

Oberstabsgefreiter

Obergefreiter
im Feldanzug,
Tarndruck

Hauptfeldwebel
im Feldanzug,
Tarndruck

Unteroffizier

Unteroffizier
Feldwebelanwärter

Fahnenjunker

Stabsunteroffizier

Stabsunteroffizier
Feldwebelanwärter

Feldwebel

Fähnrich

Oberfeldwebel

Hauptfeldwebel

Oberfähnrich

Stabsfeldwebel

Oberstabsfeldwebel

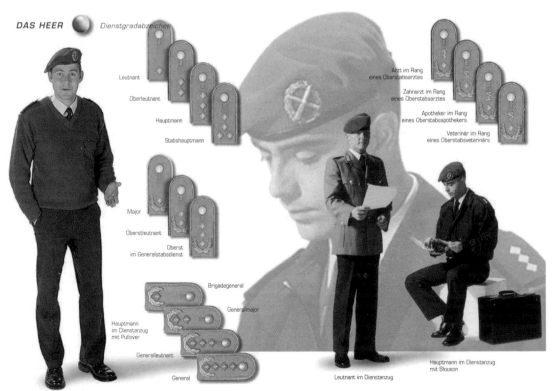

DAS HEER Dienstgradabzeichen

Leutnant

Oberleutnant

Hauptmann

Stabshauptmann

Major

Oberstleutnant

Oberst
im Generalstabsdienst

Brigadegeneral

Generalmajor

Hauptmann
im Dienstanzug
mit Pullover

Generalleutnant

General

Leutnant im Dienstanzug

Hauptmann im Dienstanzug
mit Blouson

Arzt im Rang
eines Oberstabsarztes

Zahnarzt im Rang
eines Oberstabsarztes

Apotheker im Rang
eines Oberstabsapothekers

Veterinär im Rang
eines Oberstabsveterinärs

DAS HEER — Barrett-Abzeichen

Pioniertruppe

Heeresfliegertruppe

ABC-Abwehrtruppe

Fernmeldetruppe Operative Information

Instandsetzungstruppe

Nachschubtruppe

Sanitätstruppe

Feldjägertruppe

Militärmusikdienst

Wachbataillon

Panzertruppe

Panzeraufklärungstruppe/ Feldnachrichtentruppe

Artillerietruppe

Topografietruppe

Jägertruppe

Fernspähtruppe

Fallschirmjägertruppe

Kommando Spezialkräfte

Heeresflugabwehrtruppe

Panzergrenadiertruppe

Fernmeldetruppe

1. Deutsch-Niederländisches Korps

Eurokorps

Deutsch-Französische Brigade

Hauptfeldwebel der Infanterie im Nässeschutzanzug mit Mütze

Unteroffizier der Panzertruppe in der Kombination für Panzerbesatzungen

DAS HEER — Kragenspiegel

Infanterie

Panzertruppe

Panzeraufklärungstruppe

Artillerietruppe

Heeresflugabwehrtruppe

Pioniertruppe

Fernmeldetruppe

ABC-Abwehrtruppe

Heeresfliegertruppe

Technische Truppe

Militärmusikdienst

Sanitätstruppe

Feldjägertruppe

Leutnant im Dienstanzug, hier: Artillerie

Offiziere im Generalstabsdienst

Generale

Oberleutnant im Dienstanzug

Oberfeldarzt im Dienstanzug

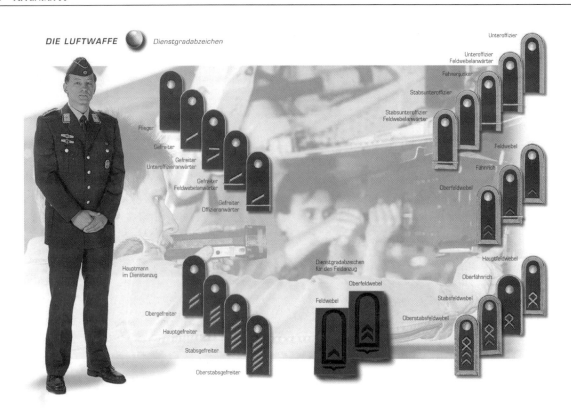

DIE LUFTWAFFE *Dienstgradabzeichen*

Flieger

Gefreiter

Gefreiter
Unteroffizieranwärter

Gefreiter
Feldwebelanwärter

Gefreiter
Offizieranwärter

Hauptmann
im Dienstanzug

Obergefreiter

Hauptgefreiter

Stabsgefreiter

Oberstabsgefreiter

Dienstgradabzeichen
für den Feldanzug

Feldwebel

Oberfeldwebel

Unteroffizier

Unteroffizier
Feldwebelanwärter

Fahnenjunker

Stabsunteroffizier

Stabsunteroffizier
Feldwebelanwärter

Feldwebel

Fähnrich

Oberfeldwebel

Hauptfeldwebel

Oberfähnrich

Stabsfeldwebel

Oberstabsfeldwebel

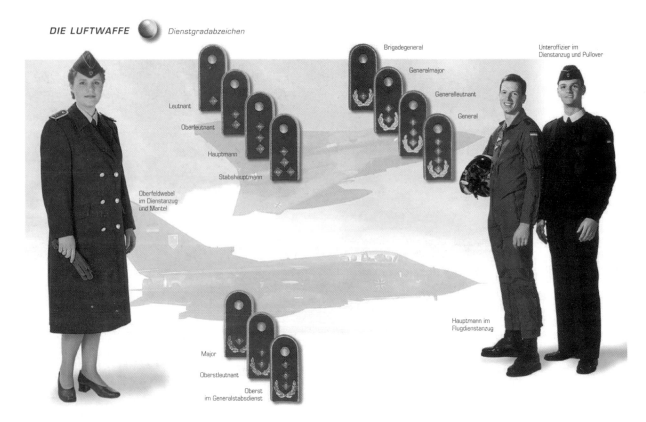

DIE LUFTWAFFE *Dienstgradabzeichen*

Leutnant

Oberleutnant

Hauptmann

Stabshauptmann

Oberfeldwebel
im Dienstanzug
und Mantel

Major

Oberstleutnant

Oberst
im Generalstabsdienst

Brigadegeneral

Generalmajor

Generalleutnant

General

Unteroffizier im
Dienstanzug und Pullover

Hauptmann im
Flugdienstanzug

DIE LUFTWAFFE — Dienstgradabzeichen und Kragenspiegel

Arzt im Rang eines Generaloberstabsarztes

Arzt im Rang eines Oberstabsarztes

Zahnarzt im Rang eines Oberstabsarztes

Apotheker im Rang eines Oberstabsapothekers

Sanitätssoldat im Rang eines Stabsunteroffiziers

Feldwebel im Feldanzug für Luftfahrzeug-technisches Personal

Kragenspiegel der Luftwaffe

Kragenspiegel für Offiziere im Generalstabsdienst

Kragenspiegel für Generale

DIE MARINE — Dienstgradabzeichen

Matrose im Sommeranzug, weiß

Matrose

Gefreiter

Gefreiter Unteroffizieranwärter

Gefreiter Bootsmannanwärter

Gefreiter Offizieranwärter

Obergefreiter

Hauptgefreiter

Stabsgefreiter

Oberstabsgefreiter

Aufschiebeschlaufe für den Bord- und Gefechtsanzug

F 219

Gefreiter

Obergefreiter

Matrose im dunkelblauen Dienstanzug

DIE MARINE Dienstgradabzeichen

Maat

Maat
Bootsmannanwärter

Seekadett

Obermaat

Obermaat
Bootsmann-
anwärter

Bootsmann

Fähnrich
zur See

Oberbootsmann

Schulterklappe für
den Sommeranzug,
sandfarben
hier: Stabsgefreiter

Stabsbootsmann
im Dienstanzug

Oberstabsbootsmann

Stabsbootsmann

Oberfähnrich zur See

Hauptbootsmann

Kapitänleutnant
im dunkelblauen
Dienstanzug

Stabskapitänleutnant

Kapitänleutnant

Oberleutnant
zur See

Leutnant zur See

DIE MARINE Dienstgradabzeichen

Korvettenkapitän

Fregattenkapitän

Kapitän zur See

Kapitänleutnant
im Militärmusikdienst

Korvettenkapitän
im Militärgeographischen Dienst

Flottillenadmiral

Konteradmiral

Arzt im Rang eines
Oberstabsarztes

Zahnarzt im Rang
eines Oberstabsarztes

Vizeadmiral

Admiral

Apotheker im Rang
eines Oberstabsapothekers

Ärztin im Rang
eines Stabsarztes
im dunkelblauen
Dienstanzug

Korvettenkapitän
im dunkelblauen
Dienstanzug
mit Blouson

TÄTIGKEITSABZEICHEN *Streitkräftegemeinsam*

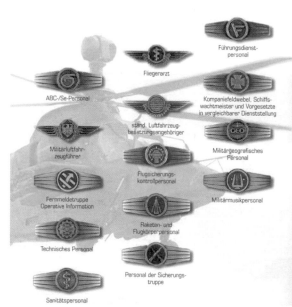

Führungsdienst-
personal

Fliegerarzt

ABC-/Se-Personal

Kompaniefeldwebel, Schiffs-
wachtmeister und Vorgesetzte
in vergleichbarer Dienststellung

stand. Luftfahrzeug-
besatzungsangehöriger

Militärluftfahr-
zeugführer

Militärgeografisches
Personal

Fernmeldetruppe
Operative Information

Flugsicherungs-
kontrollpersonal

Militärmusikpersonal

Technisches Personal

Raketen- und
Flugkörperpersonal

Sanitätspersonal

Personal der Sicherungs-
truppe

TÄTIGKEITSABZEICHEN  *Heer*

Personal im allgemeinen
Heeresdienst

Versorgungs-/
Nachschubpersonal

Kraftfahrpersonal

Rohrwaffenpersonal

Feldjäger

Taucherarzt

Taucher

TÄTIGKEITSABZEICHEN *Luftwaffe*

Waffensystemoffizier

Personal im Stabsdienst

Radarleitpersonal

Versorgungspersonal

USE OF THE ARMY-STYLE FIELD-GREY UNIFORMS BY THE GERMAN NAVY (1921–1945)

The Navy's Sea Battalions were disbanded after the end of the First World War; however, the Navy began uniforming the men of the Coast Artillery Branch along similar lines to that of the Army during the Weimar period. The field-grey uniforms and headgear were similiar; however, they wore naval-type anchor buttons, gold cap wreaths, and naval insignia on their pointed shoulder-straps. The grey double *Kapellenlitzen* had two thin bars of yellow and a thick white bar in between the two. For senior NCO ranks the collar was edged in gold braid. From 1935 to 1939 the breast eagle was silver-grey thread, and on 1 September 1939 it was changed to gold. A field-grey version of the *Bordmütze*, based on the Model 1938 Field Cap, and an Army-style service cap, as well as the Model 1943 General Issue Field Cap, were worn with the uniform. Field-grey trousers were worn with the tunic. Footwear consisted of jackboots, with the ends of the trousers tucked into the shaft of the boot, or ankle-boots with gaiters.

During the Second World War, the field-grey uniform was worn by recruits undergoing basic military training, naval Coast Artillery units, and naval Infantry units at the end of the war. Toward the end of the war, large numbers of sailors without ships or submarines to serve on were transferred to Marine Infantry divisions or to Army Infantry units. Field uniforms of Army stocks were also worn by Navy units in land combat in 1944–5. They had Army-pattern national emblems – often of the triangular Model 1944 National Emblem Pattern. The Model 1944 Field Blouse was also issued to naval personnel, but in limited numbers since the Army had priority.

Above. The naval ratings worn on the field-grey uniforms clearly distinguishes these men of the Reichsmarine from those of the Reichsheer. The naval star insignia on the sleeve is a departmental badge for sailors serving on Ships of the Line

Left. This naval Coast Artilleryman is wearing the Reichswehr 1921 Pattern Field Cap and Uniform with naval shoulder-straps. The new national emblem bearing the Nazi eagle has been applied to the uniform, therefore dating the photograph to around 1935

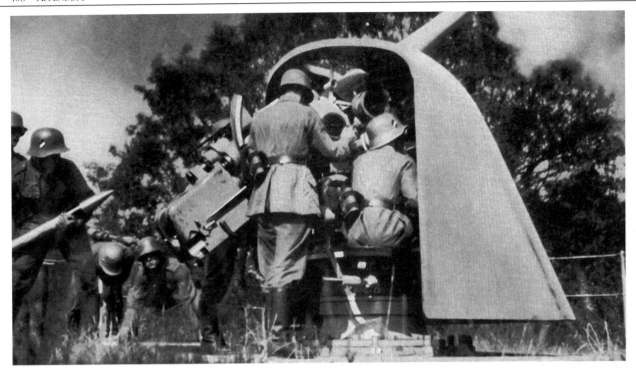

Above. Naval Coast Artillerymen in action, 1935. Many are wearing the new national emblem on their breasts that was introduced in 1935. All are wearing the Model 1918 Steel Helmets

Below. A uniform chart from the 1937–8 edition of Major W. Reibert's *Der Dienst-Unterricht im Heere: Ausgabe für den Schützen der Schützenkompanie* (Berlin: E. S. Mittler & Sohn, 1938), showing naval insignia and the field-grey uniform of the Kriegsmarine

Above left. A Marine-Artillerie-Obergefreiter wearing the field-grey Model 1940-style Tunic without the bottle-green collar. He is wearing the Coast Artillery Badge on his breast pocket. Note the Army-style service cap (Schirmmütze) with leather chinstraps. The cap insignia would have been in gold-colored metal

Above right. A Marine-Artillerie-Oberfeldwebel wearing the field-grey uniform with gold NCO lace around his collar and shoulder-straps. Note the Coast Artillery's winged flaming projectile emblem on his shoulder-straps and the piping, which is dark-green, on his service cap

Left. This enlisted man is wearing the Model 1943 Tunic and Model 1938 Field Cap. He has his Coast Artillery emblem embroidered on his shoulder-straps. Next to his Wound Badge, he is wearing the Naval Minesweeper Badge. Note the naval-style anchor buttons on his tunic

Above. An Oberfeldwebel wearing the field-grey drill uniform; however, after 1940 at was made of reed-green twill. The uniform served as summer duty dress. Note the Minesweeping and Blockade Runners Badges worn on the left pocket

Above. The Tropical Uniform in khaki being worn as a summer-dress uniform. Note the distinctive naval service cap with naval-style oakleaf wreath, which is gold-embroidered

Above. A Marine Artillery officer wearing the field-grey greatcoat with the bottle-green collar. Note the naval-style cap wreath and officer's cap cord

Above. A Marine-Artillerie-Oberfeldwebel wearing the Model 1935 Helmet with the national emblem decal in gold (Navy) rather than in silver (Army). During the Reichswehr era the helmet shield consisted of crossed yellow anchors on a white field. Note the naval pointed-style shoulder-straps

ACKNOWLEDGEMENTS

I would like to thank the following individuals who have assisted me through the years and have made this work possible: Ron G. Hickox (†); Don Miller (†); Hilary Powell; Malcolm Gordon; Thomas Brackmann; Thomas Faust; Jörn Fickart; Katrina Lattke; Ronny Van Troostenberghe; R. James Bender; Michal Jaroszynski-Wolfram; Richard Bass, Jr.; Elke Diederich and Georg Breuer; Bundesministerium der Verteidigung (German Federal Ministry of Defense); Chris Cameron; John Angolia; Lieutenant Colonel Thomas Johnson, USA (Retired); William and Lois Egan; Bolko Hartmann; Robert Tredwen; Alan Smith; David Sullivan; Lionel Leventhal; Michael Leventhal; René Chartrand; Christopher F. Seidler; Malcolm Fisher; Phillip Bühler; Ron Manion; Rick Keller and staff from Great War Militaria; Edward C. Ezell (†); Martin Windrow; Phillip Jowett; Richard Heller; SS-Sturmbannführer Walter Reder, W-SS (†); Gefreiter Hans Goebler, Kriegesmarine/U-505 (†); Dipl. Ing. Dr. Ferdinand Kirchner; Mark Salussolia; A. M. de Quesada, MD; and, to my daughter Caroline.

The following societies and its members from around the world have been gracious in providing guidance during the years researching this work: Traditionsverband ehemaliger Schutz- und überseetruppen/Freunde der früheren deutschen Schutzgebeite e.V. (FRG); Company of Military Historians (USA); Society for Army Historical Research (UK); South Africa Military Historical Society (South Africa); 8th Air Force Historical Society (USA); US Naval Institute; Garand Collector's Association (USA); Historic Naval Ships Association (USA); National Rifle Association (USA); The Sunshine Postcard Collector's Club (USA); Orders and Medals Society of America (USA); American Society of Military Insignia Collectors (USA); The Orders and Medals Research Society (UK).

I would like to gratefully acknowledge the following institutions: the Bundeswehr Museum (Dresden, Germany); Bayerisches Armeemuseum Ingolstadt (Ingolstadt, Germany); Österreichs Bundesheer; Das Heeresgeschichtliche Museum (Vienna, Austria); Rainer-Regimentsmuseum, Festung Hohensalzburg (Salzburg, Austria); Deutsches Historisches Museum (Berlin, Germany); Deutsches Klingenmuseum Solingen (Solingen, Germany); Reichsstadt-Museum (Rothenburg o.d.T., Germany); Bayerisches National Museum (Munich, Germany); Deutsches Museum (Munich, Germany); Museum Berlin Karlshorst (Berlin, Germany); Ministry of Defense (Berlin, Germany); National Archives (Washington DC, USA); Library of Congress (Washington DC, USA); National Infantry Museum (Fort Benning, USA); West Point Military Academy Museum (USA); US Army; US Navy; Imperial War Museum (London, UK); National Army Museum (London, UK); Bastogne Historical Center (Bastogne, Belgium); D-Day National Museum (New Orleans, USA); Musée de l'Armée (Paris, France); Musée du Costume Militaire (Thiaucort, France); Musée de la Bataille du Saillant de Saint-Mihiel, 1914–1918 (Thiaucourt, France). These institutions and their staff have been a treasure trove of information and much of the material they have provided have been incorporated into this work.

BIBLIOGRAPHY

Abbott, Peter. *Armies in East Africa, 1914–1918*. London: Osprey, 2002.

Ager, VerKuilen. *Friekorps Insignia*. Rochester, NY: privately published, 1979.

Ailsby, Christopher. *Hitler's Sky Warriors*. Dulles, VA: Brassey's, Inc., 2000.

Altmannsperger, Peter. *Die Soldaten unter dem Edelweiß: Die 1. Gebirgsdivision und die Bundeswehr in Bayern, Eine Bilddokumentation*. Wolfsheim, Germany: RMS-Verlag, 1998.

Angolia, John, and Schlicht, Adolf. *Die Kriegsmarine, Uniforms & Traditions*, Vols 1–3. San Jose, CA: R. James Bender Publishing, 1991–3.

Bender, Roger James. *Legion Condor: Uniforms, Organization and History*. San Jose, CA: R. James Bender Publishing, 1992.

Bleckwenn, Hans. *Unter dem Preußen-Adler: Das brandenburgisch-preußische Heer, 1640–1807*. München: C. Bertelsmann Verlag GmbH, 1978.

Das Buch der Deutschen Kolonien. Leipzig: Wilhelm Goldman Verlag, 1937.

Buchner, Alex. *The German Infantry Handbook, 1939–1945*. West Chester, PA: Schiffer, 1991.

Buchner, Alex. *Weapons and Equipment of the German Fallschirmtruppe*. Atglen, PA: Schiffer, 1996.

Bueno Carrera, José María. *La Division y la Escuadrilla Azul: Su Organizacion y sus Uniformes*. Madrid: Aldaba Ediciones, S.A., 1991.

Bueno Carrera, José María. *Uniformes Militares de la Guerra Civil Española*. Madrid: Almena Ediciones, 1997.

Bull, Stephen. *Stormtrooper*. London: Military Illustrated, 1999.

Bull, Stephen. *World War One German Army*. London: Brassy's, 2000.

Bundeswehr Heute: *Uniformen*. Bonn: Das Bundesministerium der Verteidigung, 1993.

Caballero Jurado, Carlos. *Foreign Volunteers of the Wehrmacht 1941–1945*. London: Osprey, 1983.

Caballero Jurado, Carlos. *The German Freikorps 1918–1923*. Oxford: Osprey, 2001.

Caballero Jurado, Carlos. "Los Uniformes de la División Azul". *Marton, P. and G. Vedelago. Los Uniformes Alemanes de la Segunda Guerra Mudial*. Barcelona, Spain: Editorial de Vecchi, S.A., 1981.

Cooper, Matthew. *The German Army 1933–1945*. Lanham, MD: Scarborough House, 1978.

Costley, Bill. *Obergrefrieter: Jäger Battalion Light Infantry Division*. San Diego, CA: Last 100 Days E.T.O., 1993.

Davis, Brian Leigh. *Badges & Insignia of the Third Reich 1933–1945*. Poole: Blandford Press, 1983.

Davis, Brian Leigh. *German Army Uniforms and Insignia 1933–1945*. London: Arms and Armour Press, 1992. (Second revised edition of 1971 with amendments and corrections.)

Davis, Brian Leigh. *German Combat Uniforms of World War Two*, Vols 1–2. London: Arms and Armour Press, 1984–5.

Davis, Brian Leigh. *German Uniforms of the Third Reich 1933-1945*. New York: ARCO Publishing, Inc., 1980.

Davis, Brian Leigh. *NATO Forces: An Illustrated Reference to Their Organization and Insignia*. London: Blandford Press, 1988.

de Quesada, Alejandro Manuel. "The Austrian U-Boat Service 1907–1918". *Military Trader*, Vol. 5, Issue 3 (March 1998): 46–8.

de Quesada, Alejandro Manuel. "The Austrian U-Boat Service Badge: 1910–1918". *The Military Advisor*, Vol. 7, No. 1 (Winter 1995–6): 33–5.

de Quesada, Alejandro Manuel. "Deutsche Feuerwehr Belt Buckles, 1900–1989". *Military Trader*, Vol. 7, Issue 10 (October 2000): 32–3.

de Quesada, Alejandro Manuel. *Eickhorn Export Edged Weapons, Volume One: Latin America*. Union City, TN: Pioneer Press, 1996.

de Quesada, Alejandro Manuel. "Fuerwehr Pickelhaubes of Pre-Nazi Germany". *Bits 'n' Pieces*, Vol. 1, Issue 4 (March 1993): 3, 11.

de Quesada, Alejandro Manuel. "Soldiers of the Reich in Tampa Bay". *Pastimes*, Vol. 2, No. 1 (Fall 1995): 9.

de Smet, J. L. *Uniformen des Heeres, 1933–1945*. Kedichem: Military Collectors Service, 1972.

Die Deutsche Armee vor dem Weltkriege. Leipzig: Verlag von Moritz Ruhl, 1926.

Deutsche Kämpfen in Spanien: Herausgegeben von der Legion Condor. Berlin: Wilhelm Limpert-Verlag, 1939.

Deutsche Uniformabzeichen 1900–1945. Norderstedt: Militair-Verlag Klaus D. Patzwall, 1994.

Deutsche Uniformen: Heer, Marine, Luftwaffe, Arbeitsdienst, SS, SA, NSFK, NSKK, RLB, HJ, DJ, Polizei und Gendarmerie. Leipzig: Verlag von Moritz Ruhl, 1938.

Die Deutsche Reichswehr. Leipzig: Verlag von Moritz Ruhl, 1919.

Die Deutsche Reichswehr. Leipzig: Verlag von Moritz Ruhl, 1921.

Deutsches Soldatenjahrbuch 1965. München-Lochhausen: Schild-Verlag, 1964.

Doehle, Dr Heinrich. *Die Auszeichnungen des Großdeutschen Reichs: Orden, Ehrenzeichen, Abzeichen*. Berlin: E. O. Erdmenger & Co. K.G., 1943.

Doehle, Dr Heinrich (translator: Hamelman, William E.). *Medals & Decorations of the Third Reich: Orders,*

Decorations, Badges. Denison, TX: Reddick Enterprises, 1995. (Reprint of the German 1943 edition.)

Edward, Roger. *German Airborne Troops.* Garden City, NY: Doubleday & Co., 1974.

Die ehemaligen kaiserlich Deutschen Schutztruppen. Leipzig: Verlag von Moritz Ruhl, 1910.

Eisenhart Rothe, Alexander von. *Ehrendenkmal der Deutschen Armee und Marine.* Berlin: Deutscher National-Verlag, 1931.

Ellis, Chris. *21st Panzer Division: Rommel's Afrika Korps Spearhead.* Hersham: Ian Allen, 2001.

Feist, Uwe, and Harms, Norman, *Fallschirmjäger in Action.* Carrollton, TX: Squadron/Signal Publications, Inc., 1973.

Figueroa, J. R. *Tropical Headgear of the Wehrmacht in W.W. II.* Los Angeles, CA: Figueroa Creations, 1996.

Figueroa, J. R. *Tropical Uniforms of the German Army and Airforce in W.W. II.* Los Angeles, CA: Figueroa Creations, 1993.

Fosten, D. S. V. *Cuirassiers and Heavy Cavalry: Dress Uniforms of the German Imperial Cavalry 1900–1914.* London: Almark Publishing Co., 1972.

The German Forces in the Field, November 1918. London: Imperial War Museum, 1995. (Originally published in 1918, 7th revision, by the War Office.)

Graudenz, Karlheinz, and Schindler, Hanns-Michael. *Die deutschen Kolonien.* Augsburg: Weltbild Verlag GmbH, 1988.

Die graue Felduniform der Deutschen Armee. Leipzig: Verlag von Moritz Ruhl, 1910.

Hagger, D. H. *Hussars and Mounted Rifles: Uniforms of the Imperial German Cavalry 1900–1914.* London: Almark Publishing Co., 1974.

Handbook of German Uniforms: The German Army and Luftwaffe. Harrisburg, PA: A.A.F.I.S., 1942.

Handbook of the German Army (Home and Colonial). London: Imperial War Museum, 2002. (Originally published in 1914 by the War Office.)

Handbuch Militärisches Grundwissen, NVA-Ausgabe. Berlin: Militärverlag der Deutschen Demokratischen Republik, 1988.

Harms, Norman. *German Infantry in Action.* Carrollton, TX: Squadron/Signal Publications, Inc., 1973.

Haß, Dietrich, and Hocke, Michael. *Die Prussische Polizei.* Flensburg: privately published, 1986.

Haupt, Werner. *Die Deutsche Schutztruppe 1889–1918.* Gerg am See: Türmer Verlag, 1989.

Hicks, Major James E. *German Weapons-Uniforms-Insignia 1841–1918.* La Canada, CA: James E. Hicks & Son, 1964.

Hicks, Major James E. *Notes on German Ordnance, 1841–1918.* La Canada, CA: James E. Hicks & Son, 1937.

Hoffschmidt, E. J., and Tantum, W. H., *German Army and Navy Uniforms & Insignia 1871–1918.* Old Greenwich, CT: WE, Inc., 1968.

Hormann, Jörg M. *German Uniforms of the 20th Century, Vol. 1: Uniforms of the Panzer Troops, 1917 to the Present.* West Chester, PA: Schiffer, 1989.

Hormann, Jörg M. *German Uniforms of the 20th Century, Vol. 2: Uniforms of the Panzer Troops, 1917 to the Present.* West Chester, PA: Schiffer, 1989.

Hormann, Jörg M. *Uniformen der Infanterie, 1919 bis Heute.* Friedberg: Podzun-Pallas-Verlag GmbH, 1989.

Hormann, Jörg M. *Uniformen der Panzertruppe, 1917 bis Heute.* Friedberg: Podzun-Pallas-Verlag GmbH, 1989.

Jahrbuch des deutschen Heeres 1939. Leipzig: Verlag von Breitkopf & Härtel, 1938.

Jurado, Carlos Caballero. *The German Freikorps, 1918–1923.* Oxford: Osprey, 2001.

Kaltenegger, Roland. *Weapons and Equipment of the German Mountain Troops.* Atglen, PA: Schiffer, 1995.

Keubke, Klaus-Ulrich. *Uniformen der Nationalen Volksarmee der DDR, 1956–1986.* Berlin: Brandenburgisches Verlagshaus, 1990.

Kinna, H., and Moss, D. A. *Jäger & Schützen: Dress and Distinctions 1910–1914.* Watford: Bellona Publications (Argus Books), 1977.

Das Kleine Buch vom Deutschen Heere. Leipzig: Lipsius & Tischer, 1901.

Knötel, Richard, Knötel, Herbert, and Sieg, Herbert. *Farbiges Handbuch der Uniformkunde.* Stuttgart: W. Spemann, 1985.

Knötel, Richard, Knötel, Herbert, and Sieg, Herbert. *Uniforms of the World.* New York: Charles Scribners's Sons, 1980.

Kolonialkriegerdank-Kalander für das Jahr 1917. Berlin: Verlag des Kolonialkriegerdank E.B., 1917.

Kopenhagen, Wilfried. *Die Landstreitkräfte der NVA.* Stuttgart: Motorbuch Verlag, 1999.

Large, David Clay. *Germans to the Front: West German Rearmament in the Adenauer Era.* Chapel Hill, NC: The University of North Carolina Press, 1996.

Layton, Geoff. *From Bismarck to Hitler: Germany 1890–1933.* London: Hodder & Stoughton, 2002.

Layton, Geoff. *Germany: The Third Reich 1933–45.* London: Hodder & Stoughton, 2000.

Long, Richard C. "Leibhussaren (LH) to Leibstandarte (LAH)". *The Military Advisor,* Vol. 14, No. 4 (fall 2003): 4–13.

Lorch, Carlos. *Im bunten Rock: Militärisches Zeremoniell in 16 Nationen.* Stuttgart: Motorbuch Verlag, 1997.

Marcks, Otto. *Die Bundeswehr im Aufbau.* Bonn, Germany: Athenäum-Verlag, 1957.

Marrion, R. J. *Lancers and Dragoons: Uniforms of the Imperial German Cavalry 1900–1914.* London: Almark Publishing Co., 1975.

Marton, P., and Vedelago, G., *Los Uniformes Alemanes de la Segunda Guerra Mundial.* Barcelona: Editorial de Vecchi, S.A., 1981.

Meybauer, Paul. *Die Helmwappen und Namenszüge der Deutschen Armee.* Leipzig: Verlag von Moritz Ruhl, 1910.

Nachtrage und Berichtigungen zum Deutschen Reichsheer. Berlin: Max Hochsprung, 1892.

Nash, David. *German Artillery 1914–1918.* London: Almark Publishing Co., 1970.

Die Nebeltruppe: Waffenhefte des Heeres, Herausgegeben vom Oberkommando des Heeres. München: Deutscher Volksverlag GMBH, 1939.

Neumann, Thomas F. "Modern German Army SSI Background." *The Trading Post,* Vol. 72, No. 4 (October–December 2003): 45–8.

Die Neue Deutsche Reichswehr, Die Freiwilligen-Verbände und ihre Characteristischen Abzeichen. Leipzig: Verlag von Moritz Ruhl, 1919.

Oberkommando des Heeres. *Liste der Fertigungskennzeichen für Waffen, Munition und Gerät.* Berlin: Gedruckt im Oberkommando des Heeres, 1944.

Oliver, Tony L. *D.D.R. Collectors Reference Guides, 1949–1990*, Vol. 1. Eton Wick: T.L.O. Publications, 1993.

Ortenburg, Georg. *Mit Gott für König und Vaterland: Das preußische Heer, 1807–1914.* München: C. Bertelsmann Verlag GmbH, 1979.

Palinckx, Werner. *Camouflage Uniforms of the German Wehrmacht.* Atglen, PA: Schiffer, 2002.

Pawlas, Karl R. (ed.). *Liste der Fertigungskennzeichen für Waffen, Munition und Gerät.* Nürnberg: Publizistisches Archiv für Militär- und Waffenwesen, 1977.

Pawley, Ronald. *The Kaiser's Warlords: German Commanders of World War I.* Oxford: Osprey, 2003.

Peter, Nash. *German Belt Buckles, 1845–1945: Buckles of the Enlisted Ranks.* Atglen, PA: Schiffer, 2003.

Peterson, Daniel. *Waffen SS Camouflage Uniforms & Post-War Derivatives*. London: Windrow & Greene, 1995.

Peterson, Daniel. *Wehrmacht Camouflage Uniforms & Post-War Derivatives*. London: Windrow & Greene, 1995.

Petschull, Jürgen. *Der Wahn vom Weltreich: Die Geschichte der deutschen Kolonien*. Hamburg: STERN-Buch im Verlag Gruner Jahr AG & Co., 1984.

Quarrie, Bruce. *German Airborne Troops 1939–1945*. London: Osprey, 1983.

Queen, Eric. *Red Shines the Sun: A Pictorial History of the Fallschirm-Infanterie*. San Jose, CA: R. James Bender Publishing, 2002.

Radecke, Erich. *Geschichte des Polizei-Tschakos: Von der Alten Armee zur Polizei*. Hamburg: Selbstverlag des Autors, 1995.

Ramos, Raúl Arias. *La Legión Cóndor: Imágenes inéditas para su historia*. Madrid: Agualarga Editores, S.L., 2002.

Reddick, J. Rex, Editor. *F.W. Assman & Söhne Sales Catalog*. Denison, TX: Reddick Enterprises, 1992. (Reprint of 1930s Catalog.)

Redmon, Ronald L., and Cuccarese, James F., *Panzergrenadiers in Action*. Carrollton, TX: Squadron/Signal Publications, Inc., 1980.

Reibert, Dr jur. W., Hauptmann (Heer). *Der Dienst-Unterricht im Heere: Ausgabe für den Gewehr- und L.M.G.=Schützen*. Berlin: E. S. Mittler & Sohn, 1937.

Reibert, Dr jur. W., Major (Heer). *Der Dienst-Unterricht im Heere: Ausgabe für den Nachrichtensoldaten*. Berlin: E. S. Mittler & Sohn, 1938.

Reibert, Dr jur. W., Major (Heer). *Der Dienst-Unterricht im Heere: Ausgabe für den Schützen der Schützenkompanie*. Berlin: E. S. Mittler & Sohn, 1938.

Reibert, Dr jur. W., Major (Heer). *Der Dienst-Unterricht im Heere: Ausgabe für den Schützen der Schützenkompanie*. Berlin: E. S. Mittler & Sohn, 1940.

Reibert, Dr jur. W., Hauptmann (Heer). *Der Dienst-Unterricht im Heere: Ausgabe für den S.M.G.=Schützen*. Berlin: E. S. Mittler & Sohn, 1937.

Der Reibert: Das Handbuch für den deutschen Soldaten. Hamburg: E. S. Mittler & Sohn, 1999.

Der Reibert: Das Handbuch für den Soldaten (Ausgabe Marine). Herford: E. S. Mittler & Sohn, 1979.

Der Reichsorganisationsleiter der NSDAP. *Organisationsbuch der NSDAP*. München: Zentralverlag der NSDAP, 1943.

Ripley, Tim. *The Wehrmacht: The German Army of World War II, 1939–1945*. New York: Fitzroy Dearborn, 2003.

Rosignoli, Guido. *Army Badges and Insignia of World War Two*. New York: Macmillan, 1972.

Rosignoli, Guido. *Army Badges and Insignia Since 1945*. New York: Macmillan, 1973.

Rottman, Gordon L. *Warsaw Pact Ground Forces*. London: Osprey, 1987.

Rottman, Gordon L. *World Special Forces Insignia*. London: Osprey, 1989.

Schulze, Carl. *IFOR: Allied Forces in Bosnia*. London: Windrow & Greene, 1996.

Seaton, Albert. *The Army of the German Empire, 1870–1888*. London: Osprey, 1973.

Sigel, Gustav A. (Dr. J. J. Breuilly, ed.). *German Military Forces of the 19th Century: The Armament, Insignia and Uniforms of the Army and Navy Illustrated in Full Color*. New York: The Military Press, 1989.

Sigel, Gustav A. *Germany's Army and Navy by Pen and Picture*. Chicago: The Werner Company, 1900.

Simpson, Keith. *History of the German Army*. London: Bison Books, 1985.

Smith, Digby. *NATO Uniforms Today*. London: Arms and Armour Press, 1984.

Soukup, Walter and Th. Thomas. *Uniformen und militärische Symbole des 20. Jahrhunderts*. Rastatt: Erich Pabel Verlag GmbH, 1982.

Stephens, F. J., and Maddocks, Graham J. *Uniforms and Organisation of the Imperial German Army 1900–1918*. London: Almark Publishing Co., 1975.

Steven, Andrew, and Amodio, Peter. *Waffen-SS in Colour Photographs*. London: Windrow & Greene, 1990.

Stiles, Andrina, and Farmer, Alan. *The Unification of Germany 1815–90*. London: Hodder & Stoughton, 2001.

Thomas, Nigel. *NATO Armies Today*. London: Osprey, 1987.

Thomas, Nigel. *The German Army 1939–1945 (1): Blitzkrieg*. London: Osprey, 1998.

Thomas, Nigel. *The German Army 1939–1945 (2): North Africa & Balkans*. London: Osprey, 1998.

Thomas, Nigel. *The German Army 1939–1945 (3): Eastern Front 1941–1943*. London: Osprey, 1999.

Thomas, Nigel. *The German Army 1939–1945 (4): Eastern Front 1943–1945*. London: Osprey, 1999.

Thomas, Nigel. *The German Army 1939–1945 (5): Western Front 1943–1945*. London: Osprey, 2000.

Thomas, Nigel. *The German Army in World War I (1) 1914–1915*. Oxford: Osprey, 2003.

Thomas, Nigel. *The German Army in World War I (2) 1915–1917*. Oxford: Osprey, 2004.

Thompson, Leroy. *Badge & Insignia of the Elite Forces*. London: Arms and Armour Press, 1991.

Tophoven, Rolf. *GSG 9: German Response to Terrorism*. Koblenz: Bernard & Graefe Verlag, 1984.

Uniformen und Abzeichen der deutschen Bundeswehr, 1956. (No other information to which agency published this pamphlet.)

Die Uniformen und Abzeichen der SA, SS und des Stahlhelm, Brigade Ehrhardt, Hitler-Jugend, Amtswalter, Abgeordnete, NSBO und NSKK. Berlin: Traditions-Verlag Kolf & Co., 1937.

Unsere NVA, Ausgabe 1989. Berlin: Militärverlag der DDR, 1988.

Vogenbeck, Peter, and Eugen, Pauls. *Die Adlerstempel von Deutsch-Südwestafrika*. Kalenborn-Scheuern/Münster: privately published, 1995.

Walter, John. *Military Rifles of Two World Wars*. London: Greenhill Books, 2003.

Walther, Klaus. *Uniformeffekten der bewaffneten Organe der DDR, Band I: Ministerium des Innern, 1949–1990*. Berlin: ECOTOUR Verlag GmbH, 1993.

Walther, Klaus. *Uniformeffekten der bewaffneten Organe der DDR, Band II: Ministerium für Nationale Verteidigung, 1956–1990/Ministerium für Staatssicherheit, 1957–1989*. Berlin: ECOTOUR Verlag GmbH, 1994.

Wilkins, Gary. *The Collector's Guide to Cloth Third Reich Military Headgear*. Atglen, PA: Schiffer, 2002.

Williamson, Gordon. *German Army Elite Units 1939–1945*. London: Osprey, 2002.

Woolley, Charles. *German Uniforms, Insignia & Equipment, 1918–1923: Friekorps, Reichsheer, Vehicles, Weapons*. Atglen, PA: Schiffer, 2002.

Woolley, Charles. *The Kaiser's Army in Color: Uniforms of the Imperial German Army as Illustrated by Carl Becker, 1890–1910*. Atglen, PA: Schiffer, 2000.

Woolley, Charles. *Uniforms & Equipment of the Imperial German Army as Illustrated by Carl Becker, 1900–1918*. Atglen, PA: Schiffer, 1999.

Zaloga, Steven J., and Loop, James. *Soviet Bloc Elite Forces*. London: Osprey, 1985.

Zilian, Frederick. *From Confrontation to Cooperation: The Takeover of the National People's (East German) Army by the Bundeswehr*. Westport, CT: Praeger, 1999.

GLOSSARY

Abteilung. Detachment, department, or battalion.

Abzeichen. Badge

Allerhöchste Kabinetts-Ordre (AKO). Highest Cabinet Order or Directive.

Armee. Army.

Armee-Abteilung. Army Detachment.

Armeegruppe. Army Group.

Artillerie. Artillery.

Arzt. Doctor.

Aufklärung. Reconnaissance.

Bandeau. Ribbon.

Bataillon. Battalion.

Batterie. Battery.

Baupionier. Construction Engineer

Befehlshaber der. Commander of . . .

Beil. Hatchets.

Beilpike. Pick hatchets.

Brigade. Brigade.

Brotbeutel. Bread bag or haversack.

Bundesheer. Army of the German Federal Republic.

Bundeswehr. Armed Forces of the German Federal Republic.

Chef des Generalstabes. Chief of the General Staff.

Division. Division.

Dolch. Dagger.

Einheit. Detachment or unit.

Eisenbahn. Railroad.

Ersatz. Replacement or substitute.

Fahne. Flag, standard.

Fahnenträger. Standard Bearer.

Fahrtruppen. Fast Troops.

Fallschirm. Parachute.

Fallschirmjäger. Paratrooper.

Fangschnur. Cords of aigulette.

Feld. Field.

Feldflasche. Canteen.

Feldgendarmerie. Field Police.

Feldgrau. Field-grey.

Feldjäger. Infantryman.

Feldkommandantur. Field Command.

Feldlazarett. Field Hospital.

Feldmarshall. Field Marshal.

Feldmütze. Field cap.

Feldpost. Field post.

Feldwebel. Sergeant.

Filzhaube. Felt helmet.

Flak. From Fliegerabwehrkanone, meaning anti-aircraft gun.

Flieger. Flyer, pilot.

Fliegerstutzhelm. Reinforced flight helmet.

Flügelmütze. Winged hat.

Freiwillige. Volunteer.

Führer. Leader.

Fusilier. Infantry or Heavy Infantry. A traditional term for a type of Infantryman.

Garde. Guard.

Gebirg. Mountain.

Gebirgsjäger. Mountain Trooper.

Gefreiter. Corporal.

Geheime. Secret.

GeheimeStaatspolizei (Gestapo). Secret State Police.

General. General.

Generalkommando. General Headquarters.

Generalstab des Heeres. Army General Staff.

Gepäck. Luggage.

Geschütz. Gun.

Gesellschaft. Society, organization, company.

Gewehr. Gun, rifle.

Granatwerfer. Mortar.

Grenadier. A traditional term for a type of Infantryman.

Grenztruppen. Border Guard Troops.

Gruppe. Group.

Halsbinde. A cravat of black lasting which buckles behind the neck.

Hauptmann. Captain.

Heer. Army.

Heeresgruppe. Army Group.

Helmwappen. Helmet plate.

Hut. Hat.

Jäger. Literal meaning "hunter" but usually applied to Light Infantry.

Jäger zu Pferde. Mounted Dispatch Rider.

Kaiserwehr. Armed Forces of

Imperial Germany, 1871–1918.

Kampf. Struggle.

Kavallerie. Cavalry.

Kettenkrad. Tracked motorcycle.

Knebel. Toggle.

Kochgeschirr. Individual camp kettle or mess kit.

Kokarde. Cockade.

Koller. A short boiled-wool jacket worn by members of the German heavy, Kürassier regiments.

Kolpak. Busby bag.

Kommandeur. A person commanding a unit.

Kommando. Headquarters or command.

Kompanie. Company.

Koppelschloß. Belt buckle.

Kugelhelm. Ball helmet, generic name for Artillery *Pickelhaube*.

Kürassier. Heavy Cavalry.

Krieg. War

Kriegesgefangene. Prisoner of war

Kriegsmarine. Navy during the Third Reich.

Landeskokarde. State cockade.

Landsturm. Home Guard Troops.

Landswehr. Territorial Reserve.

Lebensmittelbeutel. Ration pocket in a knapsack.

Leibriemen. Leather belt.

Leutnant. Lieutenant.

Lieb. Life.

Liebstandarte. Bodyguard Regiment.

Litewka. Jacket.

Litzen. Braid or piping.

Luftwaffe. Air Force.

Major. Major.

Nationalsozialistische Deutsche Arbeiterpartei (Nazi). German National Socialist Workers' Party.

National Volksarmee (NVA) - Armed Forces of the German Democratic Republic.

Offizier. Officer.

Orden. Decoration, orders (medals).

Patronenbehälter. Pockets for cartridges in a knapsack.

Patrontasche. Cartridge box.

Pelzmütze. Fur hat.

Perlring. Pearl ring.

Pickelhaube. Spiked helmet.

Portepee. Dagger or sword knot.

Rabatte. Covering.

Raupenhelm. Caterpillar helmet.

Regiment. Regiment.

Reichskokarde. National cockade.

Reichswehr. German Armed Forces of the Weimar Republic.

Ringkragen. Gorget.

Säbel. Saber.

Schirmmütze. Visor cap.

Schnuren. Cord or string.

Schnürschuhe. A pair of easy shoes of supple tan leather.

Schutzen. Sharpshooters.

Schutzstaffel (SS). Protection Detachment, later became the Nazi party's political army.

Schutztruppe. Literally "Protection Troops", usually applied to colonial troops.

Schwalbennester. Swallows' nests.

Seebataillon. Sea Battalion, Imperial German Naval Infantry.

Soldat. Soldier, Private.

Sonderführer. Warrant Officer.

Spaten. Spade.

Standart. Standard, regimental flag.

Stahlhelm. Helmet.

Stiefel. A pair of boots.

Tarbusch. A zinc and copper alloy.

Technik. Technology, engineering.

Tornister. Knapsack.

Tornisterbeutel. Ration bag.

Trichter. Plume holder.

Trinkbecher. Drinking cup.

Troddel. Bayonet knot.

Tropenhelm. Pith helmet.

Tschako. Shako.

Tschapka. German term for the Uhlan Helmet (Czapka).

Tuchhose. Trousers.

Unterfeldwebel. Sergeant, Non-Commissioned Officer.

Unterseeboot. Submarine.

Volk. People.

Volkspolizei (VP). People's Police of the German Democratic Republic.

Volkssturm. People's Militia.

Wäschebeutel. Compartment for clothes.

Waffen. Weapon, arms.

Waffenfarbe. Branch of Service Color.

Waffenrock. Tunic.

Wappen. Device. The "Wappen" is the state device found on the front of a *Pickelhaube*.

Wehrmacht. German Armed Forces of the Third Reich.

Werft. Dockyard.

Zelt-ausrustüng. Individual Tent.

Zeltbahn. Shelter-tent.

Zeltstock. Tent poles.

Zeltzubehörbeutel. shelter-tent accessories case in a knapsack.

Zoll. Customs.